Advanced Information and Knowledge Processing

Series Editors
Professor Lakhmi Jain
Lakhmi.jain@unisa.edu.au

Professor Xindong Wu
xwu@cems.uvm.edu

For other titles published in this series, go to
http://www.springer.com/series/4738

Jordi Nin · Javier Herranz

Editors

Privacy and Anonymity in Information Management Systems

New Techniques for New Practical Problems

 Springer

Editors

Dr. Jordi Nin
Universitat Politècnica de Catalunya
Dept. Arquitectura de Computadors
C. Jordi Girona 1-3
08034 Barcelona
Spain
nin@ac.upc.edu

Dr. Javier Herranz
Universitat Politècnica de
   Catalunya
Dept. Matemàtica Aplicada IV
C. Jordi Girona 1-3
08034 Barcelona
Spain
jherranz@ma4.upc.es

AI&KP ISSN 1610-3947
ISBN 978-1-4471-2579-2   ISBN 978-1-84996-238-4 (eBook)
DOI 10.1007/978-1-84996-238-4
Springer London Dordrecht Heidelberg New York

British Library Cataloguing in Publication Data
A catalogue record for this book is available from the British Library

Springer is part of Springer Science+Business Media (www.springer.com)

"No one shall be subjected to arbitrary interference with his privacy, family, home or correspondence, nor to attacks upon his honour and reputation. Everyone has the right to the protection of the law against such interference or attacks"
Article 12 of Universal Declaration of Human Rights (1948)

Foreword

As depicted in David Lodge's celebrated novel *Small World*, the perceived size of our world experienced a progressive decrease as jet airplanes became affordable to ever greater shares of the earth's population. Yet, the really dramatic shrinking had to wait until the mid-1990s, when Internet became widespread and the information age stopped being an empty buzzword. But small is not necessarily beautiful. We now live in a global village and, alas, some (often very powerful) voices state that we ought not expect any more privacy in it. Should this be true, we would have created our own nightmare: a global village combining the worst of conventional villages, where a lot of information on an individual is known by the other villagers, and conventional big cities, where the invidual feels lost in a grim and potentially dangerous place.

Whereas security is essential for organizations to survive, individuals and sometimes even companies also need some privacy to develop comfortably and lead a free life. This is the reason why individual privacy is mentioned in the Universal Declaration of Human Rights (1948) and data privacy is protected by law in most Western countries. Indeed, without privacy, the rest of fundamental rights, like freedom of speech and democracy, are impaired. The outstanding challenge is to create technology that implements those legal guarantees in a way compatible with functionality and security.

This book edited by Dr. Javier Herranz and Dr. Jordi Nin is devoted to edge-cutting data privacy technologies devised to cope with the huge automated private data collection inherent to the information society. Indeed, electronic transactions over the Internet, mobile phones, etc., result in vast amounts of data being collected which add to the data traditionally collected by government agencies. If no special protective action was taken, pooling all those data would allow creating fairly accurate profiles of each citizen or consumer. Yet, the (avowable) purpose of data collection is not profiling specific individuals: rather, it is conducting statistical and/or data mining analyses in view of extracting knowledge on general trends or relationships between variables. Such analytical goals must be, and they actually are, compatible with the privacy of the individual people or organizations to which the data relate.

The first part of the book gives an overview on privacy-preserving data management. Then there is a part devoted to statistical disclosure control, which aims at conciliating the utility of statistical data (whether microdata or tabular data) expected by users with a sufficiently low disclosure risk required by respondents to whom the data correspond. The last part of the book deals with preserving privacy in a number of applications, like data mining, data sharing, and social networks. Hence, the book is accessible and relevant to a broad audience, including statisticians, data managers, data miners, privacy experts, and computer scientists in general.

For a long time already, it has been my pleasure to do research with the coeditors and with several chapter contributors of this book. They are a fine blend of computer scientists doing research in database security and privacy, academic statisticians specializing in statistical disclosure control, and practitioners in data management and software development. Knowing nearly all of them professionally, I have every reason to expect that the reader will benefit from their proficiency and their communication skills in the area of private data management.

Tarragona, 6th January 2010   Josep Domingo-Ferrer
(The Three Wise Men's Day)   Chairholder
                                                        UNESCO Chair in Data Privacy
                                              Department of Computer Engineering
                                                                    and Mathematics
                                                            Tarragona, Catalonia

Acknowledgments

First of all, we want to thank the authors who accepted our invitation to prepare a chapter for this book. They did a great job, first by writing very interesting chapters and then by taking into account the comments that they got from the reviewers. They followed the guidelines and deadlines that we set, and in general, they made our editing work quite handy.

We are also indebted to the external people who helped us to review the preliminary versions of the chapters. The list of reviewers is small, but their contribution has been really big. They are Mark J. Elliot, Vicenç Torra, and Alexandre Viejo. Special thanks also go to Prof. Josep Domingo-Ferrer for writing the foreword of the book.

We would also like to thank the support that we have received from Springer, personified by Rebecca Mowat and Beverley Ford.

Regarding institutional acknowledgments, the work of the two editors is supported by different public institutions. Both of them are supported by Spanish MEC Ministry (project ARES – CONSOLIDER INGENIO 2010 CSD2007-00004). Javier Herranz enjoys a *Ramón y Cajal* grant, partially funded by the European Social Fund (ESF), from Spanish MICINN Ministry. Jordi Nin is supported by the European Community through the 7th Framework Programme Marie Curie Intra-European fellowship, contract No 235226.

Contents

Part III Preserving Privacy in Distributed Applications

Contributors

Elisa Bertino Department of Computer Science and CERIAS, Purdue University, 250 N. University Street, West Lafayette, IN, USA, bertino@cs.purdue.edu

Barbara Carminati Dipartimento di Informatica e Comunicazione, Università degli Studi dell'Insubria, Via Mazzini 5, 21100 Varese, Italy, barbara.carminati@uninsubria.it

Jordi Castro Department of Statistics and Operations Research, Universitat Politècnica de Catalunya, C. Jordi Girona 1-3, 08034 Barcelona, Catalonia, jordi.castro@upc.edu

Loredana di Consiglio Istituto Nazionale di Statistica, Roma, Italy, diconsig@istat.it

Elena Ferrari Dipartimento di Informatica e Comunicazione, Università degli Studi dell'Insubria, Via Mazzini 5, 21100 Varese, Italy, elena.ferrari@uninsubria.it

David Galindo University of Luxembourg, Luxembourg, david.galindo@uni.lu

Javier Herranz Departament de Matemàtica Aplicada IV, Universitat Politècnica de Catalunya, C. Jordi Girona 1-3, Mòdul C3, 08034 Barcelona, Catalonia, jherranz@ma4.upc.edu

Wei Jiang Department of Computer Science, Missouri Science and Technology University, 500 West 15th Street, Rolla, MO, USA, wjiang@cs.mst.edu

Vishal Kapoor Microsoft, One Microsoft Way, Redmond, WA - 98052, USA, vishal.kapoor@microsoft.com

Bernhard Meindl Department of Register, Classification and Methodology, Statistics Austria, Guglgasse 13, A-1110 Vienna, Austria, bernhard.meindl

Jordi Nin Universitat Politècnica de Catalunya, Dept. Arquitectura de Computadors, C. Jordi Girona 1-3, 08034 Barcelona, Spain, nin@ac.upc.edu

Silvia Polettini Dipartimento di Scienze Statistiche, Università degli Studi di Napoli Federico II, Napoli, Italy, s.polettini@unina.it

Pascal Poncelet LIRMM UMR CNR5 5506, 161 Rue Ada, 34392, Montpellier Cedex 5, France, poncelet@lirmm.fr

Natalie Shlomo Southampton Statistical Sciences Research Institute, University of Southampton, Southampton, SO17 1BJ, UK, n.shlomo@soton.ac.uk

Maguelonne Teisseire UMR TETIS, Maison de la Télédetection, 500, rue J.F. Breton 34093, Montpellier Cedex 5, France, teisseire@teledetection.fr

Mathias Templ Department of Statistics and Probability Theory, Vienna University of Technology, Wiedner Hauptstr. 7, A-1040 Vienna, Austria; Department of Register, Classification and Methodology, Statistics Austria, Guglgasse 13, A-1110 Vienna, Austria, templ@tuwien.ac.at

Alberto Trombetta Dipartimento di Informatica e Comunicazione, Università degli Studi dell'Insubria, Via Mazzini 5, 21100 Varese, Italy, alberto.trombetta@uninsubria.it

Francois Trousset EMA-LGI2P/EERIE, Parc Scientifique Georges Besse, 30035 Nîmes Cedex, France, Francois.Trousset@mines-ales.fr

Eric R. Verheul Radboud University Nijmegen & PricewaterhouseCoopers Advisory, The Netherlands, eric.verheul@nl.pwc.com, cs.ru.nl

Part I
Overview

Chapter 1
Introduction to Privacy and Anonymity in Information Management Systems

Javier Herranz and Jordi Nin

Abstract This first chapter is thought as a quick guide to the reader of the book. It contains a summary of the contents of each chapter. Before that, we explain the motivations that led to the edition of this book, the importance of the topics discussed in it, and the intended/expected audience.

1.1 Background and Motivation

The development of information technologies in the last years is unquestionable. Large amounts of data are collected and stored by both public institutions and private companies everyday. This collection of data has always a more or less specific goal. A first example of such goal is security: information about people, purchases, trips, personal communications, etc., is stored to decrease or detect possible security risks for the societies or to implement control policies.

Another example of a goal when collecting data is more oriented to business. Private companies collect information about clients, about other companies and products, in such a way that they can classify or predict clients' behaviors (data mining), they can compare themselves with rival companies, etc. All this information is useful to determine the market strategies to be followed.

Finally, a last canonical example of collection and storing of data is more related to research goals. Medical institutions or statistical agencies, among others, collect and disseminate data so that not only themselves but also external analysts can use this data for research purposes, for decision making, or for any other use.

All these examples illustrate the benefits that a society can globally (or partially) obtain from the development of information technologies. However, if no care is taken when collecting, storing, and disseminating data, then there are clear threats to the privacy of citizens. For example, if a hospital publicly disseminates data about

J. Herranz (✉)
Department of Matemàtica Aplicada IV, Universitat Politècnica de Catalunya,
C. Jordi Girona 1-3, Mòdul C3, 08034 Barcelona, Catalonia
e-mail: jherranz@ma4.upc.edu

J. Nin, J. Herranz (eds.), *Privacy and Anonymity in Information Management Systems*,
Advanced Information and Knowledge Processing,
DOI 10.1007/978-1-84996-238-4_1, © Springer-Verlag London Limited 2010

its patients, with the honest goal of helping pharmaceutical research and progress, confidential information about illnesses and treatments of specific patients may be leaked.

There is thus a delicate trade-off between the use of digital data (for security, progress, research, competitiveness) and the privacy of the citizens. Many documents (from the Universal Declaration of Human Rights by the United Nations to local laws) clearly protect the privacy of people, but the (non-) fulfillment of these laws is not always easy to check or detect. Ensuring privacy for individuals in a society, when dealing with digital information, is a task which involves many agents: politicians, legal authorities, managers, developers, system administrators, etc.

This book deals with the most technical part of this "privacy cycle", mostly related to computer science: the process by which different privacy mechanisms are motivated, designed, analyzed, tested, and finally implemented in companies or institutions. The intended audience of the book is sparse, although more or less centered around this technical area of computer science. On the one hand, any person working as an analyst, developer, administrator, etc. in the computer science department of a public institution or a private company which must deal with private, confidential data should be potentially interested in reading (some parts of) the book. The chapters are quite self-contained and are written with a very accessible language, also for non-experts in the area.

On the other hand, researchers from universities or from R&D departments who work in privacy and anonymity topics would clearly benefit from reading this book, because it provides a quite wide perspective of different privacy problems and solutions that are considered in real life today, in different scenarios.

1.2 Organization of the Book

Chapter 2 is really a great starting point for the book. After explaining the delicate frontier between privacy and utility of confidential information, Alberto Trombetta, Wei Jiang, and Elisa Bertino survey a large amount of techniques that are used to anonymize data and to ensure privacy when different data mining operations are performed.

The rest of chapters have been organized in two parts. Part II contains four chapters dealing with the problem of statistical disclosure control (SDC): how to modify data sets that contain statistical information before publicly releasing this modified data set, in such a way that privacy of the confidential original information is preserved? Finally, Part III contains three chapters, each of them dealing with a specific distributed application involving privacy: different agents have private inputs and they want to cooperate to run some protocol in their own interest, without revealing unnecessary parts of their private inputs.

1.2.1 Part II: Theory of SDC

Chapter 3, written by Mathias Templ and Bernhard Meindl, is a perfect combination of theoretical description of SDC protection methods and real implementations of such methods, for both microdata and tabular data. This chapter is very recommendable for both readers who want to have a first contact with SDC protection methods and developers who want to know how these methods have to be implemented.

When a data set is protected by a SDC method and then published, there is always a risk that intruders can combine this data set with other existing information and extract confidential information. There are different approaches to measure this risk.

Natalie Shlomo, in Chapter 4, and Silvia Polettini and Loredana Di Consiglio, in Chapter 5, explain, discuss, compare, and analyze some of these approaches to estimate or measure the risk associated to a protected data set. The results and recommendations in these two chapters should be very important for statistical agencies, hospitals, or any other public institution which has to release data, because a good risk estimation must always be done before publishing a protected data set.

Whereas these three chapters focus mostly on microdata (that is, standard data sets containing values for different variables of different records), Jordi Castro deals with tabular data in Chapter 6. Tabular data is data that have been obtained from standard data sets by crossing different variables; this kind of data representation is very common in statistical research. A tabular data can also leak information about the values of the original variables (before crossing). This chapter is a very nice survey of different protection techniques and risk measures that are specific to tabular data.

1.2.2 Part III: Preserving Privacy in Distributed Applications

Chapter 7 has been written by Vishal Kapoor, Pascal Poncelet, Francois Trousset, and Maguelonne Teisseire. They consider the problem of sequential pattern mining in a distributed scenario: different agents hold different parts of a database, and they want to detect sequential patterns that appear very often in the global database, without revealing anything else about the database. The authors describe and analyze a solution for this problem, PriPSec.

David Galindo and Eric Verheul consider in Chapter 8 another practical situation involving privacy and different agents. Entities collect (confidential) data from citizens into data sets and then construct pseudonymized versions of these data sets that can be sent to analysts or researchers without compromising the privacy of the citizens. Furthermore, some mechanisms can be added to allow some mining operations on different data sets. In particular, two different analysts holding different pseudonymized data sets can obtain run a protocol to obtain the information about citizens who are included in both data sets, without revealing the identity of these citizens nor information about other citizens. The solutions described in the chapter employ cryptographic primitives in a very comprehensive way.

The last chapter of this book is Chapter 9, written by Barbara Carminati and Elena Ferrari. They consider one of the hottest topics related to privacy nowadays: ensuring privacy when implementing access control policies in social networks. The chapter presents a nice survey of the state of the art in this topic, by describing the general problem and the differences between traditional access control and access control in online social networks. Authors discuss which privacy threats appear in this context, how these threats are dealt with by existing proposals offering some kind of privacy, and what is still to be done in this fascinating and currently very active research area.

Chapter 2
Advanced Privacy-Preserving Data Management and Analysis

Alberto Trombetta, Wei Jiang, and Elisa Bertino

Abstract The collection of large amounts of users' sensible data by services providers such as Google, Yahoo, or Facebook poses several relevant and challenging issues. A particularly relevant problem is how to ensure a suitable degree of statistical analysis over such data without disrupting user privacy. Toward this end, in the past few years several anonymization and privacy-preserving data mining techniques have been proposed. In this work, we propose a survey of such methodologies and techniques with a particular focus on advanced topics, such as privacy preserving management of time-varying anonymized data and privacy-preserving data mining over distributed data.

2.1 Introduction

At the present days, it is widely accepted that data repositories represent an important asset for many applications and thus their security is crucial. Data confidentiality is particularly relevant because of the value – not only monetary – that data have. For example, medical data collected by following the clinical history of the patients over several years may represent an invaluable asset that needs to be adequately protected. Such a requirement has motivated a large variety of approaches aiming at better protecting data confidentiality and data ownership. Relevant approaches include query processing techniques for encrypted data and data watermarking techniques. However, data confidentiality is not the only requirement to be addressed.

Nowadays, there is an increased concern for privacy. The availability of huge numbers of databases recording a large variety of information about individuals makes it possible to discover information about specific individuals by simply correlating a certain number of available databases. Although confidentiality and privacy are often used as synonyms, they are different concepts: data confidentiality is about the difficulty (or impossibility) by an unauthorized user to learn any information about data stored in the database. Usually, confidentiality is achieved by enforcing

A. Trombetta (✉)
Dipartimento di Informatica e Comunicazione, Università degli Studi dell'Insubria,
Via Mazzini 5, 21100 Varese, Italy
e-mail: alberto.trombetta@uninsubria.it

J. Nin, J. Herranz (eds.), *Privacy and Anonymity in Information Management Systems*,
Advanced Information and Knowledge Processing,
DOI 10.1007/978-1-84996-238-4_2, © Springer-Verlag London Limited 2010

an access policy and possibly using cryptographic tools. Privacy relates to what data can be safely disclosed without leaking sensitive information about the legitimate owner.

In the past years a wide variety of privacy-preserving techniques have been developed with the aim to making more difficult to link sensitive information to specific individuals. At a fairly abstract level, most of the proposed techniques operate some kind of transformation on the original data in order to perform privacy preservation. Typically, such techniques add some noise or perform some kind of aggregation on the original data in order to obtain an obfuscated version to be published, aiming at reducing the risk of privacy loss. This obfuscation process results in somewhat decreased data utility as well as in a decreased effectiveness in data management tasks. This is an unavoidable trade-off between data utility and privacy. In this chapter, we start by reviewing the two most relevant approaches used for such anonymization task: the (i) randomization-based approach and the (ii) aggregate-based approach, which will be briefly presented here and discussed in more depth in Section 2.2.1 and in Section 2.2.2. We then proceed to review the various approaches aimed at allowing some useful data analysis without disclosing private information.

Randomization-based anonymization techniques usually add noise (drawn from some publicly known distribution) to the data in order to mask individual values. Therefore, such techniques are designed to derive aggregate distributions from the perturbed individual values [9, 16]. Aggregate-based anonymization techniques operate over the granularity of the original data. The granularity is usually reduced by generalizing or suppressing carefully chosen values contained in the original data records. In the k-anonymization approach, the resulting anonymized data are aggregated into groups of at least k uniformly anonymized records having matching non-anonymized values [38]. In this way, the identification of single record is prevented. Subsequent enhancements – e.g., l-diversity approach [31] – of the k-anonymity approach have addressed some of its weaknesses regarding the fact that preventing the identification of single records does not necessarily amount to learn its sensitive values.

Although such approaches – both randomization-based and aggregation-based techniques – have brought significant advances of our understanding of how to protect data in order to avoid privacy loss, nevertheless they make restrictive assumptions as to whether anonymized data may change or anonymized data may be distributed across multiple, disconnected repositories. This clearly limits the effectiveness of the proposed approaches when applied in real-world scenarios, in which data may vary (and such changes have to be reported in a consistent way upon the anonymized version) or different organizations need to share and integrate the anonymized versions of their own data. These issues have recently spurred an intense research activity, whose results we survey in the second part of this chapter, in Sections 2.3 and 2.4 respectively. The techniques developed for protecting the privacy of time-varying data can be roughly divided into two broad groups, depending on whether data are continuously released in a stream and – consequently – anonymized, or whether data are produced in subsequent releases and are to be anonymized in order to prevent correlations among different releases.

Concerning the privacy-preserving data analysis techniques we present in the remaining part of this chapter, we consider the case in which the data set is vertically or horizontally partitioned and the respective owners aim at extracting some useful information from the entire data set without revealing their data. Various kind of privacy-preserving data mining tasks can be performed, such as clustering, association rule mining, decision tree computations, and set intersection [2, 8, 11]. The techniques adopted to ensure that no sensitive information is leaked during such data mining tasks are mainly cryptographic ones (e.g., homomorphic encryption or probabilistic encryption).

In Section 2.2 an overview of the main approaches deployed for anonymizing static data sets is given; in Section 2.3, the main approaches and techniques addressing the anonymization of time-varying data sets are considered; in Section 2.4 a survey of the main techniques for performing data analysis in a privacy-preserving way is presented; finally in Section 2.5 we draw our conclusions.

2.2 Managing Anonymized Data

In the recent years many data anonymization techniques has been investigated in order to preserve privacy. In the following, we survey the state of the art of the most relevant models and algorithms for anonymizing a given data set.

We will consider two broad categories of methods for anonymizing data: (i) randomization-based methods, (ii) group-based methods (of which k-anonymity is the most widely known example).

2.2.1 Randomization-Based Anonymization Techniques

Randomization approaches for anonymizing data have been proposed in contexts where it is acceptable to have imprecise, aggregate answers (up to a certain level determined by privacy concerns) based on distorted data with noise coming from certain, well-chosen probability distributions. Such approaches can be further divided into additive-based and multiplicative-based.

The additive-based randomization approach for anonymizing a given data set is the most widely adopted approach and it can be described in the following way. Consider a set of data items $DB = \{t_1, \ldots, t_n\}$. To every data item x_i noise component n_i is added, drawn from a probability distribution $f_N(y)$. Each noise component is drawn independently. The distorted data items are thus $d_1, \ldots, d_n$, where d_i denotes the perturbed data item $t_i + n_i$. It is usually assumed that the variance of the probability distribution from which noise components are extracted is large enough so that the original data items cannot by easily guessed from the distorted data set. What is published is the distorted data set $\{d_1, \ldots, d_n\}$. We denote with O the random variable associated with the distribution of the original data items, with N the random variable of the distribution of the noise components, and with

D the random variable of the distribution of the distorted data items. The relation linking such random variables is $O + N = D$ (from which, of course, one deduces $O = D - N$). Remember that n samples – that is, the distorted data items – of the distribution D are publicly known, as well as the distribution N of the noise components.

The multiplicative-based randomization approach is an alternative way to distort data items using noise components drawn from a probability distribution. The foundational work in this area is [22], in which – given a data set represented as a set of points in a (typically very high) multidimensional metric space – the authors show how to perform transformations on such data set in order to obtain a corresponding data set of reduced dimensionality in which the data items approximately maintain the distances they have in the original data set. In this way, the data set having reduced dimensionality can be used as an anonymized version of the original, high-dimensional data set in data mining tasks.

Both the additive- and multiplicative-based randomization approaches suffer from various kind of attacks aimed at reconstructing the distribution O of the original data set starting from the approximate distribution D. Regarding the additive-based approach, in order to learn information about the distribution of O (corresponding to the original data items), one starts by collecting enough distorted data items. In this way, for n large enough, the distribution of D can be well approximated. After that, it suffices to subtract N from the approximate distribution of D. There are various, more advanced techniques which are suitable for this task such as the iterative methods discussed in [2]. Note, however, that one can learn the distribution O of the original data set and individual record cannot be accessed. With respect to the multiplicative-based approach, if the attacker has some a priori knowledge about the original, non-anonymized data set – such as some linearly independent records coming from the original data set and their corresponding perturbed counterparts – then using linear algebra techniques one can gain information about the transformation. Similarly, if the attacker knows some records coming from the same distribution from which the original data set is drawn, then using principal component analysis techniques information about the original data set can be inferred.

Another randomization-based approach which does not fall into addition- and multiplication-based approaches is data swapping. Assuming that the data set to be anonymized is in tabular form, data swapping-based techniques shuffle sensitive values among different rows in order to obfuscate the relationship between such values and row identifiers. Still, such swapping preserves some useful statistics, such as those found in the marginal tables. See [10] for a recent comparison of the original proposal of data swapping with more recent techniques.

While subject to different kind of attacks, randomization-based approaches are relatively simple to implement, since the anonymization is done on a single data item basis. That is, the anonymization process is done by distorting a single data item at time, in an independent way from all the others data items. This is not true for other approaches that we will present later on, which require the entire data set in order to yield a correct anonymization.

2.2.2 Aggregation-Based Anonymization Techniques

Anonymization techniques based on perturbing data with random noise suffer from two main drawbacks, namely that (i) it is extremely difficult to effectively obfuscate outlier records and (ii) it is not considered the possibility that individual, obfuscated records can be re-identified using publicly available, background information (this is particularly true in the case of outlier records). Therefore, a substantial research effort has been done in order to devise anonymization techniques aimed at aggregate anonymized data items into different, homogeneous groups. We will start by presenting the first – and most widely known – aggregation approach, namely k-anonymization. We then proceed to illustrate subsequent techniques proposed to overcome some serious drawbacks of the k-anonymization approach.

2.2.2.1 The k-Anonymity Approach

This approach is motivated by the simple observation that a widely adopted technique for anonymizing a tabular data set consists in removing some special attributes, called unique key identifiers (e.g., social security numbers) from data records. This however does not guarantee that the obtained records cannot effectively re-identified. In fact, there is a class of attributes that can still be useful to accurately pin down the identities associated with single records, usually having access to background information. Typical examples of such attributes are age, sex, and address. Such attributes are called *quasi-identifiers* and k-anonymization aims at reducing the identifiability of data records by modifying the values stored in them. More precisely, the k-anonymization technique transforms records from the original data set in order to produce different groups of records such that, for every record in each group, there are no less than $k - 1$ other records having the same values in the quasi-identifier attributes. The attributes not considered as quasi-identifiers are left unchanged and are usually called *sensitive* attributes. Having increased in this way the granularity of the information stored in the original data set, the k-anonymized data set is publicly released. Since its initial proposal, the k-anonymity approach has been widely investigated and a comprehensive survey is [9].

Typically, the k-anonymization of a data set is performed through a *generalization* process or – as an extreme case – a *suppression* process. Using generalization, the data values contained in the quasi-identifiers are replaced with more general values. For example, address information can be replaced with zip code, or age information can be replaced with a year range. Suppression is an extreme case of generalization, in which the original value is completely cancelled out. Methods other than generalization and suppression can be deployed, such as clustering-based techniques which replace quasi-identifier values within a group with a representative value (usually the mean value).

The k-anonymization technique has been first proposed in [38], where *domain generalization hierarchies* of the quasi-identifiers are introduced in order to output k-anonymized versions of the original tabular data set. In the same work, the authors propose the concept of *minimal k-generalization*, aiming at reducing as much as possible the information loss of the anonymized data set, while guaranteeing at the same time that such data set is k-anonymous. The problem of finding a minimal k-anonymization of a tabular data set is a difficult one and in [33] the authors prove that suppression-based k-anonymization is an NP-hard problem. However, such problem can be efficiently solved using approximation algorithms (as those presented in the last cited work) or heuristic-based methods, like the ones presented in [25, 26]. Unlike heuristic-based methods, approximation-based algorithms have precise measurements on how much approximate solutions are distant from optimal ones. At the moment, the best approximation-based algorithm for k-anonymization is reported in [35] and it provides an $O(\log(k))$ approximation. Regarding anonymization techniques based on methods other than generalization, in [16] an approximation-based algorithm for clustering quasi-identifier values is shown.

2.2.2.2 The l-Diversity and t-Closeness Approaches

The main drawback of the k-anonymization approach is that, while it is effective in not allowing the re-identification of single records, it may well be the case that a k-anonymized version of a data set still releases unintended information about it. First, if the attacker has background information about the anonymized data set, such knowledge can be used to extract useful information from such anonymized data set (as in the case of the perturbation-based approach). Second, if within a group all the (unmodified) values of a sensitive attribute coincide, then a very precise information about such sensitive attribute is released. The l-diversity approach [31] is such that – while guaranteeing that at least k records within a group have the same value on quasi-identifiers – it guarantees that within a group at least l records have *different* values on sensible attributes. As the number of sensitive attributes grows, the task of finding a proper l-diverse version of the original tabular data set becomes challenging, due to the dimensionality curse. Nevertheless, for reasonably low values of l (≤ 10), the performance is acceptable and with not much overhead with respect to standard k-anonymization procedures. The l-diversity approach assumes that the values of sensitive attributes are equally distributed. This is far from true, as real data may be highly skewed. The t-closeness approach addresses this issue by requesting that the distribution of a sensitive attribute as released in a anonymized version of the data set is within a threshold t from its real distribution [27].

2.3 Managing Time-Varying Anonymized Data

All the data anonymization approaches and techniques presented in Section 2.2 assume that the anonymized data set do *not* change over time and and – as such – it is published only once. Clearly, this is a quite restrictive assumption in real-world settings, in which data item may change or may be added frequently. Taking into account time-varying data sets in the anonymization process poses several nontrivial challenges ranging from preventing linkage of data items across different anonymized data sets to keeping updated statistics about such anonymized data sets.

Therefore, various research efforts have been made recently in order to propose solutions to the problem of how to efficiently and effectively anonymize time-varying data sets. Broadly speaking, the research efforts so far have focused on two different scenarios describing how data may change. In the first scenario, data are released in subsequent batches, each updating the preceding one, as discussed in Section 2.3.1. In the second scenario (described in Section 2.3.2), the data set is viewed as a stream in which every single data item may change in a continuous way. Such scenarios present distinctive problems and different techniques has been developed in order to cope with them, as we will see in the following.

2.3.1 Anonymizing Multiple Releases

When addressing the task of anonymizing different releases of a data set, possible approaches range from publishing the newly added – anonymized – data items, once the original, anonymized data set has been published, to entirely re-anonymize the updated data set. However, these solutions suffer from the following serious drawbacks: in the former case, there is a substantial possibility of degraded data quality. In fact, the major problem is that relatively small sets of data items are anonymized independently. In this way, the anonymization process may incur in a much more significant obfuscation of the data items compared to the one in which all the newly added data items are anonymized at once. In the latter case, the entire data set is re-anonymized whenever it is augmented with new data items. Although this approach can be easily implemented by using existing techniques, it has a significant drawback. In fact, even though each released data set – when independently observed – is guaranteed to be anonymous, the combination of several released data sets may be vulnerable to different kinds of inferences, allowing data item linking across multiple anonymized data sets. Thus, non-trivial techniques are to be devised to overcome these inferences. All the approaches we will consider in the following assume that data are stored in tabular form. It is to be noted that all the existing approaches addressing the problem of anonymizing time-varying data set extend some aggregation-based (e.g., k-anonymity or l-diversity) approach previously introduced.

In [51] the problem of preventing inferences able to link different data items across multiple anonymized tables is addressed assuming that the tables' attributes in two separate releases are projections of a unique underlying table. That is, two separate releases may share common attributes. Then the authors focus their attention on unwanted information leakages that may happen when two different released tables are joined. As such, an extension of k-anonymity, termed *sequential anonymity*, is introduced in order to guarantee that two sequential releases of the same data set (possibly defined over overlapping attributes) do not leak unwanted information on the sensitive data. The basic idea behind sequential anonymity is that, given two sequential releases T_1, T_2, the first release T_1 is generalized in a way that when joined with T_2 the resulting table does not allow the re-identification of its data items. Since this approach generalizes the k-anonymity approach, the authors show that finding an optimal generalization which is sequentially anonymous is NP-hard. Nevertheless, a greedy algorithm for finding minimal sequential anonymizations is given.

In [52], the principle of m-invariance is introduced, which is a new, generalization-based anonymization technique. Basically, m-invariance guarantees that all the quasi-identifier groups which a data item is generalized to in different releases are invariant in some precise way. Such anonymization approach is effective toward arbitrary (deletions included) updates of the initially released table. In this way, it is not possible to link different versions of the same data items contained in successive releases of the original table.

In the case of incremental, successive releases [6] of an original table, the problem of identifying and preventing cross-release inferences is addressed. Toward this end, a new generalization-based anonymity notion – called (k, c)-anonymity – blending both k-anonymity and l-diversity is introduced. This new kind of anonymization will then be used in order to anonymize every single release of an initial table. Such anonymization is performed in order to withstand different attack kinds, in which an attacker may dispose in different ways of the knowledge it has about the data released in different versions of the released table. The different attack kinds considered are *difference attacks*, in which the attacker may infer additional information about data items in addition to that allowed by the (k, c)-anonymization looking at data items contained in table release and not contained in another one; *intersection attacks*, in which the inference of additional information is based on the data items contained in the intersection of two different releases; *record-tracing attacks*, in which the attacker is able to uniquely identify data items, starting from the sensitive values contained in the anonymized versions of the data items. In order to prevent such attacks, efficient algorithms for detecting whether a given sequence of released table is subject to such attacks are presented.

In [12] a quite comprehensive set of possible attacks on two incremental, k-anonymized versions T_1, T_2 of an original table are presented and formalized. An attacker is supposed to have the following knowledge on such releases, namely every data item in T_1 corresponds to some data item in T_2 but the reverse is not true, that is, there is at least one data record contained in T_2 and not in T_1. Then, the following attacks are formalized: In a *forward attack*, the attacker aims at uniquely identifying a data item in T_1, having knowledge of the data items contained in T_2. In a *cross-attack*, the attacker aims at uniquely identifying a data item in T_2, knowing that such data item has been originally released in T_1. In a *backward attack*, the attacker aims at uniquely identifying a data item in T_2, having knowledge of the data items contained in T_1. It is then presented a generalization-based anonymization technique that ensures that its output is resistant to the previously described attacks.

A different approach is taken in [48], which aims at detecting what are the views over a unique, underlying table that leak unwanted information when joined and it is shown that showing exactly those "unsafe" views is very hard to compute. More specifically, this chapter addresses the problem of how to determine whether two or more views over the same underlying table may yield unwanted disclosure of the information. k-anonymity is taken as a measure of how much information disclosure is tolerated. That is, a set of views $V_1, \ldots, V_u$ is k-anonymous over a unique, secret table T (whose schema is publicly known) if the intersection of their results with particular views called *associations* (that is, views over an identifier and a sensitive attribute) contain no less than k elements. It can be shown that if the schema of T does not contain functional dependencies, then checking whether a set of views is k-anonymous can be done in polynomial time, with respect to the size of the input views. Otherwise, in presence of functional dependencies, the checking has very high complexity, namely it is Σ_2^p-hard. On the positive side, the complexity of checking k-anonymity becomes manageable (polynomial or easily approximable) in several practical cases, such as in the presence of a single functional dependency and without common attributes in the views, or when functional dependencies do not influence k-anonymity views. However, the authors do not give suggestions on how to prevent unwanted information leakages in this setting.

Finally, in [39] the problem of how to check in a privacy-preserving fashion whether the addition of a new data item to an already released k-anonymous data set disrupts its k-anonymity. This is done without accessing the actual content of the to-be-possibly-added data item using cryptographic techniques. The proposed techniques work for both suppression- and generalization-based k-anonymous data sets.

2.3.2 Anonymizing Data Streams

The main motivation behind the introduction of a data stream-based framework to study anonymization approaches is that, in many relevant settings, data are fed in a continuous way and it is not possible to continuously release new versions of the entire data set. Compared to the previously described approaches, there are some fundamental differences, namely, in a stream-based release of anonymized data (i) data items are not republished in multiple versions (hence an attacker cannot link different versions of the same data items); (ii) time is critical, in the sense as a new data item should be anonymized and published as soon as possible; (iii) it is not possible to deploy techniques scanning multiple times the entire data set (on the contrary, all the previously described approaches assume as feasible). As such, continuous privacy-preserving data publishing has recently been acknowledged as a challenging problem and several works have appeared addressing the issues just described. The totality of the works we consider present stream-based anonymization techniques based on the k-anonymity approach.

In [28], a model of stream-based anonymous data publishing is presented, in which every anonymized data item should be released within a specified time deadline.

In [7], a stream clustering technique is used in order to form clusters on the fly, while controlling the cluster size. Once a cluster contains at least k data items, it can be generalized and released. On the other side, if all the data items contained in a cluster of size less than k are approaching the time deadline, then such cluster is merged with some neighbor cluster, generalized, and then published in order to meet the releasing time deadline. The problem of measuring the information loss derived from a missed cluster release is not addressed.

In [23] a k-anonymization-based technique for a stream of data item is presented in which the data loss is mitigated by deferring the release of a cluster, in the case that such data loss is estimated to be high enough. The decision about deferring the release or releasing an anonymized version of a data items' cluster is taken by a randomized procedure, which takes into account the distribution of the data items so far appeared in the stream.

2.4 Privacy-Preserving Data Analysis (PPDA)

In this section, the key focus on PPDA is in distributed environment where data are either horizontally or vertically distributed among more than two participating parties. Also, PPDA protocols presented here utilize cryptographic tools, e.g., probabilistic homomorphic encryption, and their tasks mainly fall into the following categories: association rule mining, clustering, decision tree computation, among others.

2.4.1 Privacy-Preserving Association Rule Mining

The association rules mining problem can be defined as follows [1]: Let $I = \{i_1, i_2, \ldots, i_n\}$ be a set of items. Let $\mathcal{D}$ be a set of transactions, where each transaction T is an itemset such that $T \subseteq I$. Given an itemset $X \subseteq I$, a transaction T *contains* X if and only if $X \subseteq T$. An association rule is an implication of the form $X \Rightarrow Y$ where $X \subseteq I, Y \subseteq I$, and $X \cap Y = \emptyset$. The rule $X \Rightarrow Y$ has *support* s in the transaction database $\mathcal{D}$ if $s\%$ of transactions in $\mathcal{D}$ contain $X \cup Y$. The association rule holds in the transaction database $\mathcal{D}$ with *confidence* c if $c\%$ of transactions in $\mathcal{D}$ that contain X also contain Y. An itemset X with k items is called k-itemset. The problem of mining association rules is to find all rules whose support and confidence are higher than certain user specified minimum support and confidence. In this simplified definition of the association rules, missing items and negative quantities are not considered. In this respect, transaction database $\mathcal{D}$ can be seen as $0/1$ matrix where each column is an item and each row is a transaction.

2.4.1.1 Horizontally Partitioned Data

The above problem of mining association rules can be extended to distributed environments. Let us assume that a transaction database $\mathcal{D}$ is horizontally partitioned among n parties where $\mathcal{D} = \mathcal{D}_1 \cup \mathcal{D}_2 \cup \cdots \cup \mathcal{D}_n$, and $\mathcal{D}_i$ resides at party i's site $(1 \leq i \leq n)$. Informally speaking, the global support is the sum of the local support of each site.

The itemset X has *local* support count of Support$(X, \mathcal{D}_i)$ at party i if Support$(X, \mathcal{D}_i)$ number of the transactions contain X. In association rule mining, an itemset is frequent only if its global support (that is, the percentage of transactions containing the itemset) is above a pre-defined threshold. That is, the *global* support count of X is given as $X.sup = \sum_{i=1}^{n}$ Support$(X, \mathcal{D}_i)$. An itemset X is *globally supported* if Support$(X) \geq s \cdot \sum_{i=1}^{n} |\mathcal{D}_i|$. Global confidence of a rule $X \Rightarrow Y$ can be given as Support$(X \cup Y)/$Support(X).

The set of large itemsets $L_{(k)}$ consists of all k-itemsets that are globally supported. The aim of distributed association rule mining is to find the sets $L_{(k)}$ for all $k > 1$ and the support counts for these itemsets, and from this, association rules with the specified minimum support and confidence can be computed. A fast algorithm for distributed association rule mining on horizontally partitioned data is given in Cheung et al. [8]. Their procedure, denoted as FDM, is summarized below.

1. *Candidate sets generation*: Generate candidate sets $CG_{i(k)}$ based on $GL_{i(k-1)}$, itemsets that are supported by the S_i at the $(k-1)$th iteration, using the classic a priori candidate generation algorithm. Each party generates candidates based on the intersection of globally large $(k-1)$ itemsets and locally large $(k-1)$ itemsets.
2. *Local pruning*: For each $X \in CG_{i(k)}$, scan the database $\mathcal{D}_i$ at party i to compute Support$(X, \mathcal{D}_i)$. If X is locally large S_i, it is included in the $LL_{i(k)}$ set. It is clear that if X is supported globally, it will be supported in one party's database.
3. *Support count exchange*: $LL_{i(k)}$ are broadcast, and each party computes the local support for the items in $\cup_i LL_{i(k)}$.
4. *Broadcast mining results*: Each party broadcasts the local support for itemsets in $\cup_i LL_{i(k)}$. From this, each party is able to compute $L_{(k)}$.

In [24], authors discuss how to convert the FDM algorithm to a privacy-preserving association rule mining algorithm. As discussed in this chapter, to enable privacy-preserving version, it is enough to privately check whether a local large itemset $LL_{i(k)}$ is globally supported. To achieve this, each site first obtains a union of $LL_{i(k)}$ using commutative encryption techniques. Then $L_{(k)}$ is calculated via secure sum and secure comparison protocols based on the following observations:

$$\text{Support}(X, \mathcal{D}) \geq s * |\mathcal{D}| = s \cdot \sum_{i=1}^{n} |\mathcal{D}_i|,$$

$$\sum_{i=1}^{n} (\text{Support}(X, \mathcal{D}_i) - s \cdot |\mathcal{D}_i|) \geq 0.$$

Using the secure sum and secure comparison protocols, frequent association rules can be generated. Note that this protocol requires that the number of participating parties should be at least three. In addition, it is not *completely* secure under the semi-honest model since the protocol discloses the number of commonly supported itemsets.

2.4.1.2 Vertically Partitioned Data

Given the transaction database $\mathcal{D}$ as 0/1 matrix, where each column is an item and each row is a transaction, the $\mathcal{D}$ is considered vertically partitioned if different parties know different columns of the $\mathcal{D}$. To mine association rules over vertically partitioned data, it has been shown that you need to calculate a dot product with 0/1 vectors, where each vector represents whether a certain set of items are present in a transaction or not [40]. To compute the dot product securely, probabilistic homomorphic public key encryptions can be adopted, e.g., Paillier [34]. Suppose E is such an encryption scheme, it has the following properties:

- The encryption function is injective, i.e., $\forall x_1, x_2 \in X$, $E(x_1) = E(x_2) \Rightarrow x_1 = x_2$;
- The encryption function is additive homomorphic, i.e., $\forall x_1, x_2 \in RX$, $E(x_1) \times E(x_2) = E(x_1 + x_2)$;
- The encryption function has semantic security as defined in [15], e.g., a set of ciphertexts do not provide additional information about the plaintext to an adversary with polynomial-bounded computing power.

Using these properties, detailed privacy-preserving protocols on mining association rules in vertically partitioned environment are presented in [13, 53]. These protocols are secure under the semi-honest model and work for two or more participating parties. Using zero-knowledge proofs [14] under the random oracle model [5], these protocols can be transformed into secure protocols under the malicious model and the accountable computing (AC) framework [20, 21], where the AC framework does not enforce honest behaviors but it can detect any malicious behaviors after the execution of a secure protocol.

A related problem is to mine frequent patterns without inference problem, and a specific example is given in [3, 4]. Informally speaking, given the pattern $a_1 \wedge a_2 \wedge a_3 \wedge a_4$ holds for 80 individuals and the pattern $a_1 \wedge a_2 \wedge a_3$ holds for 81 individuals, we can infer that there is only one individual in the data set for whom the pattern $a_1 \wedge a_2 \wedge a_3 \wedge \neg a_4$ holds. The knowledge inferred poses potential threat to the anonymity of that individual. To solve this problem, privacy-preserving protocols were proposed in [18] based on the DkA framework [19] to mine frequent association rules without the inference problems described above.

2.4.2 Privacy-Preserving Classification

Classification plays an important role in data mining. In general, a model or model parameters are learned from training data, and the learned models will be used to classify new data into pre-defined classes. Here, we assume data that are represented in relational format where each row is one data record or tuple and each column is an attribute describing certain properties or information of each data tuple. One of the attribute is called the class attribute. To learn or build a classifier, the class attribute is known in the training data set. Then the classifier is used to predict the value of the class attribute of a new data tuple based on other attributes. Common classification learning methods are decision tree, Naive Bayes, and support vector machine.

2.4.2.1 Decision Tree Classifier

Horizontally Partitioned Data

A well-known classification algorithm is ID3 [36] used to generate a decision tree classifier. Each node in a decision tree is an attribute. The tree is built from top to bottom recursively, and the key at each stage is to pick the best attribute to classify the data based on information gain. Let T denote a set of data tuples with a set of attributes $A = \{A_1, A_2, \ldots, A_m, A_c\}$, where A_c is the class attribute having k distinct values $a_{c1}, a_{c2}, \ldots, a_{ck}$. Let $T(a_{ci})$ denote the set of tuples with class value a_{ci}, and suppose A_j has l distinct values $a_{j1}, a_{j2}, \ldots, a_{jl}$. The entropy of T and the conditional entropy of T given A_j are defined as follows:

$$H(T) = -\sum_{i=1}^{k} \frac{|T(a_{ci})|}{|T|} \log \frac{|T(a_{ci})|}{|T|} \qquad H(T|A_j) = \sum_{i=1}^{l} \frac{|T(a_{ji})|}{|T|} H(T(a_{ji})).$$

Information gain is computed by $G(A) = H(T) - H(T|A_j)$. The attribute with the highest information gain is selected as the tree node at the current recursive call. Key steps of an ID3 algorithm is highlighted in Algorithm 1.

Algorithm 1: ID3-Tree(T, A)

  if $(A - \{A_c\} = \emptyset)$ **then**
    └ return a leaf-node with the majority class value in T.

  if *(all tuples in T have the same class value)* **then**
    └ return a leaf-node with the class value.

  else
    Suppose A_j, with attribute values $a_{j1}, \ldots, a_{jl}$, is the best attribute to classify tuples in T. Partition T into $T(a_{j1}), \ldots, T(a_{jl})$ such that every tuple in $T(a_{ji})$ has the attribute value a_{ji}.
    Return a tree with root labeled A_j and edges labeled $a_{j1}, \ldots, a_{jl}$ such that the edge a_{ji} goes to the tree ID3-Tree($T(a_{ji})$, $A - \{A_j\}$).

A privacy-preserving two-party protocol to generate an ID3 tree was proposed in [29, 30]. The protocol is secure under the semi-honest model. To build a tree securely, the key is to securely compute $(x_1 + x_2) \ln(x_1 + x_2)$ where x_b is the party P_b's private input. The computation returns two random shares y_1, y_2 such that $y_1 + y_2 \mod |\mathcal{F}| = (x_1 + x_2) \ln(x_1 + x_2)$. Using the protocol that securely computing $(x_1 + x_2) \ln(x_1 + x_2)$ with Yao's secure circuit evaluation techniques [29], the participating parties can find the best attribute without disclosing their private data. Although during each round, one attribute is disclosed to both parties, this does not affect the security of the protocol because these attributes are part of the tree, the final results. Therefore, the protocol completely secure under the semi-honest model.

Vertically Partitioned Data

To build a decision tree securely is more complicated when data are vertically partitioned. Privacy-preserving protocols to produce such a decision tree were presented in [43, 45]. In this problem domain, the schema information is assumed to be private, and only one site knows the class attribute. Each site has an identifier attribute that serves as a join key. The final tree is also privately distributed across individual sites. The main protocol consists of several sub-protocols, each of them is responsible for one particular task in Algorithm 1.

To accomplish the first step, the participating parties can use the secure sum protocol [24, 37] as follows: one party initiates the protocol by selecting a large random number and adds this number to the number of remaining attributes. At the end, this party and the last party use commutative encryption to check if $A - \{A_c\} = \emptyset$. To check if all tuples in T have the same class, each site needs to know how its data are partitioned at the current node. The concept of a constraint set is used to find a subset of the local data that needs to be considered at current iteration or node. Informally, a constraint set contains attribute values that defines a local/partial path of the tree leading to the current node. Then from the subset of the local data, class distribution counts at the current node can be collaborative computed. To protect individual site's privacy, secure set intersection protocols [11, 44] are adopted in calculating each class' distribution count. Note that class distribution counts are known to all sites. From this information, each site can determine the majority class and whether all tuples at the current node have the same class. In addition, information gain of a specific attribute can also be derived from the class distribution counts.

Since some intermediate results released are not part of the final results, additional approaches were given to make the protocol more secure. Also, because the final decision tree is privately distributed, classification steps were proposed to utilize the tree. Note that these protocols work for two or more participating parties.

2.4.2.2 Naive Bayes Classifier

The Naive Bayes classifier [32] is an effective learning method. Suppose data instances or tuples are in relational format $\langle a_1, \ldots, a_m \rangle$ (a_i denotes a particular value of attribute A_i). Based on a set of training data (the data with an additional class attribute A_c), using the classifier, we can predict the class value of a new data tuple. The Bayes classifier assigns the class value to the new data tuple if the class value c_j maximize the following probability: $P(c_j) \times \Pi_{i+1}^{m} P(a_i|c_j)$, where $P(a_i|c_j)$ is estimated from the training data and prior probability $P(c_j)$ can also be decided in certain way. For example, $P(a_i|c_j) = \frac{n_{ai}}{n_{cj}}$, where n_{cj} denotes the number of tuples having class value c_j, and n_{ai} denotes that among those n_{cj} tuples, the number of tuples having attribute value a_i. To securely build the Naive Bayes classifier, the key is to estimate $P(a_i|c_j)$ and $P(c_j)$ securely.

Horizontally Partitioned Data

In [46], protocols are proposed to securely build this classifier. Under this distributed environment, each party holds partial information for n_{ai} and n_{cj}. To compute these values securely, the participating parties can use the secure sum protocol. Once these values are available to all the parties, the corresponding probabilities can be derived easily. Since every party knows the schema of the data set, the parties are able to classify a new data tuple independently. However, because the values n_{ai} and n_{cj} are disclosed to all the parties, so this process of building a Naive Bayes classifier is not completely secure under the semi-honest model. To satisfy the security requirement, the key is to use the secure protocol for computing $\ln x$ [30]. Although the secure protocol computing $\ln x$ only works for two-party case, it is still applicable by transforming the multiparty computation of n_{ai} and n_{cj} into a two-party computation.

Vertically Partitioned Data

The protocol presented in [42, 46] assumes that only one party has the class attribute. The main idea is that at the end of the execution of the protocol, each party has shares of the conditionally independent probabilities that constitute the parameters of the classifier. The challenge is to compute these shares and classify a new tuple with these shares. Note that the individual probability $P(a_i|c_j)$ can be computed by $\frac{n_{ai}}{n_{cj}}$. Suppose Alice has the attribute A_i and Bob owns the class attribute. Initially, Alice constructs a vector corresponding to the entries in the training data. Set the entry value to 1 if the corresponding tuple has the value a_i, and set it to 0 otherwise. Bob sets up a similar vector with $\frac{1}{n_{cj}}$ for the entries with class value c_j and 0 for other entries. Then a secure dot product protocol can be adopted to generate random shares of the probability, and the secure protocol to compute $\ln x$ will be used to classify a new instance.

2.4.2.3 Support Vector Machines

Privacy-preserving support vector machine (SVM) protocols are proposed in [47, 49, 50]. Here, we only present their main ideas related to a linear kernel. In a linear binary classification task, an SVM identifies a separating plane/hyperplane that maximizes the margin, the distance from the closest points to the plane. To maximize the margin and minimize the error, the SVM solution can be formulated to the following dual problem by utilizing lagrange multipliers:

$$\min_{a} \left\{ \frac{1}{2} a^T Q a - e^T a \right\}, \quad \text{such that} \quad (0 \le a_i \le v) \wedge \left(\sum_{i=1}^{m} d_i a_i = 0 \right),$$

where d_i and a_i are the class label and the coefficient for a data vector x_i, and Q is an $m \times m$ matrix computed by the scalar product of every data tuple pair, i.e.,

$Q_{ij} = K(x_i, x_j)d_id_j$ and $K(x_i, x_j) = x_i \cdot x_j$ for linear SVM. The support vector x_i correspond to the positive coefficient a_i.

Vertically Partitioned Data

When data are vertically partitioned, the key is to compute the matrix Q secure, which is the same as computing $K(x_i, x_j)d_id_j$ securely. Since K is a Gram matrix, it can be computed from the local Gram matrices. For example, the data $m \times n$ matrix A is vertically partitioned into A_1 and A_2. Let K_1 and K_2 be the $m \times m$ Gram matrices of A_1 and A_2, i.e., $K_1 = A_1 \times A_1^T$ and $K_2 = A_2 \times A_2^T$. Then $K = K_1 + K_2$. Under the assumption that there are at least three participating parties, K can be securely generated using the secure sum protocol. K is released to every party, and each party will derive Q from K. Then the global SVM model can be computed at each individual party.

Using the SVM model to classify new data instances, dot products need to be computed between the support vectors and the new data instances. The classification function is defined as $f(x) = \sum_{i=1}^{m} a_i d_i K(x_i, x) - \varepsilon$, where x_i is the support vector and x is the new data instance. After training, each party has a_i, d_i, ε (the bias), and partial support vectors. Thus, to securely compute the dot product, secure addition of vectors is needed, and these vectors are dot products between a partial support vector and the new data instance.

Horizontally Partitioned Data

In this setting, training data are partitioned and distributed across multiple parties, assuming the class labels are the same for all these parties. To securely compute the Gram matrix Q, it is possible to use secure dot product protocols. An efficient secure dot product protocol was given in [49], which is used to produce Q.

2.4.3 Privacy-Preserving Clustering

Clustering is one of the most commonly adopted approach in data mining and can be roughly defined as the process of grouping different objects that are similar in some way. A cluster is then a group of object which are pair-wise similar and not similar to objects contained in other clusters. There is a huge number of clustering techniques and algorithms. We present here algorithms that have been modified in order to perform clustering over a data set, without directly accessing to it.

2.4.3.1 k-Means Clustering

Given a data set, the k-means algorithm first selects k data records, based on certain criteria, as the initial cluster centers. The remaining data are clustered depending on their distance to the current cluster centers. In general, a record is assigned to the closest cluster. Once all data are clustered, new cluster centers are computed. These steps are repeated until the new cluster centers are "close enough" to the previous cluster centers. The key to develop a secure k-means protocol includes securely computing the distance between a data record with each cluster centers, securely identifying the closest cluster and securely checking the stopping conditions.

Vertically Partitioned Data

A secure k-mean protocol was proposed in [41]. The protocol is secure under the semi-honest model and the number of participating parties should be at least three. During the execution of the protocol, each party knows a partial value of the current cluster centers. Let μ_{ij} denotes this partial value at jth cluster of party i. μ_{ij} is related to the attributes the party has. Thus, each party has partial information of the cluster centers. Initially, the parties arbitrarily assign values to μ_{ij} based on their local values. Then a secure sub-protocol is called on each data record to find the closest cluster to which it belongs. This sub-protocol works as follows: a party creates a column vector with k entries. The values at the jth entry indicate the distance of a given record t to the jth cluster center. Imagining that we combine these column vectors to generate a $k \times i$ matrix, and the goal is to find a row such that the sum of all its values is the smallest among all the rows. Then t will be assigned to the cluster corresponding to this row.

The following steps are necessary to find such a row: disguise the distance values of each vector with random values in a way that when the values at each row are summed up, these random values are cancelled out; when distances are compared, the parties only know the comparison results but not individual distance; the order of clusters are permuted so that the comparison results are meaningless. Detailed techniques, e.g., permutation algorithm, random value generation, are given in [41]. In addition, all the secure comparisons are done using Yao's technique. Once every t is clustered, new μ_{ij} can be computed locally. To check the stopping condition, a secure sum can be used along with a secure comparison.

Arbitrarily Partitioned Data

Suppose a data set has m attributes $A = \{A_1, \ldots, A_m\}$ and n records $t_1, \ldots, t_n$. The data set is arbitrarily partitioned between two parties if a party owns a portion of t projected on any subset of A. For example, let t be a record, Alice could own $t[A_1, \ldots, A_k]$ and Bob owns $t[A_{k+1}, \ldots, A_m]$. Alice could own t and Bob does not know t at all.

A two-party secure k-means protocol is proposed in [17]. The protocol is secure under the semi-honest model and assumes that the data are arbitrarily partitioned. The protocol consists of three sub and secure protocols: computing the closest cluster, recomputing the mean, and checking the termination condition. Initially, the cluster centers are shared between the two parties. Each party holds a random share of the center; that is, the sum of the shares will produce the correct cluster center. To find the closest cluster for a given tuple t, both parties need to compute the distance of t from each cluster center. The k distance values are also shared between the two parties in the same way as the cluster centers. The main components of the distance calculation involve a secure dot product protocol [13]. Once all the shares are computed, Yao's secure circuit evaluation technique [29] is used to find the minimum distance. Then t is assigned to the cluster with the minimum distance.

After all data are clustered, new cluster centers need to be derived. Since there are m attributes, each cluster center has m components. Let μ_{ij} denotes the jth component of cluster i. μ_{ij} can be computed by $\mu'_{ij} = \frac{p_j + q_j}{n_j^A + n_j^B}$, where p_j denotes the sum of the values corresponding to attribute A_j of all records in cluster i and n_j^A denotes the number of records in cluster i having values for attribute A_j. q_j and n_j^B are defined similarly for the other party. μ'_{ij} is computed by Yao's secure circuit evaluation technique. The protocol for checking termination status can also be achieved using Yao's technique.

2.4.3.2 Customized Clustering Algorithms

The recluster algorithm proposed in [16] is particularly designed in a way that it is easy to be transformed to a privacy-preserving clustering protocol. Recluster is a recursive algorithm. It first horizontally divides data into two halves, and each half will produce $2k$ clusters. At the end, the $2k$ clusters from each half is merged based on their proposed error metric into $2k$ clusters. Then these $2k$ clusters are merged again to produce the final k clusters.

To covert recluster into a two-party secure protocol, both parties initially call recluster to produce k local clusters on their data (Data are assumed to be horizontally partitioned). Then the local clusters are merged securely to produce k global clusters, and these cluster centers are shared between the two parties. Using additive homomorphic encryption techniques, e.g., [34], each party obtains random shares of the other party's local k cluster centers. From these shares and using Yao's secure circuit evaluation technique [29], the parties can find the best pair of clusters to merge to eventually produce k global cluster centers.

So far, we have shown techniques/protocols for association rule mining, classification, and clustering in the domain of privacy-preserving data mining. These are not meant to be complete but to provide some insight on the design of privacy-preserving protocols. In summary, many secure protocols use secure sub-protocols, such as secure sum, dot product, and secure comparison. If the functionality is simple and the input size is small, Yao's secure circuit evaluation technique can be used to implement secure protocols.

2.5 Conclusions

In the first part of this chapter we have reviewed the basic approaches and techniques employed for the anonymization of data sets. We have thus presented a variety of data obfuscation approaches such as randomization and generalization-based approaches. Such approaches have been thoroughly investigated and many variants of the most fundamental techniques have been presented. We then presented the most recent proposals dealing with the problem of data set anonymization in the context of time-varying data. Although the impressive progress is made in the very recent years, still much is to be done in order to have a general enough and usable approach. In the second part of the chapter, the most relevant privacy-preserving data mining techniques have been presented. This is a consolidated research area, as should be clear from the variety and depth of the proposed solutions.

References

1. Agrawal R. and Srikant R. Fast algorithms for mining association rules. In: *Proceedings of the 20th International Conference on Very Large Data Bases, 12–15 September, Santiago, Chile*, pp. 487–499, 1994.
2. Agrawal R. and Srikant R. Privacy preserving data mining. In: *Proceedings of the ACM SIG-MOD Conference*, Dallas, Texas, USA, 2000.
3. Atzori M., Bonchi F., Giannotti F., and Pedreschi D. Blocking anonymity threats raised by frequent itemset mining. In: *Proceedings of the 5th IEEE International Conference on Data Mining (ICDM 2005), 27–30 November 2005, Houston, Texas, USA*, IEEE Computer Society, Washington, DC, pp. 561–564, 2005.
4. Atzori M., Bonchi F., Giannotti F., and Pedreschi D. k-anonymous patterns. In: *Knowledge Discovery in Databases: PKDD 2005, 9th European Conference on Principles and Practice of Knowledge Discovery in Databases, Porto, Portugal, October 3–7, 2005, Proceedings*, Lecture Notes in Computer Science, Springer, Berlin, pp. 10–21, 2005.
5. Bellare M. and Rogaway P. Random oracles are practical: A paradigm for designing efficient protocols. In: *Proceedings of the First ACM Conference on Computer and Communications Security*, Fairfax, Virginia, USA, pp. 62–73, 1993.
6. Byun J.W., Li T., Bertino E., Li N., and Sohn Y. Privacy-preserving incremental data dissemination. *Journal of Computer Security* 17(1):43–68, 2009.
7. Cao J., Carminati B., Ferrari E., and Tan K.L. Castle: A delay-constrained scheme for k-anonymizing data streams. In: *Proceedings of IEEE ICED Conference*, Penang, Malaysia, 2008.
8. Cheung D.W.-L., Han J., Ng V., Fu A.W.-C., and Fu Y. A fast distributed algorithm for mining association rules. In: *Proceedings of the 1996 International Conference on Parallel and Distributed Information Systems (PDIS'96), December 1996, Miami Beach, Florida, USA*, IEEE, pp. 31–42.
9. Chin F. and Ozsoyoglu G. Auditing for secure statistical databases. In: *Proceedings of the ACM'81 Conference*, Los Angeles, California, USA, 1981.
10. Fienberg S. and McIntyre J. Data swapping: Variations on a theme by Dalenius and Reiss. In: *Proceedings of Privacy in Statistical Databases*, Barcelona, Spain, 2004.
11. Freedman M.J., Nissim K., and Pinkas B. Efficient private matching and set intersection. In: *Eurocrypt 2004, Interlaken, Switzerland, 2–6 May. International Association for Cryptologic Research (IACR)*, Interlaken, Switzerland, 2004.
12. Fung B.C.M., Wang K., Fu A.W.C., Pei J. Anonymity for continuous data publishing. In: *Proceedings of EDBT, ACM, ACM International Conference Proceeding Series*, Nantes, France, vol. 261, pp. 264–275, 2008.
13. Goethals B., Laur S., Lipmaa H., and Mielikainen T. On secure scalar product computation for privacy-preserving data mining. In: *The 7th Annual International Conference in Information Security and Cryptology (ICISC 2004), Seoul, Korea, 2–3 December* (eds. C. Park and S. Chee), pp. 104–120, 2004.

14. Goldreich O., Micali S., and Wigderson A. Proofs that yield nothing but their validity or all languages in NP have zero-knowledge proof systems. *Journal of the ACM*, 38:690–728, 1991.
15. Goldwasser S., Micali S., and Rackoff C. The knowledge complexity of interactive proof systems. In: *Proceedings of the 17th Annual ACM Symposium on Theory of Computing, Providence, Rhode Island, USA, 6–8 May*, pp. 291–304, 1985.
16. Jagannathan G., Pillaipakkamnatt K., and Wright R.N. A new privacy preserving distributed k-clustering algorithm. In: *Proceedings of the 2006 SIAM International Conference on Data Mining (SDM06)*, Bethesda, Maryland, USA, 2006.
17. Jagannathan G. and Wright R.N. Privacy-preserving distributed k-means clustering over arbitrarily partitioned data. In: *Proceedings of the 2005 ACM SIGKDD International Conference on Knowledge Discovery and Data Mining, Chicago, IL, 21–24 August*, pp. 593–599, 2005.
18. Jiang W. and Atzori M. Secure distributed k-anonymous pattern mining. In: *Sixth IEEE International Conference on Data Mining (ICDM06), Hong Kong, China, 18–22 December*, pp. 319–329, 2006.
19. Jiang W. and Clifton C. A secure distributed framework for achieving k-anonymity. *Special Issue of the VLDB Journal on Privacy-Preserving Data Management*, September 2006.
20. Jiang W. and Clifton C. AC-framework for privacy-preserving collaboration. In: *SIAM International Conference on Data Mining, Minneapolis, Minnesota, 26–28 April*, 2007.
21. Jiang W., Clifton C., and Kantarcioglu M. Transforming semi-honest protocols to ensure accountability. *Data and Knowledge Engineering*, 65(1):57–74, 2008.
22. Johnson W. and Lindenstrauss J. Extensions of Lipshitz mapping into Hilbert space. *Contemporary Mathematics*, 26:189–206, 1984.
23. Han Y., Pei J., Jiang B., Tao Y., and Jia Y. Continuous privacy preserving publishing of data streams. In: *Proceedings of EDBT, ACM, ACM International Conference Proceeding Series*, Saint-Petersburg, Russia, vol. 360, pp. 648–659, 2009.
24. Kantarcioglu M. and Clifton C. Privacy-preserving distributed mining of association rules on horizontally partitioned data. *IEEE Transactions on Knowledge and Data Engineering*, 16(9):1026–1037, September 2004.
25. LeFevre K, DeWitt D, and Ramakrishnan R. Incognito: Full domain k-anonymity. In: *Proceedings of ACM SIGMOD Conference*, Chicago, Illinois, USA, 2006.
26. LeFevre K., DeWitt D., and Ramakrishnan R. Mondrian multidomain k-anonymity. In: *Proceedings of IEEE ICDE Conference*, Istanbul, Turkey, 2007.
27. Li N., Li T., and Venkatasubramanian S. t-closeness: Privacy beyond k-anonymity and l-diversity. In: *Proceedings of IEEE ICED Conference*, 2007.
28. Li J., Ooi B.C., Wang W. Anonymizing streaming data for privacy protection. In: *Proceedings of IEEE ICDE Conference*, 2008.
29. Lindell Y. and Pinkas B. Privacy preserving data mining. In: *Advances in Cryptology – CRYPTO 2000, Springer-Verlag, Berlin, 20–24 August*, pp. 36–54, 2000.
30. Lindell Y. and Pinkas B. Privacy preserving data mining. *Journal of Cryptology*, 15(3): 177–206, 2002.
31. Machanavajjahala A., Gehrke J., Kifer D., and Venkitasubramanian M. l-diversity: Privacy beyond k-anonymity. In: *Proceedings of IEEE ICDE Conference*, 2006.
32. Mitchell T. *Machine Learning*. McGraw-Hill Science/Engineering/Math, New York, NY, 1st edition, 1997.
33. Meyerson A. and Williams R. On the complexity of optimal k-anonymity. In: *Proceedings of ACM PODS Conference*, 2006.
34. Paillier P. Public key cryptosystems based on composite degree residuosity classes. In: *Advances in Cryptology – Eurocrypt '99 Proceedings, Prague, Czech Republic, 2–6 May*, LNCS 1592, pp. 223–238, Springer-Verlag, Berlin, 1999.
35. Park H. and Shim K. Approximate algorithms for k-anonymity. In: *Proceedings of ACM SIGMOD Conference*, Beijing, China, 2007.
36. Quinlan J.R. Induction of decision trees. *Machine Learning*, 1(1):81–106, 1986.
37. Schneier B. *Applied Cryptography*. Wiley, New York, NY, 2nd edition, 1995.

38. Sweeney L. Achieving k-anonymity privacy protection using generalization and suppression. *International Journal of Uncertainty, Fuzziness and Knowledge-Based Systems*, 10(5): 571–588, 2002.
39. Trombetta A., Jiang W., Bertino E., Bossi L. Privately updating suppression and generalization based k-anonymous databases. In: *Proceedings of ICDE, IEEE*, Cancun, Mexico, pp. 1370–1372, 2008.
40. Vaidya J. and Clifton C. Privacy preserving association rule mining in vertically partitioned data. In: *The Eighth ACM SIGKDD International Conference on Knowledge Discovery and Data Mining, Edmonton, Alberta, Canada, 23–26 July*, pp. 639–644, 2002.
41. Vaidya J. and Clifton C. Privacy-preserving k-means clustering over vertically partitioned data. In: *The Ninth ACM SIGKDD International Conference on Knowledge Discovery and Data Mining, Washington, DC, 24–27 August*, pp. 206–215, 2003.
42. Vaidya J. and Clifton C. Privacy preserving naïve Bayes classifier for vertically partitioned data. In: *2004 SIAM International Conference on Data Mining, Lake Buena Vista, Florida, 22–24 April*, pp. 522–526, 2004.
43. Vaidya J. and Clifton C. Privacy-preserving decision trees over vertically partitioned data. In: *The 19th Annual IFIP WG 11.3 Working Conference on Data and Applications Security, Storrs, Connecticut, 7–10 August*, Springer, Berlin, 2005.
44. Vaidya J. and Clifton C. Secure set intersection cardinality with application to association rule mining. *Journal of Computer Security*, 13(4):593–622, November 2005.
45. Vaidya J., Clifton C., Kantarcioglu M., and Scott Patterson A. Privacy-preserving decision trees over vertically partitioned data. *ACM Transactions on Knowledge Discovery in Data*, 2(3):1–27, October 2008.
46. Vaidya J., Kantarcioglu M., and Clifton C. Privacy preserving naive Bayes classification. *International Journal on Very Large Data Bases*, 17(4):879–898, July 2008.
47. Vaidya J., Yu H., and Jiang X. Privacy preserving SVM classification. *Knowledge and Information Systems*, 14(2):161–178, February 2008.
48. Yao C, Wang XS, Jajodia S. Checking for k-anonymity violation by views. In: *Proceedings VLDB Conference*, Trondheim, Norway, 2005.
49. Yu H., Jiang X., and Vaidya J. Privacy-preserving SVM using nonlinear kernels on horizontally partitioned data. In: *SAC '06: Proceedings of the 2006 ACM Symposium on Applied Computing, ACM Press, New York, NY, USA*, pp. 603–610, 2006.
50. Yu H., Vaidya J., and Jiang X. Privacy-preserving SVM classification on vertically partitioned data. In: *Proceedings of PAKDD '06, volume 3918 of Lecture Notes in Computer Science, Springer-Verlag, Berlin, January*, pp. 647–656, 2006.
51. Wang K. and Fung B. Anonymizing sequential releases. In: *Proceedings ACM KDD Conference*, Philadelphia, Pennsylvania, USA, 2006.
52. Xiao X. and Tao Y. M-invariance: Towards privacy preserving re-publication of dynamic datasets. In: *Proceeding of SIGMOD Conference, ACM*, pp. 689–700, 2007.
53. Zhan J., Matwin S., and Chang L.W. Privacy-preserving collaborative association rule mining. In: *Proceedings of the 19th Annual IFIP WG 11.3 Working Conference on Database and Applications Security, Storrs, Connecticut, 7–10 August*, 2005.

Part II
Theory of SDC

Chapter 3
Practical Applications in Statistical Disclosure Control Using R

Mathias Templ and Bernhard Meindl

Abstract The aim is to show how statistical disclosure methods can be applied to data using the R-packages sdcMicro and sdcTable.

The reader of this chapter should be advised how popular methods in microdata protection and tabular protection can be applied within these packages to real-world data.

sdcMicro supports an exploratory approach for the anonymization of both categorical key variables and numerical variables. Hereby, global recoding, local suppression, and risk estimation can be applied interactively. Furthermore, various popular methods for microdata protection will be briefly described, but also some new methods for microdata protection and disclosure risk estimation considering real-life data problems will be introduced.

Additionally, a description of how tabular protection can be applied using the R-package sdcTable is given. The most challenging part from the user point of view is the preliminary data preparation before tabular protection can be applied. In this case, meta information about the hierarchical variables defining the table must be provided by the user.

3.1 Microdata Protection Using sdcMicro

Microdata protection has proved to be extremely popular and has grown extensively in the last few years, because of the significant rise in the demand for *scientific-use files* among researchers and institutions.

The aim and in many cases the legal obligation of data holders which want to disseminate microdata is to provide data for which it may only be possible to identify statistical units by disproportional costs and time resources.

M. Templ (✉)

Department of Statistics and Probability Theory, Vienna University of Technology, Wiedner Hauptstr. 7, A-1040 Vienna, Austria; Department of Register, Classification and Methodology, Statistics Austria, Guglgasse 13, A-1110 Vienna, Austria

e-mail: templ@tuwien.ac.at

J. Nin, J. Herranz (eds.), *Privacy and Anonymity in Information Management Systems*,   31
Advanced Information and Knowledge Processing,
DOI 10.1007/978-1-84996-238-4_3, © Springer-Verlag London Limited 2010

The aim of SDC is to reduce the risk of disclosing information on statistical units (individuals, enterprises, organizations) and on the other hand to provide as much information as possible by minimizing the amount of data modification.

3.1.1 Software Issues

R-package sdcMicro includes the most popular techniques for microdata protection. It is designed to protect survey data including sampling weights but it can also be applied to data without survey weights (e.g., population data). The underlying code is open source and freely available on the comprehensive R archive network (CRAN, see http://cran.r-project.org). The installation can be easily achieved by typing the following command into R (the text after the # only comments the operation for additional information to the readers)

Listing 3.1 Installing the package sdcMicro

```
install.packages('sdcMicro')
```

The installation of sdcMicro comes with a manual including help files for all functions. These help files are structured standard documents which describe the parameters and usage of each function. Furthermore, a section with examples on how to apply the corresponding function is included. To be aware of possible interactions of the functions, a package vignette is also available. The help index together with the description of the package can be easily displayed by

Listing 3.2 Loading sdcMicro, displaying the help index and the package vignette

```
require(sdcMicro)
help(package=sdcMicro)
vignette('sdcMicroPaper')
```

The software is designed to be flexible and to provide reproducibility.

3.1.2 The sdcMicro GUI

The package features also a graphical user interface (GUI). gWidgetsRGtk2 [46] was used to generate the GUI and must be installed when using it. This package allows the gWidgets API to use the RGtk2 package [24] to allow the use of the powerful Gtk2 libraries within R. The Gtk2 libraries usually come with a standard Linux installation. When installing the gWidgetsRGtk2 R-package, a very easy-to-use built-in install routine pops up when Gtk2 is not installed. After installation, R has to be restarted once.

Reproducibility and flexibility are also provided within the GUI. The graphical user interface (see Fig. 3.1) can be loaded by typing the following command into R:

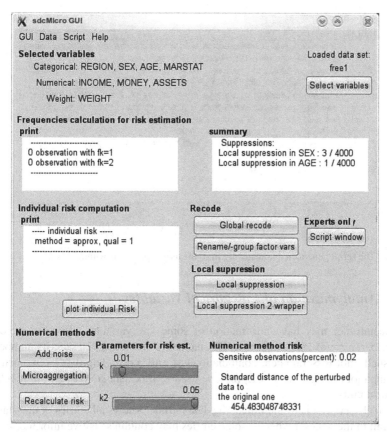

Fig. 3.1 The graphical user interface of sdcMicro. The summaries of a possible anoymization of the μ-Argus test data are shown

Listing 3.3 Starting the GUI

```
sdcGUI ()
```

Within the GUI, data can be easily loaded, variables can be selected, and different methods can be easily applied. The GUI provides interaction between all possible objects, i.e., all measures of information loss and disclosure risk as well as frequency counts, effects of recordings, etc., are automatically updated after an operation has been applied.

Each effect of a mouse click and each operation performed is saved in a script (see Fig. 3.2). This script can later easily be modified and re-applied to the data and/or run only up to a specific line.

Unfortunately, the following examples of the methods applied in this section cannot be shown with the GUI to stay in the limits of pages. It seems to be more elegant to demonstrate the examples via the command line language of R instead of showing a lot of snapshots from the GUI. Nevertheless, each operation which is shown can also be applied easily by using the GUI of sdcMicro.

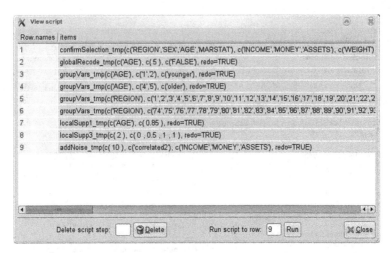

Row.names items

Row.names	items
1	confirmSelection_tmp(c('REGION','SEX','AGE','MARSTAT'), c('INCOME','MONEY','ASSETS'), c('WEIGHT')
2	globalRecode_tmp(c('AGE'), c(5), c('FALSE'), redo=TRUE)
3	groupVars_tmp(c('AGE'), c('1','2), c('younger'), redo=TRUE)
4	groupVars_tmp(c('AGE'), c('4','5), c('older'), redo=TRUE)
5	groupVars_tmp(c('REGION), c('1','2','3','4','5','6','7','8','9','10','11','12','13','14','15','16','17','18','19','20','21','22',2
6	groupVars_tmp(c('REGION), c('74','75','76','77','78','79','80','81','82','83','84','85','86','87','88','89','90','91','92','9:
7	localSupp1_tmp(c('AGE'), c(0.85), redo=TRUE)
8	localSupp3_tmp(c(2), c(0 , 0.5 , 1 , 1), redo=TRUE)
9	addNoise_tmp(c(10), c('correlated2'), c('INCOME','MONEY','ASSETS'), redo=TRUE)

Delete script step: [ ] Delete   Run script to row: 9 Run   Close

Fig. 3.2 The script generated automatically from the users operations within the GUI

3.1.3 Anonymization of Categorical Variables

A data intruder may have information of some key variables. Whereas direct identifying variables, such as IDs, names, addresses, social security numbers, are usually not disseminated, combinations of indirect identifiers, such as denomination, age class, NACE, may be used to link data sources and to identify statistical units.

If an observation is re-identified, the data intruder knows all entries of this statistical unit in the data set whereas some entries may contain sensitive information.

3.1.3.1 Frequency Counts and Disclosure Risk

Consider a random sample of size n drawn from a population of size N. Let $\pi_i, i = 1, \ldots, N$ be the (first-order) inclusion probabilities, i.e., the probability that the element u_i of a population of the size N is chosen in a sample of the size n. Imagine that the re-identification of statistical units could be performed by using external samples or registers with equal variables, called (categorical) *key variables*.

All possible combinations of categories in the key variables $X_1, \ldots, X_m$ can be calculated by cross-tabulation of these categorical variables. Let $f_k, k = 1, \ldots, n$ be the frequency counts obtained by cross-tabulation and let F_k be the frequency counts of the population which belong to the same category. If $f_k = 1$ applies the corresponding observation is unique in the sample. If $F_k = 1$ applies then the observation is unique in the population.

Unfortunately, F_k is usually unknown since in statistics usually information on samples is collected and only few information about the population is known from registers and/or external sources.

3.1.3.2 Estimation of F_k

F_k may be estimated by using the sampling weights. Whenever an observation has a sampling weight equal to 100 it can be assumed that 100 observations do have the same characteristics in the population related to the stratification variables of a (complex) sampling design.

The estimation of the frequency counts in the population is given by the sum of the weights associated with the observations which belong to the corresponding category. F_k may then be estimated by

$$\hat{F}_k = \sum_{i \in \{j | x_{j.} = x_{k.}\}} w_i \quad , \qquad (3.1)$$

with $x_{i.}$ denotes the ith row of the key variables.

Please note that this definition is again different from the classical one which expresses F for each category and not for each observation.

Example 3.1 In order to demonstrate both the calculation of frequency counts in the sample and the estimation of frequency counts in the population a simple data set for demonstration is used which is included in R-package sdcMicro [42, 43].

Listing 3.4 Loading and subsetting a data set for demonstration. This subset includes the categorical key variables and the sampling weights

```
data(francdat) x <- francdat[,c(2,4,5,6,8)]
print(x)
R>    Key1 Key2 Key3 Key4      w
R> 1    1    2    5    1   18.0
R> 2    1    2    1    1   45.5
R> 3    1    2    1    1   39.0
R> 4    3    3    1    5   17.0
R> 5    4    3    1    4  541.0
R> 6    4    3    1    1    8.0
R> 7    6    2    1    5    5.0
R> 8    1    2    5    1   92.0
```

Please note that this data set is also used in [5] and [44].

The frequency calculation can be done by using the R-function freqCalc():

Listing 3.5 Calculating the frequency counts and displaying the results

```
ff <- freqCalc(x, keyVars=1:4, w=4)
print(cbind(x, ff$fk, ff$Fk))
R>    Key1 Key2 Key3 Key4      w ff$fk ff$Fk
R> 1    1    2    5    1   18.0     2   110
R> 2    1    2    1    1   45.5     2  84.5
R> 3    1    2    1    1   39.0     2  84.5
R> 4    3    3    1    5   17.0     1    17
R> 5    4    3    1    4  541.0     1   541
R> 6    4    3    1    1    8.0     1     8
R> 7    6    2    1    5    5.0     1     5
R> 8    1    2    5    1   92.0     2   110
```

The values of observations 1 and 8 are equal in the underlying key variables, for example. Thus $f_1 = 2$ and $f_8 = 2$. The frequency in the population $\hat{F}_1$ and $\hat{F}_8$ can be estimated with the sum of their sampling weights, w_1 and w_8, which equals 110. Hence, two observations with $x_{k.} = (1, 2, 5, 1)'$ exist in the sample and 110 observations with these entities can be expected to exist in the population.

freqCalc() includes three parameters which could be displayed in R either using

Listing 3.6 Displaying the arguments of function freqCalc()

```
args(freqCalc)
R> function (x, keyVars = 1:3, w = 4)
```

or typing ?freqCalc which displays the whole help file. x is an object of class data.frame or matrix, keyVars is a vector specifying the column index of the key variables, and w defines the column index of the weight variable. The resulting output of the function is the frequency counts of the sample and the estimated frequency counts of the population.

The function is implemented in C and integrated into R using the R/C interface. For this reason the computation is very fast and is able to deal also with large data sets and many key variables (for runtime issues, see [42]).

Please note that the frequency counts are usually obtained by cross-tabulation of the key variables which differs from the notation used in this chapter. Usually, each cell $k = 1, \ldots, K$ is the cross-product of the categories of the key variables, with K being the amount of different categories of the cross-product. Thus the new notation provides theoretically the same information but it is more applicable when implementing methods into software, since the overall aim is to perform all operations on individual level and not only on aggregated information. This is especially true when estimating re-identification risks for each observation.

To obtain the original definition for each category the information must only be aggregated using R's aggregate() function, for example.

3.1.3.3 Global Risk Measures

A global measure of the re-identification risk is given by the number of uniqueness which occurs in both the sample and the population. It can be expressed in the following way:

$$\tau_1 = \sum_{k=1}^{n} \mathbb{I}(F_k = 1, f_k = 1) \, , \tag{3.2}$$

where $\mathbb{I}$ denotes the indicator function.

Another well-known global risk measure is given by

$$\tau_2 = \sum_{k=1}^{n} \mathbb{I}(f_k = 1)\frac{1}{F_k} \quad , \tag{3.3}$$

in which the indicator is weighed with the reciprocal value of the population frequency counts. The higher the population frequency count the lower the risk of re-identification. If F_k is particularly high, the data intruder cannot be sure if he is able to assign correctly the observation for which he holds information.

F_k must be estimated when estimating τ_1 and/or τ_2. τ_1 and τ_2 are estimated by

$$\hat{\tau}_1 = \sum_{k=1}^{n} \mathbb{I}(f_k = 1)E(P(F_k = 1|f_k = 1)) \quad , \quad \hat{\tau}_2 = \sum_{k=1}^{n} \mathbb{I}(f_k = 1)E(\frac{1}{F_k}|f_k = 1).$$
$$\tag{3.4}$$

Unfortunately, it is not reasonable to use $\hat{F}_k$ as given in Formula (3.1) to estimate a global disclosure risk. A certain distribution of F_k must be assumed in order to formulate a realistic measure of global risk.

The use of prior assumptions for distributions to estimate the individual risk can be found in [2, 27, 29, 30].

However, all these authors do not provide arguments for why Formula (3.1) should not be used for the estimation of the individual risk. For better understanding of this problem the following example is given.

Example 3.2 In this example which was also used in [44] the global risk τ_1 is not only calculated (from a synthetic population) but also estimated (from a sample of the synthetic population). The synthetic population allows to know the true values of F_k and the global risk measures, for example.

First, a population including four categorical key variables is generated.

Listing 3.7 Generation of a synthetic population

```
set.seed(1234)
pop <- data.frame(cat1=sample(1:4, 100, replace=TRUE),
                  cat2=round(rnorm(100,6)),
                  cat3=sample(1:3, 100, replace=TRUE),
                  cat4=sample(1:2, 100, replace=TRUE))
```

From this population consisting of 100 observations, a sample with simple random sampling without replacement is drawn. No stratification is considered to keep the example as simple as possible. The inclusion probabilities are fixed to $\frac{1}{8}$, and therefore the sampling weights are fixed to 8

Listing 3.8 Drawing a sample

```
s1 <- round(nrow(pop)/8)        # --> 12
sp <- sample(1:nrow(pop), s1)   # choose 12 out of 100
s <- pop[sp, ]                  # the sample
s[,"w"] <- rep(8, nrow(s))      # the sampling weights
```

In the next step, the frequency counts in the sample are calculated and the frequency counts in the population are estimated.

Listing 3.9 Calculation and estimation of the frequency counts in the synthetic population. The population frequency counts are known in this example but they are also estimated from the drawn sample

```
popf <- freqCalc(pop, keyVars=1:4, w=NULL)
samplef <- freqCalc(s, keyVars=1:4, w=5)
```

The global risk τ_1 can be calculated easily.

Listing 3.10 Calculation of the global risk τ_1

```
sum(popf$Fk[sp] == 1)
R> 5
```

The true value is 5, but the estimated risk $\hat{\tau}_1$ is zero.

Listing 3.11 Estimation of the global risk τ_1 from the sample

```
sum(samplef$fk == 1 & samplef$Fk == 1)
R> 0
```

This results because the estimated population frequency counts are ≤ 8.

The previous example has shown that other concepts for risk estimation should be considered. The most popular one is the Benedetti–Franconi model [1], which is also implemented in the R-package sdcMicro.

3.1.3.4 Superpopulation Models

To estimate the frequencies of the population F_k, it is assumed that the population is drawn from a superpopulation. In fact, this means that either the frequencies in the population will be generated synthetically by drawing from a specific distribution of the frequency counts or quantiles of the assumed distribution of F_k are used. Using quantiles of the prior assumed distribution of F_k makes it possible to estimate the risk of each statistical unit. However, this estimation is just as good as the frequency counts of the population are modeled and how well the model assumption is fulfilled. Many suggestions exist in literature: the use of a Poisson-Gamma superpopulation model [2], the Dirichlet-multinomial model [38], the negative binomial model [1, 18], a log-linear model [35, 36], a multinominal model [17], the Poisson-inverse Gaussian model [6], and references therein.

3.1.3.5 The Benedetti–Franconi Model for Risk Estimation

For the popular Benedetti–Franconi model [1, 18] $F_k|f_k$ has to be estimated, i.e., the frequency counts in the population given the frequency counts in the sample. A common assumption is $F_k \sim \text{Poisson}(N\pi_k)$ (independently) (see, e.g., [18]), where N is assumed to be known and with π_k the inclusion probabilities. (Binomial) Sampling from F_k means that $f_k|F_k \sim \text{Bin}(F_k, \pi_k)$. By standard calculations (see, e.g., [2]) one gets

$$f_k \sim \text{Poisson}(N\pi_k) \quad \text{and} \quad F_k|f_k \sim f_k + \text{Poisson}(N(1-\pi_k)) \ .$$

Concerning the risk calculation, the uncertainty on the frequency counts of the population is accounted in a Bayesian fashion by assuming that the population frequency given the sample frequency, $F_k|f_k$, is drawn from a negative binomial distribution with success probabilities p_k and the number of successes f_k [27, 30]. By using this assumption [1] estimated the risk τ_2 by the well-known and so-called "model from Benedetti and Franconi." Using this background [5] estimated the individual risk $\hat{r}_k$ for each observation as follows:

$$\hat{r}_k = \left(\frac{\hat{p}_k}{1-\hat{p}_k}\right)^{f_k} \left\{ A_0 \left(1 + \sum_{j=0}^{f_k-3} (-1)^{j+1} \prod_{l=0}^{j} B_l \right) + (-1)^{f_k} \log(\hat{p}_k) \right\} \ , \quad (3.5)$$

whereas

$$\hat{p}_k = \frac{f_k}{\hat{F}_k} = \frac{f_k}{\sum_{i \in \{j|x_{j.}=x_{k.}\}} \pi_i} \ ,$$

while

$$B_l = \frac{(f_k - 1 - l)^2}{(l+1)(f_k - 2 - l)} \frac{\hat{p}_k^{l+2-f_k} - 1}{\hat{p}_k^{l+1-f_k} - 1} \quad \text{and} \quad A_0 = \frac{\hat{p}_k^{1-f_k} - 1}{f_k - 1} \ .$$

If $f_k = 1$ [5] use

$$\hat{r}_k = \frac{\hat{p}_k}{1-\hat{p}_k} \log\left(\frac{1}{\hat{p}_k}\right) \ ,$$

while if $f_k = 2$ they use

$$\hat{r}_k = \frac{\hat{p}_k}{1-\hat{p}_k} - \left(\frac{\hat{p}_k}{1-\hat{p}_k}\right)^2 \log\left(\frac{1}{\hat{p}_k}\right) \ ,$$

If the sample is large the computation in formula (3.5) becomes infeasible, but the following approximation works reasonable [5]:

$$\hat{r}_k = \frac{\hat{p}_k}{f_k - (1-\hat{p}_k)} \ .$$

From our previous example we obtain the following risk by using our developed R-package *sdcMicro* and the function indivRisk(). The individual risk $\hat{r}_k$ is estimated below and its result is shown in the last column of the following table. The method for the estimation of the individual risk in package *sdcMicro* is based on the concept of [5] which was outlined in the previous text.

Listing 3.12 Estimation and display of individual risks

```
rk <- indivRisk(ff)$rk
print(cbind(x, ff$fk, ff$Fk, rk))

R>   Key1 Key2 Key3 Key4       w  ff$fk  ff$Fk      rk
R> 1    1    2    5    1    18.0      2    110   0.017
R> 2    1    2    1    1    45.5      2   84.5   0.022
R> 3    1    2    1    1    39.0      2   84.5   0.022
R> 4    3    3    1    5    17.0      1     17   0.177
R> 5    4    3    1    4   541.0      1    541   0.011
R> 6    4    3    1    1     8.0      1      8   0.297
R> 7    6    2    1    5     5.0      1      5   0.402
R> 8    1    2    5    1    92.0      2    110   0.017
```

It follows that the individual risk is large for observations 4, 6, and 7.

Function `indivRisk()` has only one parameter which must be an object of class `freqCalc`, which is typically a output of function `freqCalc()`.

Further research has already been done in this topic. Newest approaches consider the neighborhood of each category within log-linear models [30].

Although all the concepts for risk estimation require a lot of assumptions which may not hold in practice, the most important assumption which is often used, $F_k \sim \text{Poisson}(N\pi_k)$ and $f_k \sim \text{Poisson}(N\pi_k)$, may be reasonable in theory but may not be valid in practice. Although other distributions for F_k have been discussed by other authors, the best modeling of F_k depends on the underlying data, i.e., each data set requires different assumptions. The lack of all these methods is that they are not data-driven approaches, but prior assumptions about distributions are taken.

3.1.3.6 Global Recoding and Local Suppression

Typically, categorical key variables with categories including only few entries lead to uniqueness and high risk. Thus recoding into broader categories (e.g., age-to-age classes) or combining categories (e.g., combining two NACE 2-digit levels) may reduce the risk.

The output of the previous example shows, for example, that observation 7 has a high risk of disclosure. This is not surprising because it is unique in the sample and it is estimated that only five observations with the same entries in the key variables exist in the population.

Therefore, the estimated individual risk must be reduced, e.g., by global recoding of a variable. Here, the categories of certain variables are assigned to broader categories. As mentioned before, it is very likely that, after the recoding, more observations are equal in the key variables and so $\hat{F}_k$ increases and $\hat{r}_k$ decreases.

Recoding the values of the first key variable to only four possible labels (1 to 4) reduces the risk dramatically for some observations.

Listing 3.13 Global recoding of one key variable

```
x[,1] <- globalRecode(x[,1], breaks=c(0,1,2,3,6),
                      labels=c(1,2,3,4))
```

Note that the usage of global recording is much easier within the GUI of sdcMicro.

After recoding it is possible that the risk of re-identification is not reduced or not reduced significantly for several observations. Then, usually, local suppression is applied. In this method, certain values in the key variables are suppressed in order to reduce the risk. This should be done in an optimal way, i.e., to suppress as few values as possible on the one hand and to guarantee low risk of re-identification on the other hand. An iterative algorithm is implemented in the package *sdcMicro* [43] to search for an optimal solution [43]. The user can also assign weights to the key variables, because often some variables seem to be less important (such as *age*) than others (such as economic branch classification in business data). The probability of local suppressions in variables with high weights is then higher as for variables with small importance/weights.

Listing 3.14 Obtaining k-anonymity (here: $k = 2$)

```
localSupp2Wrapper(x, keyVars=1:4, w=5, kAnon=2)
R> 2-anonymity has been reached.
```

Another possibility is to apply function localSupp() which may be more applicable due to such a small data example.

Anyway, it is easy to see when the value in the second entry in the fourth variable is suppressed that the risk is highly reduced:

	Key1	Key2	Key3	Key4	π_k	f_k	$\hat{F}_k$	$\hat{r}_k$
1	1	2	5	1	18.0	2	110.0	0.017
2	1	2	1	1	45.5	2	84.5	0.022
3	1	2	1	1	39.0	2	84.5	0.022
4	4	3	1	5	17.0	3	30.0	0.048
5	4	3	1	4	541.0	2	549.0	0.003
6	4	3	1	NA	8.0	4	571.0	0.002
7	4	3	1	5	5.0	3	30.0	0.048
8	1	2	5	1	92.0	2	110.0	0.017

The data now only imply low risk of re-identification for each observation.

3.1.3.7 Post-randomization Method (PRAM)

By applying PRAM [19, 23], values of categorical variables may change to different categories, according to a pre-defined probability mechanism which is given in the form of a specific transition matrix.

Function pram() provides the invariant PRAM methodology [19, 23] and produces objects from class *pram*. A print method and a summary method are provided for objects of this class.

In the following, the variable MARSTAT is perturbed from the μ-Argus test data set which is included in package sdcMicro. A lot of information is stored in the resulting object MARSTATpram, e.g., the invariant transition matrix. Summary and print methods are provided as well.

Listing 3.15 An application of PRAM and a selected output of the summary method

```
data(free1)
MARSTATpram <- pram(free1[,''MARSTAT''])
summary(MARSTATpram)


    original frequencies            transition Frequency
     1     2     3     4        1      1 --> 1      2448
   2547   162   171  1120       2      1 --> 2        27
                                3      1 --> 3        28
                                4      1 --> 4        44
   frequencies after perturb.:  5      2 --> 1        33
                                6      2 --> 2       118
     1     2     3     4        7      2 --> 3         4
   2571   160   178  1091       8      2 --> 4         7
                                9      3 --> 1        20
                               10      3 --> 2         3
                               11      3 --> 3       130
                              ...     ...            ...
```

Further parameters of the function are as follows:

Listing 3.16 Parameters for pram()

```
args(pram)
R> function (x, pd = 0.8, alpha = 0.5)
```

pd is the minimum diagonal entries for the generated transition matrix and alpha is the amount of perturbation used for the invariant PRAM method. The output of this function is not presented here, but it is well described in the manual of the package [43].

3.1.3.8 Summary

A short description of the most popular methods for the protection of categorical microdata was presented and the corresponding software implementation in sdcMicro was shown, i.e., functions

- freqCalc() for frequency calculation
- indivRisk() for individual risk estimation
- globalRecode() for recoding
- localSupp() and localSupp2Wrapper() for local suppression
- pram() for post-randomization
- and various print, summary, and plot methods

All these functions can be applied within the sdcMicro GUI as well, simply by clicking the corresponding buttons.

3.1.4 Anonymization of Numerical Variables

Almost every combination of continuous scaled variables is unique in the sample. Thus, the concept of uniqueness used in the previous chapter does no longer work whenever continuous scaled variables are observed.

Unfortunately, a data intruder may have information about a value of a statistical unit. If this value matches with the anonymized data, then he can be quite sure that the re-identification was successful. The intruder then knows all the information about this unit in the data set, i.e., the values of each variable of this unit. Unfortunately, this information can be very sensitive, for example, information about cancer, taxes, or competitors.

Unfortunately, an intruder may also use *record linkage techniques* (also known as statistical matching) to identify already perturbed values. If a value is not perturbed sufficiently a successful re-identification is then possible. Thus, the re-identification risk should be also estimated.

3.1.4.1 Adding Noise Methods

One possible procedure is to add *additive* noise to each numerical variable

$$Y = X + \varepsilon \ ,$$

where $X \sim (\mu, \Sigma), \varepsilon \sim N(0, \Sigma_\varepsilon), \ \Sigma_\varepsilon = \alpha \cdot \mathrm{diag}(\sigma_1^2, \sigma_2^2, \ldots, \sigma_p^2), \alpha > 0,$ $\mathrm{Cov}(\varepsilon_i \neq \varepsilon_j) \ \forall i \neq j$, and p is equal to the dimension of the numerical variables which should be perturbed (see, e.g., also in [4]). Let x be a subset of data consisting of the numerical key variables, then adding additive noise to continuous scaled variables can easily performed with package sdcMicro:

Listing 3.17 Adding additive noise to numerical key variables

```
addNoise(x)
```

The amount of noise for each variable can be specified by changing specific parameters of the function addNoise().

Multivariate measures such as the correlation coefficient cannot be preserved when adding additive (uncorrelated) noise. Correlation coefficients can, however, be preserved if correlated noise is added. In this case the covariance matrix of the masked data is $\Sigma_Y = (1 + \alpha)\Sigma_X$ (see, e.g., in [4]).

Kim [22] uses $d = \varepsilon(1 - \alpha^2)$ and then $x_j d + \alpha z_j$ is calculated where z_j are random numbers drawn from $N(\frac{(1-d)\bar{x}_j}{\alpha}, s_j)$, with s_j being the standard deviation of X_j.

The restricted correlated noise method (implemented as method *restr* in *sdcMicro*) is a similar method which takes the sample size into account ([4]).

Listing 3.18 Adding noise by simple correlated noise, Kim's approach and restricted correlated noise

```
addNoise(x, method='correlated')
addNoise(x, method='correlated2')
addNoise(x, method='restricted')
```

ROMM (random orthogonal matrix masking, [45]) applies the transformation $Y = AX$ where A is randomly generated and fulfills the orthogonality condition $A^{-1} = A^T$. To obtain a orthogonal matrix as described in [45] the Gram–Schmidt procedure was chosen in the implementation of method *ROMM*.

Listing 3.19 Applying ROMM using default parameters

```
addNoise(x,  method='ROMM')
```

However, all these methods either are influenced by outliers (method correlated, restricted and ROMM) or do not preserve outliers sufficiently (additive noise) (see [41]). To deal with inhomogeneous data sets including outliers a method in which outliers are detected may be adequate. Observations with large robust Mahalanobis distances may be treated as outliers.

Outliers should be much more protected than the rest of the observations because outlying observations have a higher risk for re-identification than non-outliers. In package *sdcMicro* a method called `outdect()` is implemented which considers this fact.

3.1.4.2 Rank Swapping and Microaggregation

Rank swapping [9] sorts the entries of one variable by their numerical values (ranking). Each ranked value is then swapped with another ranked value that has been chosen randomly within a restricted range. The rank of two swapped values cannot differ by more than p percent of the total number of observations. Rank swapping must be applied to each variable separately and therefore the multivariate data structure is not preserved very well. Nevertheless, this popular method can be easily applied by using package sdcMicro for a given data matrix x. In the implementation the rank swapping is applied columnwise.

Listing 3.20 Rank swapping using a 15% swapping range

```
swappNum(x,  p=15)
```

A familiar definition of microaggregation can be found at http://neon.vb.cbs.nl/casc/Glossary.htm: "Records are grouped based on a proximity measure of variables of interest, and the same small groups of records are used in calculating aggregates for those variables. The aggregates are released instead of the individual record values."

The choice of the "proximity" measure is the most challenging and most important part in microaggregation. The multivariate structure of the data is only preserved if similar observations are aggregated. Sorting data based on one single variable in ascending or descending order (method *single* in *sdcMicro*), sorting the observations in each cluster (after clustering the data) by the most influential variable in each cluster (method *influence*, see [39]), and sorting (and re-ordering the data after aggregation) in each variable (individual ranking method, see [10]) are considered not to be optimal for multivariate data (see [40]).

Projection methods typically sort the data according to the first principal component (method *pca*) or its robust counterpart (method *pppca*), whereas the methods used to obtain the principal components can differ a lot. Usually, all principal components must be estimated when using standard approaches for PCA, but method pppca avoids this and estimates the first (robust) principal component by projection pursuit without the need of estimating the covariance.

While pca methods are fast, the maximum distance to average vector (MDAV) often provides better results. This method is an evolution of the multivariate fixed-size microaggregation (see [14], for example). However, this method (*mdav* in *sdcMicro*) is based on Euclidean distances in a multivariate space.

The algorithm has been improved by replacing Euclidean distances with robust Mahalanobis distances. In [39] a new algorithm called RMDM (**R**obust **M**ahalanobis **D**istance-based **M**icroaggregation) was proposed for microaggregation where MDAV [14] is adapted in several ways.

Microaggregation can be easily applied with package sdcMicro:

Listing 3.21 General procedure to apply microaggregation

```
microaggregation(x, method='METHOD', k=3)
```

For parameter 'METHOD' more than 10 different methods are available [42]. Parameter k determines the aggregation level used.

3.1.4.3 Information Loss

One measure of information loss, called IL1s (see, e.g., in [48] or [25]), is based on aggregated distances from original data points to corresponding values from the perturbed data divided by the standard deviation for each variable. Unfortunately, this measure is large even if only one outlier is highly perturbed but all values are exactly the same as in the original data set.

Other measures are considered in [20] and [39]. Measures of information loss which compare univariate statistics of the original data and the perturbed data are, for example, the sum of the differences of the mean or medians. Measures which compare multivariate statistics of the original data and the perturbed data evaluate differences of the correlation matrices or loadings obtained by principal component analysis. Improved measures of information loss have been suggested by [25] and are also implemented in *sdcMicro* as well as robust measures (see in the package manual of *sdcMicro*).

To apply it one uses the original data and the masked data.

Listing 3.22 Calculation of the IL1 data utility measure

```
dUtility(x, xm, method=''IL1'')
```

When calling functions for measuring data utility or risk, expected input parameters include x, the original data set, and xm, the masked data set.

The implemented summary method includes more than 10 measures of information loss. It can be easily applied to objects of class "micro" (which are typically calculated using functions addNoise() and microaggregation()).

Methods can finally be compared using function valTable() which calls the summary method for each anonymization method chosen.

Listing 3.23 Comparing methods using function valTable() and displaying a subset of the calculated output

```
v <- valTable(Tarragona, method=c(''simple'',''onedims'',
    ''pca'',''clustpppca'',''mdav'', ''addNoise: additive '',
    ''addNoise: correlated2'', ''swappNum''))
v[,c(1,3,5,9)]
R>                      method amedian   devvar acors
R> 1                    simple   3.497    3.638 5.119
R> 2                   onedims   0.033    0.605 0.006
R> 3                       pca   2.617    2.765 9.567
R> 4                 clustpppca   3.640    2.797 7.399
R> 5                      mdav   1.982    2.523 5.681
R> 6                       rmd   0.864    1.662 1.392
R> 7        addNoise: additive  42.892  379.889 6.318
R> 8     addNoise: correlated2   2.993    0.151 1.426
R> 9                  swappNum   0.114    8.500 1.096
```

3.1.5 Disclosure Risk

In [13] a measure of disclosure risk is proposed which is based on distances. It is assumed that an intruder can link the masked record of an observation to its original value (see, e.g., [25]). Given the value of a masked variable it is checked whether the corresponding original value falls within an interval centered on the masked value. The width of the interval itself is based on the rank of the variable or on its standard deviation [13]. However, this interval does not depend on the scale of the actual value and therefore the length of the interval is equal for non-outlying and outlying values. However, [41] shows that outlying observations should be much more perturbed than non-outliers.

By using distance-based record linkage methods one tries to find the nearest neighbors between observations from two data sets. Reference [13] has shown that these methods outperform probabilistic methods.

Reference [41] suggests new and more realistic measures of disclosure risk which accounts for outlying observations by using robust Mahalanobis distances. The robustification was done using the MCD estimator [31].

The aim is now to measure the distance of each observation to the center of the data in a multivariate space. For a p-dimensional multivariate sample x_i ($i = 1, \ldots, n$) the Mahalanobis distance is defined as

$$MD_i = (x_i - t)^T C^{-1}(x_i - t) \quad \text{for } i = 1, \ldots, n \ , \tag{3.6}$$

where t is the estimated multivariate location and C the estimated covariance matrix. In robust statistics, usually, t is a robust estimate of location (e.g., via MCD) and C is the sample covariance matrix obtained by the MCD estimator, for example.

Multivariate outliers may simply be defined as observations featuring large (squared) Mahalanobis distances.

Observations whose robust Mahalanobis distances (RMD_i) are greater than $\chi^2_{(0.975, p)}$ may be defined as outliers.

The intervals for each data value should now depend on these robust distances, i.e., the intervals may be defined as $k_j \times (RMD_i)^{1/2}$, $j \in \{1, \ldots, p\}$. Following this approach we obtain a disclosure risk for each observation by checking if any value of an observation falls into the corresponding interval or not. Then the percentage of observations featuring high risk can be calculated.

However, if we assume that we have applied microaggregation with high aggregation level, e.g., 10, the methods described previously lead to a high risk of disclosure if the original value and the microaggregated value are close to each other. But these measures are unrealistic for this simple microaggregation example since 10 observations possess the same value in the microaggregated variable, and data intruder can never be sure which one is the correct link. Especially, if this observation is near the center of the data cloud the previous measures fail to provide a meaningful measure of disclosure risk.

An observation which is marked as unsafe is thus considered safe if m observations are very close to the masked observation.

All the mentioned disclosure risk methods can again be applied within the package sdcMicro by function dRisk() and dRiskRMD() or by using the results from above, already stored in object v.

Listing 3.24 Showing additional output from function valTable()

```
v[,c(1,17,20,21)]
R>                         method   risk0    wrisk1    wrisk2
R>  1                      simple   0.000   621.445     0.000
R>  2                     onedims   0.799   626.591   616.920
R>  3                         pca   0.000   622.762     0.000
R>  4                   clustpppca   0.000   626.337     0.000
R>  5                        mdav   0.000   623.839     0.000
R>  6                         rmd   0.000   626.099     0.000
R>  7        addNoise:  additive   0.000   549.716   549.716
R>  8  addNoise:  correlated2   0.000   613.749   613.749
R>  9                    swappNum   0.000   622.762   615.199
```

In 3.24, risk0 refers to the method of [25], wrisk1 and wrisk2 to the measures proposed by [41].

It is not possible to interpret wrisk1 and wrisk2 in a probabilistic way. However, they can be used for comparison of methods.

3.1.6 Case Study Using Real-World Data

In the following an anonymized scientific-use file for the continuing vocational training survey (CVTS2) data set is created in order to display the functionality of package sdcMicro to real-world complex data.

This survey includes information on internal measures which enterprises have taken and (partly) payed for on advanced vocational training for employees. The raw survey data consist of 2613 enterprises for which a total of 197 variables has been recorded.

Further information on the CVTS2 data can be found at Statistics Austria's web-page at http://www.statistik.at.

The difficulty in generating a scientific-use file for these data is the large number of categorical variables and the fact that a combination of these variables might be used by an attacker to correctly identify an enterprise. One scenario is considered using a subset of the available categorical variables as key variables. It has to be noted that the decision on the choice of categorical key variables (from subject matter specialists) is always subjective while the methods for statistical disclosure control are applied afterward in a non-subjective manner.

Before actually starting to apply anonymization methods, 29 variables which either were direct identifiers or were including non-relevant information have been deleted from the data set. We skipped this part of code and continue with the corresponding subset, called cvts.

We started by comparing different scenarios and several combinations of possible key variables by having a look at the corresponding individual risks for re-identification [18] as well as the number of unique combinations of the characteristics in the key variables.

This can be easily carried out by repeatedly running a slightly modified script until both a great reduction in risk and an acceptable loss of information are obtained.

In such a situation, the graphical user interface of sdcMicro is advantageous because the results are automatically updated and displayed in the GUI after an action has been performed out (see Fig. 3.1).

It is in fact very convenient to compare different scenarios using sdcMicro because the user only has to specify the desired key variables and re-run the code. Finally, we decided to use the following key variables:

- **economic classification of the enterprise:** 10 categories
- **number of employees:** 4 categories
- **generated revenues for vocational training:** 2 categories
- **expenses for vocational training:** 2 categories

It should be noted that all of these key variables are modified in an explorative manner by using the globalRecode() function.

We always looked at the number of unique combinations of the key variables, the number of observations with a given combination of the key variables that occur only twice as well as the individual risk for re-identification. We observed 58 unique observations and 50 observations whose combination of values of the key variables occurred exactly two times, see 3.25.

Listing 3.25 Calculation of frequency counts

```
fr <- freqCalc(x, keyVars=c(5,10,12,13), w=51)
fr
R> 58 observations with fk = 1
R> 50 observations with fk = 2
```

One aim is to provide k-anonymity [33, 34, 37] and low risk of re-identification. This means that for any combination of key variables at least k observations must exist in the data set sharing that combination. Additionally, low individual re-identification risk of every observation must be guaranteed. The sdcMicro function localSupp() or localSupp2wrapper() can be used to suppress values in the key variables. We find 3-anonymity in combination with the other anonymization methods (e.g., microaggregation) applied to be a sufficient protection to publish this data set.

If one observation still reports high risk, one can set interactively from the corresponding plot of the individual risks (using plot(x) where x must be an output object of function indivRisk()) a threshold which is needed by function localSupp(). By applying function localSupp2Wrapper() one can guarantee k-anonymity.

Listing 3.26 Ensuring k-anonymity (here $k = 2$)

```
supps <- localSupp2Wrapper(x, keyVar=c(5,10,12,13),
          w=51, importance=c(0.1, 0.6, 1, 1))
print(supps$supp)
R> classif.     emp     revenues    expenses
R>     2         6        49          33
```

In listing 3.26 we assume that the variable *economic classification of enterprises* (classif.) is more important as others, i.e., less values will be suppressed in this variable. Thus, in this example, only two values have been suppressed in the first key variable.

After dealing with categorical variables and indirect identifiers, we took additional precautions by microaggregating the available continuous scaled key variables.

Listing 3.27 Microaggregation of the continuous scaled key variables with nums being the index of the key variables

```
cvts[, nums] <- microaggregation(x[,nums], k=3)
```

After these steps the resulting scientific-use file may be considered safe since 3-anonymity and low individual risk is provided and the continuous scaled key variables have been microaggregated.

In this section a short overview of the possibilities to protect continuous scaled key variables using R-package sdcMicro was presented. The main functions are summarized in the following:

- `swappNum()` to apply rank swapping.
- `addNoise()` to add noise. Different methods can be chosen.
- `microaggregation()` microaggregates the data. Again, different methods can be chosen.
- `valTable()` can be used to compare methods and reports their corresponding information loss and disclosure risk after perturbation.

3.2 Tabular Data Protection Using `sdcTable`

Statistical agencies generally do not publish microdata, but disseminate information in the form of aggregated data. Aggregated data are usually represented as statistical tables with totals in the margins.

3.2.1 Frequency and Magnitude Tables

A statistical table is constructed from microdata. According to the characteristics of one or more dimensional variables, all statistical units (e.g., persons, enterprises, or legal entities) that possess the same set of characteristics for each of the dimensional variables are grouped.

If the number or units for each combination of the dimensional variables is listed, the resulting table is referred to as frequency table. If some aggregated measure (usually the sum of a continuous scaled variable) is listed, the table is called magnitude table.

However, it should be noted that each statistical table is defined by a set of linear constraints connecting inner and marginal cells. In order to illustrate theses relations, the following simple, two-dimensional frequency Table (Table 3.1) is considered (see also in [7]).

In Table 3.1 the number of persons featuring some kind of characteristic living in certain zip-codes and age classes is shown. It is easy to see that in this simple example the linear constraints are just the sum of the rows and the columns. This means that the number of persons living in zip-code 5021 and the number of people living in zip-code 5022 sum up to the total number of people living in zip-code 502 since this larger area consists only of those two zip-codes. Therefore, the 14 people between 56 and 60 years in zip-code 5021 and the 12 persons in the same age class in zip-code 5022 sum up to the total number of persons in this age-group in zip-code 502. Additionally, summing up over the age-groups for any zip-code results in the linear restrictions which form the age-totals.

Table 3.1 Two-dimensional frequency table with margins

	1–55	56–60	61–65	Total
5021	1529	14	1	1544
5022	2985	12	2	2999
502	4514	26	3	4543

Table 3.2 Magnitude two-dimensional table

	1–55	56–60	61–65
5021	47,556	44,281	45,302
5022	41,852	37,952	39,040

Even though statistical tables present aggregated information of individuals contributing to the table cells, the risk of identifying single statistical units using tables is present and can in fact be high.

Consider now in addition to Table 3.1, Table 3.2 in which the median income is listed for each combination of zip-code and age classes. This table illustrates a disclosure situation. From the frequency Table (Table 3.1) it is clear that only one statistical unit contributes to the cell defined by zip-code 5021 and age class 61–65. Therefore, a data intruder gains the knowledge that the income of this single person is $45,302$. Disclosure would definitely occur if the data intruder manages to identify this person based on the dimensional variables. For example, he knows that his colleague is living in the corresponding zip-code and is between 61 and 65 years of age.

However, by looking at Table 3.2 we can state another possibly disclosure problem, because any of the two persons that contribute to the table cell with zip-code 5022 and age class 61–65 can calculate the income of the other contributing person by using the information on his own income which he certainly knows.

Since laws on data privacy are strict in almost all countries, national statistical offices do not only protect microdata but also aggregated data such as statistical tables in order to avoid disclosure of sensitive information.

Popular methods of protecting aggregated output to avoid possible re-identifications of statistical units or attribute disclosure feature cell suppression, rounding, or table reorganization by collapsing categories. Generally speaking, this means that some cells have to be suppressed or modified.

3.2.2 Primary Sensitive Cells

The first step when protecting tabular output is to determine table cells that need to be protected. These cells are referred to as primary sensitive cells.

The *minimum frequency rule* is the most popular rule to identify primary unsafe table cells. Using this rule, any table cell for which n or less statistical units contribute is considered to be primary unsafe. The parameter n is often set to 3 or 4.

Further popular methods are based on the idea that a cell should be protected if one or two statistical units *dominate* the cell. An example would be a table showing turnover by region of some businesses. If, for example, an enterprise is responsible for the vast majority of the generated turnover in its corresponding cell, this enterprise dominates this cell. If this fact is well known, the turnover of the enterprise can be estimated quite well by data intruders and thus, the cell needs to be protected.

Popular rules for identifying primary sensitive cells based on dominance criteria are the (n, k)-rule and the $p\%$-rule. According to the (n, k)-rule a table cell is unsafe if the total contribution of the n largest contributors exceeds $k\%$ or the total cell value. k is often set to 85% in practice. Using the p-rule, a cell needs to be protected if the cell total minus the two largest contributors is less than $p\%$ of the largest contribution. Generally, the $p\%$-rule should be preferred over the (n, k)-rule which has been shown by many authors (see, e.g., [8, 26, 47]).

3.2.3 Secondary Cell Suppression

Due to the linear relationships which are typical for statistical tables it is not sufficient to protect tables by identifying primary sensitive cells and suppressing its values. In order to avoid the recalculation or the possibility to gain good estimates for sensitive cells, additional cells need to be suppressed. The problem of finding additional cells for suppression is called *secondary cell suppression problem*. It is a quite complex and computer-intensive task to find and identify cells which are needed to be suppressed or changed in order to protect the primary sensitive cells since statistical tables are often hierarchical, multidimensional, and/or linked in practice.

Optimal solutions exist which are based on minimizing a pre-defined cost-function taking the linear relationships of the hierarchical tables into account (see e.g., [15]). The objective function is often chosen to minimize the total number of additional suppressions or similar criteria. The computational costs to solve the resulting complex combinatorial optimization problems are enormous for large hierarchical tables. Therefore, different heuristic solutions for two- and three-dimensional tables have been proposed (see, e.g., [4, 11, 16, 21]).

However, it should be noted that often the tables from statistical agencies are multidimensional with more than three dimensions. A practical implementation with up to four dimensions is implemented in the software τ-Argus. Details on its implementation are given in [26, 32].

Reference [12] proposes a heuristic solution to solve the problem by splitting a possible large statistical table into subtables and solving several smaller linear problems instead of trying to solve the complete program in one step. This method is often referred as the *Hitas* method.

3.2.4 Software Issues

R-package sdcTable is a newly written package to protect tabular data. The package is developed within an open-source project and can be downloaded from the comprehensive R archive network (CRAN, see http://cran.r-project.org).

3.2.4.1 Installation and Dependencies

The installation of the package can also be done directly in R.

Listing 3.28 Installation of the sdcTable package

```
install.packages('sdcTable')
```

The package itself depends on the R-package `lpSolve` ([3]) which provides an interface to call the free and open linear programming solver *lpSolve* within the R environment.

The installation of `sdcTable` provides online help for all the functions included as well as test data and examples which can be copied by the user and directly pasted and run in the R scripting window. To view the available help, the user needs to type the following command:

Listing 3.29 Displays the help index of package `sdcTable`

```
help(package=sdcTable)
```

Figure 3.3 shows the workflow needed to use package `sdcTable`. After reading the microdata into R, it is needed to standardize the data in a specific way so that it is possible to apply suppression or perturbation algorithms. By using the function *createFullData()* an object of class *fullDat* is created which can be used for further processing. The function *protectTable()* is a wrapper function which can be used to call different suppression algorithms. A successful run of *protectTable()* results in an object of class *safeTable*. For objects of class *safeTable* a summary function is provided which prints useful information such as the protection algorithm used to protect the statistical table, the number of primary and additional suppression, or the running time of the algorithm.

General Workflow

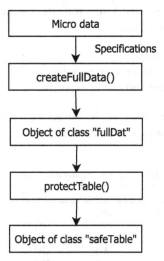

Fig. 3.3 Workflow needed in order to use package `sdcTable`

3.2.4.2 Capabilities of the Package

The user is able to protect tabular data which have to be transformed into a specific format by using either the GHMITER algorithm ([28]) or the Hitas algorithm. Both heuristic algorithms can be called within *protectTable()*. Initial work has started to support rounding algorithms in this package. In the published version, algorithms for simple, random, and controlled rounding have been implemented for subtables.

In the next section, the usage of sdcTable is explained by explaining all the steps mentioned above.

3.2.5 Anonymizing Tables Using sdcTable – A Guided Tour

In this section, it will be shown how to use sdcTable to protect hierarchical tables.

3.2.5.1 Standardizing Input

Suppose we have input microdata available and the statistical table we need to protect is defined by three dimensional variables, namely *sex*, *age*, and *region*. The first few entries of the microdata set are displayed in Table 3.3.

It should be noted here that prior to any further data manipulations it is required to remove already pre-calculated totals from the microdata set – they will be calculated by createFullData() anyway. If, for example, the sum of income for males and females for combinations of *age* and *region* would be included in the data, these entries need to be removed.

In order to be able to continue working with sdcTable, it is necessary to standardize the input. In practice, this step can be quite time consuming considering the great amount of different input and output formats or variable codings. Standardizing the input data consists of basically three steps:

1. removing pre-calculated totals,
2. defining the hierarchical structure of each dimensional variable,
3. recoding each dimensional variable in a specific way.

The first step is trivial and therefore no further explanation is needed. The latter two steps will now be explained in detail.

Table 3.3 Underlying microdata

	Sex	Age	Region	Income
4914	Male	AG1	SR13	20,273.96
26,412	Female	AG12	SR111	25,791.30
29,410	Female	AG3	SR22	25,462.63
6713	Male	AG10	SR13	28,005.68
1258	Male	AG3	SR16	25,426.51
4437	Male	AG6	SR32	22,252.87

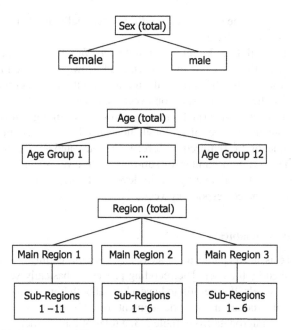

Fig. 3.4 Hierarchical structure of dimensional variables

In Fig. 3.4 the hierarchical structure of the three dimensional variables is visualized. One can observe that variables *sex* and *age* have two levels (this means that there is only one total) while variable *region* has a total of three levels. The grand total consists of three main regions and each of these main regions consists of several sub-regions.

The hierarchical structure is saved as a list-object in R. For each dimensional variable a vector is specified. The required number of elements of each vector is defined by the number of levels. The values of each vector element are defined by the number of digits that are needed in this level to sequentially number the characteristics in this level.

Listing 3.30 Hierarchical structure of dimensional variables

```
dimStruct <- list()
dimStruct[[1]] <- c(1,1)      # sex
dimStruct[[2]] <- c(1,2)      # age
dimStruct[[3]] <- c(1,1,2)    # region
```

In this code-listing a list-object *dimStruct* is defined. For each dimensional variable the standardized hierarchical structure is given as a vector.

We are now considering variable *sex*. As we can see from Fig. 3.4, this dimensional variable has only two levels. Thus, the required number of elements is 2. Since the total number of characteristics in the first level ("Total") is one, only one digit is required for sequentially numbering. Therefore, the 1 is written as the first vector element. In the second level, we observe two characteristics, namely *male* and *female*. Since only one digit is required for sequentially numbering, the second element for this vector is also 1.

The situation is slightly different for variable *age*. Variable *age* features also two levels. For the total, also only one digit is required. However, as seen in Fig. 3.4, a total of 12 age-groups exists. Therefore, the required digits for sequential numbering are 2 which is also the value of the second vector element.

For the third dimensional variable *region* we observe from Fig. 3.4 that three levels exist. Therefore, the number of vector elements needs to be 3. As in the previous examples, only one digit is required for level 1 (the total) and level 2 (the three main regions). But the maximum number of sub-regions in level 3 is 11; two digits are required for sequentially numbering within level 3 of variable *region*. This is why the third element of the corresponding vector is set to 2.

3.2.5.2 Recoding Variables

Since `sdcTable` is not capable to process any variable codings, standardization needs to be applied by the user. The recoding process is basically sequential numbering within sub-levels. It is helpful to have a look at both Fig. 3.4 and the definition of the hierarchical structure in the code segment from above.

Considering the microdata from Table 3.3, a total of three dimensional variables exists defining the statistical table which need to be standardized. The easiest variable to recode is obviously *sex* since this variable has only two characteristics. The necessary digits needed can be calculated easily by summing up the vector defining the hierarchical structure.

Listing 3.31 Required digits for standardized variables

```
# digits needed for standardized variables
# sex, age and region

unlist(lapply(dimStruct, sum))
R> 2 3 4
```

As we can see from 3.31, we obviously only need two digits to standardize variable *sex* and three or rather four digits are required for the standardized variables *age* and *region*, respectively.

The first digit of any standardized variable always equals zero, since the coding for the grand total consists of zeros only. In all further levels, all characteristics are sequentially numbered within their upper levels. This leads to the standardized codes of "01" for males and "02" for females when considering variable *sex*. We note that codes for totals ("00" in this case) do not need to be created since these observations have already been excluded from the minimal data set. To clarify, one could transform the hierarchical variable *sex* using the following R-statements:

Listing 3.32 Recoding of Variable "sex" into standardized form

```
# minDat is the minimal dataset without totals
minDat$sex[which(minDat$sex=='male')]     <- '01'
minDat$sex[which(minDat$sex=='female')]   <- '02'
```

The missing totals will be calculated automatically from the minimal data set using function *createFullData()* and codes for missing (sub)totals will be automatically generated.

Similarly, the automatic recoding for variable *age* is done. The only difference is that three digits are needed for the standardized variable and the characteristic "000" represents the total value over all age-groups, while "005" and "011"represent the fifth and eleventh age-group, respectively.

Considering variable *region* the situation becomes slightly more complicated because *region* consists of three levels. From 3.31 we know that a total of four digits is required for the standardization of this variable. As above, "0000" would represent the grand total over all areas, while "0200" represents the second main area and "0203" its third sub-area.

3.2.5.3 Creating a Complete Data set

Having standardized all the dimensional variables, it is now possible to create a complete data set featuring all possible (sub)totals that can be calculated from variables defining the table.

Listing 3.33 Creating a complete data set for further processing

```
indexVars <- 1:3

complDat <- createFullData(minDat, indexvars, dimStuct)
print(class(complDat))
R> ''fullData''
```

Code-listing 3.33 shows how to create a data set using `createFullData()` function. We suppose that the data set `minDat` was changed in a way that the first three columns are now the standardized variables *sex*, *age*, and *region* and the fourth column represents the number of observations for a given combination of the dimensional variables. Furthermore, variable `indexVars` specifies the position of the dimensional variables within `minDat`, and `dimStuct` is defined as in 3.30.

The output of this function is an object `complDat` which is of class *fullData*. It would be possible to ask the procedure for simple primary suppression of cells using a minimum frequency rule which can be specified in the function call. We note that any object of this class is a list-object with the list-elements being the complete data set with all possible (sub)totals and with an additional column added stating if a cell was marked as primary suppressed. Another list-object lists the indices of the cells that should be protected. Therefore, it is possible to manually set cells as primary suppressions based on a specific rule by directly modifying an object of class `fullData`.

3.2.5.4 Protecting the Data

Given an object of class *fullData* it is then possible to protect table cells whose indices are listed in the list-object `supps2check` of an object of class `fullDat` by running function `protectData()` as it is shown in code-listing 3.34.

Listing 3.34 Protecting a data set using different algorithms

```
safeDatHypercube <- protectData(complDat,
                                method=''HYPERCUBE'')
safeDatHitas <- protectData(complDat, method=''HITAS'')
```

Running function `protectTable()` requires only two input parameters. The first one is an object of class *fullData* that has previously been calculated. The second required argument is the choice of the suppression algorithm. Currently, only two choices are possible: *HYPERCUBE* and *HITAS*.

Furthermore, it is possible to set additional arguments depending on the choice of the suppression algorithm. Without specifying further arguments, the default values which are documented in the included online help are used. It is also possible to specify whether empty cells should be allowed to be included in suppression patterns when using the HYPERCUBE algorithm or changing the upper and lower protection levels when using the HITAS method.

3.2.5.5 Comparing and Analyzing Results

Having protected an object of class *fullData* using function `protectTable()`, the resulting object is of class `safeTable`. A summary function for objects of this class has been implemented, showing useful information such as the number of primary suppressed cells, the number of additionally suppressed cells, the complete running time of the procedure, or the necessary runs to protect against differencing for secondary suppressions which is necessary in heuristic procedures such as the HYPERCUBE algorithm. Code-listing 3.35 shows the corresponding output based on the results of 3.34.

Listing 3.35 Comparing results using the included summary function

```
print(summary(safeDatHypercube))
R> The dataset was protected using HYPERCUBE !
R> Necessary runs: 5
R> Total duration: 5.453931
R> Primary suppressions: 24 (1.78 %)
R> Secondary suppressions: 144 (10.67 %)

print(summary(safeDatHitas))
R> The dataset was protected using HITAS !
R> Necessary runs: 1
R> Total duration: 5.315442
R> Primary suppressions: 24 (1.78 %)
R> Secondary suppressions: 125 (9.26 %)
```

The results displayed in 3.35 show that the HITAS algorithm results in a total of 125 additional suppressions. In contrast, the HYPERCUBE algorithm suppresses a total of 144 cells to protect the primary cells sufficiently. However, the algorithms are not directly comparable since the choice of protection intervals and the choice if empty cells may be included in the supression patterns when using the

HYPERCUBE algorithm influence the results. Also, the more complex the statistical tables to protect, the HITAS algorithm tends to run much longer than HYPERCUBE.

3.2.6 Summary

In this section a short overview of the possibilities to protect hierarchical tabular data using R-package sdcTable was presented. The main steps to apply protection using the package are as follows:

- Standardization: the resource-intensive process of reshaping data so that it can be used within the package can be done easily within R.
- createFullData() to create a data object suitable as an input object for further processing.
- protectTable() for secondary cell suppression using different algorithms.

3.3 Summary

Statistical disclosure control is a subject of amazingly many uses due to existing laws on data privacy and surprisingly few effective practitioners. The road to practical applications of statistical disclosure limitation methods was blocked, mostly because methods have not been available in software or only available in closed-source software. The problem with closed-source software is that it is simply not possible to enhance, modify, contribute code, or fix bugs since no access to the source code is provided. The main philosophy of the proposed two R-packages is open-source development under a general public license. Given such a license, the Intellectual rights of every author who contributes to the packages with code is respected.

In the first part of the chapter, an application of the most popular methods for statistical disclosure control to protect microdata from official statistics was shown using the sdcMicro package. It was shown how to apply methods from sdcMicro to protect categorical data by recoding, suppression, and randomization. Furthermore, it was outlined that recoding of variables is a highly explanatory process which is supported by the software. Finally, an example based on real-world data was given to show the anonymization of both categorical variables and continuous scaled variables.

In the second part of the chapter the open-source package sdcTable was presented. This software could be used for protecting hierarchical tables. A detailed description was given of how the data must be structured to allow to apply the available protection methods. This detailed structure is necessary to provide all information about the hierarchies in the tables. After this data preparation step the application of protection methods for complex hierarchical tables becomes easy, just by applying functions createFullData() and protectTable(). In comparison with existing closed-source software to protect tables, sdcTable does not need any additional commercial software – it is based on an open-source solver to solve linear programs.

References

1. Benedetti R. and Franconi L. Statistical and technological solutions for controlled data dissemination. In: *Pre-Proceedings of New Techniques and Technologies for Statistics*, Sorrento, Italy, pp. 225–570, 1998.
2. Bethlehem J.G., Keller W.J., and Pannekoek J. Disclosure control of microdata. *Journal of the American Statistical Association*, 85(409):38–45 1990.
3. Berkelaar M. lpSolve: Interface to Lp solve v. 5.5 to solve linear/integer programs. R Package Version 5.6.4, 2008.
4. Brand R. Microdata protection through noise addition. In: *Privacy in Statistical Databases*. Lecture Notes in Computer Science, vol. 3050, Springer, New York, NY, pp. 347–359, 2004.
5. Capobianchi A., Polettini S., and Lucarelli M. Strategy for the implementation of individual risk methodology into m-ARGUS In: Report for the CASC project. No 1.2-D1, 2001.
6. Carlson M. Assessing microdata disclosure risk using the Poisson-inverse Gaussian distribution. *Statistics in Transition*, 5:901–925, 2002.
7. Castro J. and Baena D. Using a mathematical programming modelling language for optimal CTA. In: *Privacy in Statistical Databases*. Lecture Notes in Computer Science, vol. 5262, Springer, New York, NY, pp. 1–12, 2008.
8. Cox L.H., Linear sensitivity measures in statistical disclosure control. *Journal of Statistical Planning and Inference,* 75:153–164, 1981.
9. Dalenius T. and Reiss S.P. (1982) Data-swapping: A technique for disclosure control. *Journal of Statistical Planning and Inference*, vol. 6, pp. 73–85, 1982.
10. Defays D. and Nanopoulos P. Panels of enterprises and confidentiality: The small aggregates method. In: *Proceedings of the 1992 Symposium on Design and Analysis of Longitudinal Surveys, Statistics Canada, Ottawa*, pp. 195–204, 1993.
11. Defays D. and Anwar M.N. Masking microdata using micro-aggregation. *Journal of Official Statistics*, 14:449–461, 1998.
12. DeWolf P.P. HiTaS: A heuristic approach to cell suppression in hierarchical tables. In: *Inference Control in Statistical Databases*, Lecture Notes in Computer Sciences, vol. 2316, Springer, New York, NY, pp. 81–98, 2002.
13. Domingo-Ferrer J., Mateo-Sanz J.M. and Torra V. Comparing SDC methods for microdata on the basis of information loss and disclosure risk In: *Pre-proceedings of ETK-NTTS, Springer, New York, NY*, vol. 2, pp. 807–826, 2001.
14. Domingo-Ferrer J. and Mateo-Sanz J.M. Practical data-oriented microaggregation for statistical disclosure control. *IEEE Transcations on Knowledge and Data Engineering*, 14(1):189–201, 2002.
15. Fischetti M. and Salazar-Gonz´alez J.J. Models and algorithms for optimizing cell suppression in tabular data with linear constraints. *Journal of the American Statistical Association,* 95:916–928, 1999.
16. Fischetti M. and Salazar-Gonz´alez J.J. Complementary cell suppression for statistical disclosure control in tabular data with linear constraints. *Journal of the American Statistical Association,* 95:916–928, 2000.
17. Forster J.J. and Webb E.L. Bayesian disclosure risk assessment: Predicting small frequencies in contingency tables. *Journal of the Royal Statistical Society*, C 56:551–570, 2007.
18. Franconi L. and Polettini S. Individual risk estimation in m-Argus: A review. In: *Privacy in Statistical Databases*. Lecture Notes in Computer Science, vol. 3050, Springer, New York, NY, pp. 262–272, 2004.

19. Gouweleeuw J., Kooiman P., Willenborg L. and DeWolf P-P. Post-randomisation for statistical disclosure control: Theory and implementation. *Journal of Official Statistics*, 14(4):463–478, 1998.
20. Hundepool A., Domingo-Ferrer J., Franconi L., Giessing S., Lenz R., Longhurst J., Schulte Nordholt E., Seri G., and De Wolf P. Handbook on Statistical Disclosure Control, 2007. http://neon.vb.cbs.nl/casc/Handbook.htm
21. Kelly J.P., Golden B.L., and Assad A.A. Using simulated annealing to solve controlled rounding problems. *Annals of Operations Research*, 2(2):174–190, 1990.
22. Kim J.J. A method for limiting disclosure in microdata based on random noise and transformation. In: *Proceedings of the Section on Survey Research Methods, American Statistical Association*, Alexandria, Louisiana, USA, pp. 303–308, 1986.
23. Kooiman P., Willenborg L., and Gouweleeuw J. A method for disclosure limitation of microdata. In: Research Paper 9705, Statistics Netherlands, Voorburg, 1997.
24. Lawrence M. and Temple Lang D. R bindings for Gtk 2.8.0 and above. R Package Version 2.12.7, 2008.
25. Mateo-Sanz J.M., Domingo-Ferrer J., and Sebé F. Probabilistic information loss measures in confidentiality protection of continuous microdata. *Data Mining and Knowledge Discovery*, 11:181–193, 2004.
26. Merola G. Generalized risk measures for tabular data. In: *Proceedings of the 54th Session of the International Statistical Institute*, Berlin, Germany, 2003.
27. Polletini S. and Seri G. Strategy for the implementation of individual risk methodology into m-ARGUS. Report for the CASC Project No 1.2-D1, 2004.
28. Repsilber D. Sicherung persönlicher Angaben in Tabellendaten. *Statistische Analysen und Studien Nordrhein-Westfalen* 1:24–35, 2002.
29. Rinott Y. On models for statistical disclosure risk estimation. In: *Proceedings of the joint ECE/Eurostat Work Session on Statistical Data Confidentiality*, Luxembourg, pp. 275–285, 2003.
30. Rinott Y. and Shlomo N. A generalized negative binomial smoothing model for sample disclosure risk estimation. In: *Privacy in Statistical Databases*. Lecture Notes in Computer Science, vol. 4203, Springer, New York, NY, pp. 82–93, 2006.
31. Rousseeuw P. Multivariate Estimation with High Breakdown Point. Privacy in Statistical Databases. Mathematical Statistics and Applications. Akademiai Kiado, Budapest, pp 283–297, 1985.
32. Salazar-Gonz´alez J.J. Controlled rounding and cell perturbation: Statistical disclosure limitation methods for tabular data. *Mathematical Programming*, 105:583–603, 2005.
33. Samarati P. and Sweeney L. Protecting privacy when disclosing information: k-anonymity and its enforcement through generalization and suppression. In: SRI Intl. Tech. Report, 1998.
34. Samarati P. Protecting respondents' identities in microdata release. *IEEE Transactions on Knowledge and Data Engineering*, 13(6):1010–1027, 2001.
35. Skinner C.J. and Holmes D.J. Estimating the re-identification risk per record in microdata. *Journal of Official Statistics*, 14:361–372, 1998.
36. Skinner C.J. and Shlomo N. Assessing identification risk in survey microdata using loglinear models. In: S3RI Methodology Working Papers, M06/14, University of Southampton, Southampton Statistical Sciences Research Institute, 2006.
37. Sweeney L. k-anonymity: A model for protecting privacy. *International Journal on Uncertainty Fuzziness and Knowledge-based Systems* 10(5):557–570, 2002.
38. Takemura A. Statistical Data Protection Eurostat, Luxembourg, pp. 45–58, 1999.
39. Templ M. Software development for SDC in R. In: *Privacy in Statistical Databases*. Lecture Notes in Computer Science, vol. 4203, Springer, New York, NY, pp. 347–359, 2006.
40. Templ M. sdcMicro: A new flexible R-package for the generation of anonymised microdata – design issues and new methods. In: Joint UNECE/Eurostat Work Session on Statistical Data Confidentiality, Manchester, UK, 2007.

41. Templ M. and Meindl B. Robustification of microdata masking methods and the comparison with existing methods. In: *Privacy in Statistical Databases*. Lecture Notes in Computer Science, vol. 5262, Springer, New York, NY, pp. 177–189, 2008.
42. Templ M. Statistical disclosure control for microdata using the R-package sdcMicro. *Transactions on Data Privacy*, 1(2):67–85, 2008.
43. Templ M. sdcMicro: Statistical Disclosure Control methods for the generation of public- and scientific-use files. Manual and Package. R Package Version 2.6.3, 2009.
44. Templ M. *New Developments in Statistical Disclosure Control and Imputation: Robust Statistics Applied to Official Statistics*. Suedwestdeutscher Verlag fuer Hochschulschriften, 2009.
45. Ting D., Fienberg S., and Trottini M. ROMM methodology for microdata release. In: *Monographs of Official Statistics, Work Session on Statistical Data Confidentiality*. Eurostat, Luxembourg, 2005.
46. Verzani J. and Lawrence M. gWidgetsRGtk2: Toolkit implementation of gWidgets for RGtk2. Published online <http://cran.r-project.org/web/packages/gWidgetsRGtk2/index.html>, 2009.
47. Willenborg L. and De Waal T. Elements of statistical disclosure control. Springer-Verlag, New York, NY, 2000.
48. Yancey W.E., Winkler W.E., and Creecy R.H. Disclosure risk assessment in perturbative microdata protection. In: *Inference Control in Statistical Databases*. Lecture Notes in Computer Science, Springer, New York, NY, pp. 49–60, 2002.

Chapter 4
Disclosure Risk Assessment for Sample Microdata Through Probabilistic Modeling

Natalie Shlomo

Abstract Disclosure risk occurs when there is a high probability that an intruder can identify an individual in released sample microdata and confidential information may be revealed. For some social surveys, the population from which the sample is drawn is generally not known or only partially known through marginal distributions. The identification is made possible through the use of a key, which is a combination of indirectly identifying variables, such as age, sex, and place of residence. Disclosure risk measures are based on the notion of population uniqueness in the key. In order to quantify the disclosure risk, probabilistic models are defined based on distributional assumptions about the population counts according to the observed sample counts. The parameters for the distribution are estimated through log-linear models. The model selection criteria is based on a 'minimum error' test using a forward search algorithm. The methods are expanded to cover the case of complex survey designs and misclassification on the key variables, either arising from the survey process or as a result of perturbative disclosure control techniques that may have been applied to the data. Variance and confidence intervals of estimated disclosure risk measures are also addressed. The methods are demonstrated on real data drawn from extracts of the 2001 UK Census. Possible extensions to the probabilistic modeling are presented based on a local polynomial regression smoothing technique in neighborhoods of the cells of the key.

4.1 Introduction

Statistical agencies face growing demands for the release of microdata while under legal, moral, and ethical obligations to preserve the confidentiality of respondents. The microdata released are generally based on samples arising from social surveys where the statistical unit is a household or an individual. Microdata from business

---

N. Shlomo (✉)
Southampton Statistical Sciences Research Institute, University of Southampton,
Southampton, SO17 1BJ, UK
e-mail: n.shlomo@soton.ac.uk

J. Nin, J. Herranz (eds.), *Privacy and Anonymity in Information Management Systems*,
Advanced Information and Knowledge Processing,
DOI 10.1007/978-1-84996-238-4_4, © Springer-Verlag London Limited 2010

surveys are typically not released because of their disclosive nature due to high sampling fractions and skewed distributions.

Many statistical agencies have set up provisions for providing access to sample microdata arising from social surveys for research purposes under different modes of access, for example, public-use files, microdata under contract, special license agreements, on-site data labs, and data archives. Each of these modes of access might have different levels of disclosure risk protection depending on who is requesting the data. New developments in remote access and remote computation servers are possible solutions for data release and pose specific challenges for applying web-based disclosure risk techniques 'on the fly' for statistical outputs.

In order to preserve the privacy and confidentiality of individuals in statistical data, statistical agencies must assess the disclosure risk in sample microdata and if required choose appropriate statistical disclosure control (SDC) methods to apply to the data. Measuring disclosure risk involves assessing and evaluating numerically the risk of re-identifying statistical units. SDC methods perturb, modify, or summarize the data in order to prevent re-identification by a potential attacker. To make informed decisions about the release of microdata, objective disclosure risk measures are needed. These measures are compared to tolerable risk thresholds which may vary according to the mode of access. Higher levels of protection through SDC methods impact negatively on the utility and quality of the data. The SDC decision problem involves finding the optimal balance between managing and minimizing disclosure risk and ensuring high utility in the data.

In this chapter, we focus on quantifying the disclosure risk for sample microdata arising from social surveys. Microdata is released only after taking out directly identifying variables, such as names, addresses, and identity numbers. Disclosure risk arises from attribute disclosure where small counts on cross-classified indirect identifying key variables can be used to identify an individual and confidential information may be learnt. The key variables are typically variables that are visible and traceable and are accessible to the public or to potential intruders. They include variables such as sex, age, occupation, place of residence, country of birth, family structure. In the kinds of social survey applications of concern here, we assume that the key variables are categorical. Sensitive variables are often continuous ones but can also be categorical. We define the 'key' as the set of combined identifying key variables, typically presented as a contingency table spanned by key variables containing the counts from the microdata.

One disclosure risk scenario often used at statistical agencies is the ability of an intruder to match the released microdata to external sources containing the target population based on a common key. Following several authors (e.g., [2, 7, 16]), consider a microdata file consisting of records for a sample of individuals from a finite population. The disclosure risk scenario is based on the assumption that an intruder has access to the file as well as auxiliary information on the values of the key variables for some known individuals in the population. The intruder matches the two data sources in order to identify one or more records in the microdata. We suppose the intruder assesses whether there is a microdata record and a known individual for which the probability that the former belongs to the latter is high.

The basic definition of identification risk is the value of this probability when the microdata record does indeed belong to the known individual. External sources can be either in the form of prior knowledge that the intruder might have about a specific population group or individuals or by having access to outside files containing information about the population, such as a National Population Register, Electoral Role, or private databases (for example, customer, or market research databases).

The probability of identification risk is conditional on the data which might reasonably be assumed available to the intruder and defined with respect to a model and assumptions, which are justifiable from analysis of the data and from knowledge of the processes (sample selection, measurement error etc.) generating the data. The key variables are treated as given according to a specified scenario, as in [16].

A literature review of methods for assessing disclosure risk for sample microdata arising from social surveys can be classified into four types:

- Heuristics that identify records as 'special uniques' on a set of cross-classified key variables, i.e., sample uniques that are likely to be population uniques (see [9, 29]).
- A global disclosure risk measure developed by Skinner and Elliot [25] which takes into account the sample design and does not need parametric assumptions for its estimation.
- Probabilistic record linkage on a set of key (matching) variables that can be used to link the microdata to an external population file. Disclosure risk is quantified by the number of correct matches (see [6, 28, 30]).
- Probabilistic modeling of disclosure risk which has been developed under two approaches: a full model-based framework taking into account all of the information available to 'intruders' and modeling their behavior (see [7, 15, 18]), and a more simplified approach that restricts the information that would be known to intruders (see [1, 2, 8, 10, 19, 24]).

In this chapter, the focus is on the simplified probabilistic modeling approach for assessing disclosure risk in microdata and specifically the risk of identifying an individual which can lead to the disclosure of sensitive attributes. Using probabilistic modeling we obtain consistency between record-level and global-level disclosure risk measures. Record-level disclosure risk measures can be used to target high-risk records in the microdata for localized applications of SDC techniques. Global disclosure risk measures are aggregated from record-level risk measures and are essential for informing decisions about the release of microdata. To quantify the disclosure risk, a frequency table of counts spanned by the identifying categorical key variables is produced from the microdata. The corresponding table for the population is assumed unknown as is the case for typical social surveys where samples may be drawn from address lists or area-based sampling frames. Some partial information may be known about the population in the form of marginal distributions. Disclosure risk arises from cells of the table where both the sample and the population counts are small. This allows an intruder who has the sample data and access to some information on the population to identify an individual with high probability thereby exposing sensitive information. We restrict our attention to these high-risk records only.

The framework for disclosure risk assessment based on the simplified probabilistic modeling approach is set out in Section 4.1 where global and individual disclosure risk measures are defined based on classical distributional assumptions of count data. We initially assume that variables may have undergone some recoding to reduce the disclosure risk. Section 4.2 presents the use of log-linear modeling to estimate the parameters of the distribution and estimates of the disclosure risk measures. A model selection technique is also described based on a goodness-of-fit criteria that assures good estimates of the disclosure risk measures. Section 4.3 discusses extensions to the case of complex survey designs and Section 4.4 to the case where the microdata has been exposed to measurement error, either arising naturally in the survey processes or as a result of a perturbative method of disclosure control that may have been applied to the microdata. Section 5 discusses variance estimation and confidence intervals for the global disclosure risk measures. Section 6 provides examples of applying the methods described in the previous sections on samples drawn from the 2001 UK Census data. Finally, Section 7 introduces some possible extensions to the probabilistic modeling for assessing disclosure risk.

4.2 Disclosure Risk Measures and Their Estimation

4.2.1 Notation and Definitions

To introduce measures of disclosure risk, let F_k be the population count and f_k be the sample count in cell k of the multiway contingency table formed by cross-classifying the key variables (with cells labeled $k = 1, \ldots, K$). Disclosure risk arises from cells in which both f_k and F_k are positive and small and, in particular, when $f_k = F_k = 1$ (sample and population uniques). Skinner and Holmes defined in [24] a risk measure given by $E(1/F_k) = \sum_r P(F_k = r)/r$, where $P(F_k = r)$ denotes the probability that $F_k = r$ under the model ($r = 1, 2, \ldots$). This is based on the assumption that the intruder would not know values of the population (especially for small counts) and the assumption of the exchangeability on the selection of records in cell k. We focus on those records in the sample that are sample unique $f_k = 1$ for a cell k since these cells will provide the highest risk measure. Assuming that the pairs (F_k, f_k) are independent, we define $P(F_k = 1 | f_k = 1)$ the conditional probability that $F_k = 1$ and $E(1/F_k | f_k = 1)$ the conditional expectation of $\frac{1}{F_k}$. These are referred to as record-level disclosure risk measures [29] since they vary between records. Global disclosure risk measures are typically aggregations of the record-level risk measures which can be normalized by some measure of the total size of the table, by the number of sample uniques, or by some measure of the information value of the data.

Here, we consider simply summing the record-level measures across sample unique records to give

$$\tau_1 = \sum_{SU} P(F_k = 1 | f_k = 1), \tag{4.1}$$

the expected number of sample uniques that are population unique and

$$\tau_2 = \sum_{SU} E(1/F_k | f_k = 1), \tag{4.2}$$

the expected number of correct matches for sample uniques, where $SU = \{k : f_k = 1\}$ denotes sample unique cells. As global disclosure risk measures aggregate across individual record-level disclosure risk measures, we obtain consistency between the two types of disclosure risk measures. The focus will be on situations where K is large (and the (F_k, f_k) may be treated as independent) so that τ will closely approximate, $\tau_1^* = \sum_k I(f_k = 1, F_k = 1)$, the number of sample uniques that are population uniques, or $\tau_2^* = \sum_k I(f_k = 1)\frac{1}{F_k}$, the expected number of correct matches for sample uniques, respectively. The problem of disclosure risk assessment becomes one of statistical inference if the f_k are observed but the F_k are not. Using probabilistic modeling when population frequencies F_k are unknown, we can infer from the sample to obtain the estimates:

$$\hat{\tau}_1 = \sum_{SU} \hat{P}(F_k = 1 | f_k = 1) \text{ and } \hat{\tau}_2 = \sum_{SU} \hat{E}[1/F_k | f_k = 1]. \tag{4.3}$$

4.2.2 Estimating the Disclosure Risk

Models are required not only for the explicit definition of most of the disclosure risk measures in the previous section but also for inference about these measures. Following standard methods for contingency tables (e.g. [3]), we assume that F_k are realizations of independent Poisson random variables with means λ_k $(k = 1, \ldots, K)$, where $\lambda_k = N\gamma_k$ $(\gamma_k \geq 0$ and $\sum_{k=1}^{K} \gamma_k = 1)$: $F_k \sim P(\lambda_k)$. We assume that the sample is drawn by Bernoulli sampling where individuals in cell k have the same known inclusion probability π_k so that the sample counts f_k are also independent Poisson random variables: $f_k \sim P(\pi_k \lambda_k)$. Under the Bernoulli sampling assumption, we have $F_k | f_k \sim P[\lambda_k(1 - \pi_k)] + f_k$ so that the record-level measures may be expressed as

$$P(F_k = 1 | f_k = 1) = \exp[-(1 - \pi_k)\lambda_k]$$

and

$$E(1/F_k | f_k = 1) = \{1 - \exp[-(1 - \pi_k)\lambda_k]\} / [(1 - \pi_k)\lambda_k]. \tag{4.4}$$

The contingency table spanned by the key variables is typically very large and therefore the problem of estimating $\{\lambda_k\}$ is a hard problem, especially when we focus specifically on those cells where the observed sample count f_k is equal to one.

In the approach of [2], the parameters $\lambda_k = N\gamma_k$ are assumed to be realizations from a Gamma prior distribution $\gamma_k \sim \text{Gamma}(\alpha, \beta)$. Since under the constraint $\sum_{k=1}^{K} \gamma_k = 1$, we obtain $E\gamma_k = \alpha\beta = \frac{1}{K}$ and $\sum_{i=1}^{K} E\gamma_k = 1$ and therefore only the hyperparameter β needs to be estimated from the sample. The parameter β determines the amount of dispersion of the parameters γ_k around their mean $\frac{1}{K}$. This simplistic assumption of a Gamma prior with one hyperparameter assumes that the population is exchangeable with respect to the cells of the key and all cells have the same disclosure risk. It follows that the marginal distribution of the sample counts f_k under the Bernoulli sampling scheme follows the negative binomial distribution: $f_k \sim \text{NB}(\alpha, p_k = \frac{1}{1+N\pi_k\beta})$ with a mean of $E(f_k) = \frac{\alpha(1-p_k)}{p_k} \equiv \mu_k$ and a variance of $\text{Var}(f_k) = \frac{\alpha(1-p_k)}{p_k^2} \equiv \mu_k + \frac{\mu_k^2}{\alpha}$. With the above parameterization we have $E(f_k) = N\pi_k\alpha\beta$ and $\text{Var}(f_k) = N\pi_k\alpha\beta(1 + N\pi_k\beta)$. Further calculations in [19] yield $F_k|f_k \sim f_k + NB(\alpha + f_k, \rho_k = \frac{N\pi_k+1/\beta}{N+1/\beta})$, $(F_k \geq f_k)$.

As $\alpha \to 0$ (and hence $\beta \to \infty$), we obtain $F_k|f_k \sim f_k + \text{NB}(f_k, \pi_k)$, which is the negative binomial assumption in the model proposed by Benedetti et al. [1]. As $\alpha \to \infty$ and $\alpha\beta \to$ constant, we obtain the Poisson model described in [8, 24] and presented below. In this sense the negative binomial distribution with parameter α subsumes both models. In Section 7 we describe an extension of probabilistic modeling using the negative binomial distribution and based on local neighborhoods.

The original model proposed in [2] was based on only one hyperparameter β to model the parameters $\{\lambda_k\}$ and therefore did not accurately reflect the underlying structure in the data. Different researchers [8, 24] propose using log-linear modeling to estimate the parameters $\{\lambda_k\}$. The parameters $\{\lambda_k\}$ are related via the log-linear model:

$$\log \lambda_k = x_k' \beta \tag{4.5}$$

where x_k is a $q \times 1$ design vector, depending on the values of the key variables in cell k and β is a $q \times 1$ parameter vector. Typically, x_k specifies the main effects and low-order interactions of the categorical key variables [3]. Since the f_k are the outcomes of independent $P(\pi_k\lambda_k)$ random variables, the maximum likelihood (ML) estimator $\hat{\beta}$ are obtained by solving the score equations:

$$\sum_k [f_k - \pi_k \exp(x_k'\beta)]x_k = 0, \tag{4.6}$$

using numerical techniques. The risk measures in (4.1) and (4.2) can then be estimated by replacing λ_k by $\hat{\lambda}_k = \exp(x_k'\hat{\beta})$ in the expressions (4.4) and then aggregating to (4.3).

4.2.3 Model Selection and Goodness-of-Fit Criteria

Authors of [27] have developed a diagnostic criteria and model selection technique known as the minimum error test which can deal with the very large and spare contingency tables that are typical in disclosure risk assessment for sample micro-data. The criteria is related to similar tests for over-or under-dispersion of count data under the Poisson regression model (see [5]), i.e., testing the assumption that the conditional mean is equal to the conditional variance. The minimum error test approach involves (i) specifying the key variables, (ii) selection of one or more log-linear models which fit well according to these criteria, and (iii) using the well-fitting models to obtain disclosure risk estimates.

The problem of estimating the parameters using log-linear modeling for a very large and sparse contingency table based on sample counts is to ensure that the zero cell counts are modeled accurately. Random (non-structural) zeros are defined for the case where $f_k = 0$ and $F_k \neq 0$. These occur when the selection of the sample does not include a member in cell k due to a small population count and a small sampling rate. Structural zeros are defined for the case where $f_k = 0$ and $F_k = 0$. These occur when impossible combinations of categories of key variables are cross-classified, for example, 'young children' combined with the category of 'married' would result in a structural zero count.

The impact of trying to model both the random and structural zero cell counts correctly in a large and sparse contingency table leads to problems of over-fitting when the models are 'too complex' or under-fitting when the model is 'over-smoothed.' For example, if high-order interactions are used to estimate the parameters $\{\lambda_k\}$ (for example, the saturated model where $\lambda_k = f_k/\pi_k$), the marginal totals that are used to fit the models would have many random zero counts, resulting in estimating the expected cell count as zero when in fact there could be population associated to those cells. On the other hand, if the model only includes main effects (the independence model), there is little chance of marginal totals having sample counts of zeros. This would result in the incorrect modeling of the structural zeros since they would have non-zero-fitted cell counts when in fact there is no population associated to these cells. The under-fitting of the model leads to an under-estimation of disclosure risk, while over-fitting leads to an over-estimation of disclosure risk.

Because the contingency table includes both random and structural zeros counts, the aim is to define the main effects and appropriate interactions in the model that take into account both types of zeros and models them appropriately. This would provide a model of equal dispersion and good estimates of disclosure risk measures.

The minimum error test proposed by Skinner and Shlomo [27] is as follows: Denote the two record-level risk measures: $h_1(\lambda_k) = \exp[-(1 - \pi_k)\lambda_k]$ and $h_2(\lambda_k) = \{1 - \exp[-(1 - \pi_k)\lambda_k]\}/[(1 - \pi_k)\lambda_k]$, where $h(\lambda)$ is a monotonic decreasing function of λ. The goodness-of-fit criterion for choosing a specification of model (4.5) minimizes the error of $\hat{\tau} = \sum_k I(f_k = 1)h(\hat{\lambda}_k)$ as an estimator of $\tau = \sum_k I(f_k = 1)h(\lambda_k)$ or as a predictor of $\tau^* = \sum_k I(f_k = 1)g(F_k)$ which takes the particular forms: $\tau_1^* = \sum_k I(f_k = 1, F_k = 1)$ or $\tau_2^* = \sum_k I(f_k = 1)/F_k$, respectively.

Changing the notation from [27], the test statistic is approximated by

$$B = \sum_k E[I(f_k = 1)][h(\hat{\lambda}_k) - h(\lambda_k)] = \sum_k \pi_k \lambda_k \exp(-\pi_k \lambda_k)[h(\hat{\lambda}_k) - h(\lambda_k)].$$

$$(4.7)$$

A Taylor expansion of h leads to the approximation:

$$h(\hat{\lambda}_k) \approx h(\lambda_k) + h'(\lambda_k)(\hat{\lambda}_k - \lambda_k) + h''(\lambda_k)(\hat{\lambda}_k - \lambda_k)^2/2, \qquad (4.8)$$

using a quadratic expansion of $h(\hat{\lambda}_k)$ around λ_k. For example, when $h(\lambda) = h_1(\lambda)$, $h'(\lambda_k) = -(1 - \pi_k)h_1(\lambda_k)$ and $h''(\lambda_k) = (1 - \pi_k)^2 h_1(\lambda_k)$.

Substituting approximation (4.8) into (4.7) gives

$$B \approx \sum_{k\pi} \pi_k \lambda_k \exp(-\pi_k \lambda_k)[h'(\lambda_k)(\hat{\lambda}_k - \lambda_k) + h''(\lambda_k)(\hat{\lambda}_k - \lambda_k)^2/2]. \qquad (4.9)$$

Since $E(f_k) = \mu_k = \pi_k \lambda_k$ and $E[(f_k - \pi_k \hat{\lambda}_k)^2 - f_k] = \pi_k^2 (\lambda_k - \hat{\lambda}_k)^2$ under the null hypothesis of a Poisson model fit, it follows that, for a large number of cells, expression (4.9) is approximated by

$$\hat{B} = \sum_k \lambda_k \exp(-\mu_k)\{-h'(\lambda_k)(f_k - \pi_k \hat{\lambda}_k) + h''(\lambda_k)[(f_k - \pi_k \hat{\lambda}_k)^2 - f_k]/(2\pi_k)\}.$$

$$(4.10)$$

$\hat{B}$ is written as $\hat{B}_1$ or $\hat{B}_2$ when $h(\lambda) = h_1(\lambda)$ or $h(\lambda) = h_2(\lambda)$ respectively, for example

$$\hat{B}_1 = \sum_k \hat{\lambda}_k \exp(-\hat{\lambda}_k)(1 - \pi_k)\{(f_k - \pi_k \hat{\lambda}_k) + (1 - \pi_k)[(f_k - \pi_k \hat{\lambda}_k)^2 - f_k]/(2\pi_k)\}$$

$$(4.11)$$

The bias estimates are standardized under the assumption that the model is correctly specified. In this case, $\hat{B}$ has zero expectation, and using standard results for the first four moments of a Poisson random variable, $\text{var}(\hat{B}) = \sum_k a_k^2(\pi_k \lambda_k) + 2b_k^2(\pi_k \lambda_k)^2$, where $a_k = -\lambda_k \exp(-\pi_k \lambda_k)h'(\lambda_k)$ and $b_k = \lambda_k \exp(-\pi_k \lambda_k)h''(\lambda_k)/(2\pi_k)$.

A natural estimator of $\text{var}(\hat{B})$ is given by

$$v = \sum_k \hat{a}_k^2 \hat{\mu}_k + 2\hat{b}_k^2 \hat{\mu}_k^2, \qquad (4.12)$$

where $\hat{\mu}_k = \pi_k \hat{\lambda}_k$, and

$$\hat{a}_k = -\hat{\lambda}_k \exp(-\hat{\mu}_k)h'(\hat{\lambda}_k), \qquad (4.13)$$

and

$$\hat{b}_k = \hat{\lambda}_k \exp(-\hat{\mu}_k)h''(\hat{\lambda}_k)/(2\pi_k). \qquad (4.14)$$

For $h(\lambda) = h_1(\lambda)$, we have $a_k = (1 - \pi_k)\lambda_k \exp(-\lambda_k)$ and $b_k = (1 - \pi_k)^2\lambda_k$ $\exp(-\lambda_k)/(2\pi_k)$. For $h(\lambda) = h_2(\lambda)$, $a_k = \exp(-\pi_k\lambda_k)h_2(\lambda_k) - \exp(-\lambda_k)$ and $b_k = \{\exp(-\pi_k\lambda_k)h_2(\lambda_k) - \exp(-\lambda_k)[1+(1 - \pi_k)\lambda_k/2]\}/[\pi_k\lambda_k]$.

Given the assumptions above, $\hat{B}/\sqrt{v}$ has an approximate standard normal distribution under the hypothesis that the expected value of $\hat{B}$ is zero. These minimum error tests are designed to assess whether a model displays evidence of under-fitting or over-fitting for estimation purposes and not to test whether a given model is correct.

As mentioned, for typical data sets arising from social surveys, the independence log-linear model tends to under-fit and leads to over-estimation of the disclosure risk measures. At the other extreme, the all 3-way interaction model tends to over-fit and leads to under-estimation of the risk measures. A reasonable solution typically lies between these extremes and indeed the all 2-way interactions log-linear model often leads to good estimates of the risk measures for the types of data sets and size of tables spanned by key variables that are used in practice.

Skinner and Shlomo [27] suggest a practical approach using a forward search algorithm: compute the minimum error tests for the independence model and the all 2-way interactions model. If the latter model shows no sign of under-fitting, then start with the independence model and add in the 2-way interaction terms for different pairs of key variables, chosen sequentially in order to reduce $\hat{B}$, until a model is identified which is judged to show no evidence of under-fitting. On the other hand, if the all 2-way interactions model is found to exhibit under-fitting, then start a similar forward model search algorithm from this model as the initial model, adding 3-way interaction terms for different triples of key variables. As in any model search algorithm for a hierarchical log-linear model, the inclusion of a higher order term containing an interaction implies that all lower order effects are also included. In addition, it is sensible to produce disclosure risk estimates for each of a number of 'reasonable models' and to use the differences between the estimates as a diagnostic to check the sensitivity of the measures to the specification of the model. Section 8.1 provides examples of how this approach can be carried out in practice.

4.3 Complex Survey Designs

Social surveys will generally employ complex sampling schemes, especially stratification and multi-stage sampling, and use of survey weights. The authors of [27] describe how the probabilistic method approach described in Section 4.2 can be adapted to take into account the complex survey design.

The greatest variations in individual inclusion probabilities tend to arise from differences between major strata, especially geographical strata. It is common to include such major stratification variables as key variables since they will typically be very visible, e.g., state of residence. In this case, there will be no between-stratum component to the variation in inclusion probabilities within cells. Even if there are design variables, which are not natural key variables, but do lead to major variations in inclusion probabilities, they should be included as key variables to ensure that a single inclusion probability π_k is defined in each cell k.

Another factor in a complex survey design is the possibility that the sampling of individuals within same cells is clustered. In practice, the number of sample individuals in a primary sampling unit in a social survey is usually limited in order to avoid loss of precision. The cross-classification of key variables, such as sex, age group, ethnicity, religion, place of residence, or occupation, will typically cut across the primary sampling units and divide them by many more cells than the sample sizes within the primary sampling units. There still might be individuals from the same cell within a common cluster, e.g., few key variables in practice would split twin children of the same sex living in the same family, but based on empirical work the degree of clustering in cells tends not to lead to departures from the 'working assumption' that the (F_k, f_k) are independent resulting in the bias of the disclosure risk measures.

In order to estimate the $\{\lambda_k\}$ consistently under complex sampling, pseudo maximum likelihood estimation techniques can be employed [17]. The estimating equation in (4.6) is modified by replacing f_k by $\hat{F}_k$, obtained by summing the survey weights across sample individuals in cell k, and by removing π_k. The resulting estimates $\hat{\lambda}_k$ are plugged into the expressions in (4.4). The value of π_k in these expressions is replaced by the estimate $\hat{\pi}_k = f_k/\hat{F}_k$. Note that the risk measures only depend on π_k for sample unique cells and the value of $\hat{\pi}_k$ in this case is simply the reciprocal of the weight for the sample unique case, and this will be the inclusion probability of that case if inverse inclusion probability weighting is employed. If the only variation in inclusion probabilities is between major strata, the λ_k could be consistently estimated alternatively by simply ensuring that the strata are represented by a key variable and that the main effects of this key variable are included in the model, with π_k in (4.4) replaced by $\hat{\pi}_k$. For the minimum error test criteria for carrying out the model selection, we use the same expression for $\hat{B}$ as in (4.10) with π_k replaced by $\hat{\pi}_k$ and with $\hat{\lambda}_k$ estimated as above. The term $(f_k - \pi_k \hat{\lambda}_k)$ may alternatively be expressed as $\hat{\pi}_k(\hat{F}_k - \hat{\lambda}_k)$, i.e., a multiple of the term featuring in the pseudo score equation. The final term $(f_k - \pi_k \hat{\lambda}_k)^2 - f_k$ can be expressed as $(\hat{\pi}_k \hat{F}_k - \hat{\pi}_k \hat{\lambda}_k)^2 - \hat{\pi}_k \hat{F}_k$.

4.4 Measurement Error Models for Disclosure Risk Measures

The probabilistic model described above as well as other probabilistic models proposed by various authors (see [1, 2, 20, 21] assumes that there is no measurement error in the way the data is recorded. Kuha and Skinner [13] discuss errors that take the form of misclassification of categorical variables that arise naturally in surveys. In the statistical disclosure control setting, key variables can be purposely misclassified as a disclosure control technique, for example, through record swapping or the post-randomization method (PRAM).

The authors of [26] adapt the estimation of risk measures to take into account measurement errors. Denoting the cross-classified key variables in the population and the microdata as X, we assume that X in the microdata have undergone some misclassification or perturbation error denoted by the value $\tilde{X}$ and determined independently by a misclassification matrix M,

$$\Pr(\tilde{X} = k | X = j) = M_{kj}. \tag{4.15}$$

To assess the disclosure protection provided by misclassification, Skinner and Shlomo [26] assume that the intruder observes a match between a specific sample unit A and a target population unit B, i.e., observes $\tilde{X}_A = X_B$ (where $\tilde{X}_A$ is the value of $\tilde{X}$ for unit A and X_B is the value of X for unit B), and measures disclosure risk in terms of the uncertainty as to whether $A = B$.

Writing $\tilde{X}_a = k$ and $X_b = j$ and using the assumption of (4.15) about the misclassification mechanism, they define a record-level disclosure risk measure based on a match with a sample unique under measurement error as

$$\Pr(A = B | \text{data}) = ([M_{kk}/(1 - \pi_k M_{kk})]/[\sum_j F_j M_{kj}/(1 - \pi_k M_{kj})] \tag{4.16}$$

It follows that $\Pr(A = B | \text{data}) \leq 1/F_k$ with equality holding if there is no misclassification. The extent to which the left-hand side of this inequality is less than the right-hand side measures the impact of misclassification on disclosure risk.

If the sampling fraction is small the measure (4.16) can be approximated by

$$\Pr(A = B | \text{data}) \approx M_{kk}/\sum_j F_j M_{kj}.$$

Moreover, if the population size is large, then approximately $\sum_j F_j M_{kj} \approx \tilde{F}_k$, where $\tilde{F}_k$ is the number of units in the population which would have $\tilde{X} = k$ if they were included in the microdata (with misclassification). Hence a simple approximate expression for the disclosure risk, natural for many social surveys, is

$$\Pr(A = B | \text{data}) \approx M_{kk}/\tilde{F}_k. \tag{4.17}$$

An alternative approximation to expression (4.16) is obtained by assuming that the misclassification is small, say $M_{kk} = (1 - \delta)\phi_{kk}$ and $M_{kj} = \delta\phi_{kj}$ $(j \neq k)$, where the ϕ are fixed and $\delta \to 0$. In this case,

$$\Pr(A = B | \text{data}) \approx F_k^{-1}\{1 - [\tilde{F}_k - F_k M_{kk}]/[F_k M_{kk}/(1 - \pi_k M_{kk})]\} \tag{4.18}$$

or

$$\Pr(A = B | \text{data}) \approx [M_{kk}/(1 - \pi_k M_{kk})]/[(F_k \pi_k M_{kk}^2)/(1 - \pi_k M_{kk}) + \tilde{F}_k]. \tag{4.19}$$

Note that none of the approximations in (4.17), (4.18), or (4.19) depend on M_{kj} for $k \neq j$ and so knowledge of these probabilities is not required in the estimation of disclosure risk if 'acceptable' estimates of M_{kk} and $\tilde{F}_k$ are available. Expressions (4.18) and (4.19) also require estimates of F_k.

The definition of risk in (4.16) applies to a specific record. It is of interest also to define aggregate measures. In particular, Skinner and Shlomo [26] consider the sum of these record-level measures across sample unique records defined from (4.16) as

$$\tau = \sum_{k \in SU} [M_{kk}/(1 - \pi_k M_{kk})/[\sum_j F_j M_{kj}/(1 - \pi_k M_{kj})], \qquad (4.20)$$

where SU is the set of key variable values which are sample unique. This measure may be interpreted as the expected number of correct matches among sample uniques.

A related measure which could be used if the misclassification status of microdata records is known can be defined as follows: Let SUCC denote the set of key variable values which are sample unique and where these sample unique values have been correctly classified. The measure is given by

$$\tau_{CC}^* = \sum_{k \in SUCC} 1/F_k \qquad (4.21)$$

and again may be interpreted as the expected number of correct matches among sample uniques.

An agency wishing to apply an SDC method to survey microdata will generally not know the values of $\tilde{F}_k$ or F_k appearing in the disclosure risk expressions. The values of M_{kj} are assumed known. Expression (4.17) provides a simple way to extend the Poisson log-linear modeling approach in Sections 2.1 and the estimation of disclosure risk measures in Section 4.2.2 for the case of misclassification provided that M_{kk} is known. Since the $\tilde{f}_k, k = 1, \ldots, K$, represents the available data, all that is required is to ignore the misclassification and estimate $1/\tilde{F}_k$ from the $\tilde{f}_k, k = 1, \ldots, K$ as shown in Section 4.2.1, that is, by fitting a log-linear model to the $\tilde{f}_k, k = 1, \ldots, K$ following the same criteria as before. This results in an estimate $\hat{E}(1/\tilde{F}_k | \tilde{f}_k = 1)$ which can then be multiplied by the M_{kk} values and summed if aggregate measures of the form in (4.20) are needed. Section 6.2 presents an example of an application of this method.

4.5 Variance Estimation for Global Disclosure Risk Measures

In the context of this probabilistic method approach for estimating disclosure risk measures, Rinott and Shlomo [22] considered the variance of a global risk estimator and its related confidence interval. They point out that calculating precise estimates and confidence intervals for global disclosure risk measures is a hard problem due to the fact that risk measures are not ordinary parameters. In fact, they depend both on the sample counts (random, observable data) and on the population counts (unobservable parameters), and therefore they are not the parameters in the classical sense. Given the sample and a risk measure estimate, its variability and the need for a confidence interval is due to the fact that the population is unknown and assumed random in the model while the sample is fixed. A confidence interval should provide information on how precise the disclosure risk estimate is for a particular sample and not across all possible random samples. Therefore, conditional (or credible) confidence intervals (e.g., [14]) are considered with a coverage probability which is conditional on the given sample based on the posterior distribution of the parameter. For a discussion and references on the issue of estimating parameters of the type considered here which involve both the known sample and unknown parameters, with a brief discussion of the relevance to disclosure control, see [31].

Consider first $\tau_1 = \sum_{SU} P(F_k = 1 | f_k = 1)$ from (4.1) where SU represents the set of sample uniques. Given the sample counts $f = \{f_k\}$ the measure is a sum of Bernoulli random variables over sample uniques, taking the value one with probability $P(F_k = 1 | f_k = 1)$. Thus

$$\text{Var}(\tau_1 | f) = \sum_k I(f_k = 1) P(F_k = 1 | f_k = 1)(1 - P(F_k = 1 | f_k = 1)) \quad (4.22)$$

and is estimated by

$$\overset{\wedge}{\text{Var}}(\tau_1 | f) = \sum_k I(f_k = 1) \hat{P}(F_k = 1 | f_k = 1)(1 - \hat{P}(F_k = 1 | f_k = 1)), \quad (4.23)$$

provided it is possible to estimate the indicated conditional probabilities. In a similar way, for $\tau_2 = \sum_{SU} E(1/F_k | f_k = 1)$ in (4.2):

$$\text{Var}(\tau_2 | f) = \sum_k I(f_k = 1) \text{Var}(1/F_k | f_k = 1), \quad (4.24)$$

which is estimated by replacing the latter conditional variance by its estimate based on the estimated conditional distribution of $\{F_k | f_k\}$ to yield

$$\overset{\wedge}{\text{Var}}(\tau_2 | f) = \sum_k I(f_k = 1) \overset{\wedge}{\text{Var}}(1/F_k | f_k = 1). \quad (4.25)$$

In order to construct confidence intervals, the approximation that conditionally on $f = \{f_k\}$, $\tau_i - E(\tau_i | f)$ ($i = 1, 2$), is normally distributed with variance as in (4.22) for τ_1 and (4.24) for τ_2 can be used. Since $E(\tau_i | f)$ is not observed, we replace them by their estimates $\hat{\tau}_i$, $i = 1, 2$ given in (4.3). Following details in Section 4.2.3 and assuming the Poisson log-linear model, a model is selected which minimizes the bias (or rather an estimate thereof):

$$B_i = \hat{\tau}_i - E(\tau_i|f) \tag{4.26}$$

and then use the approximate confidence interval of the type:

$$\hat{\tau}_i \pm Z_{\alpha/2}\sqrt{\hat{\text{Var}}(\tau_i|f)} \tag{4.27}$$

for $i = 1, 2$, where the variance estimates are those of (4.3) and (4.5), respectively. Since $E(\tau_i|f)$ is replaced by $\hat{\tau}_i$, this is a reasonable approximation provided B_i is indeed small, and thus the utility of this approximation depends on the quality of the model selection and parameter estimation.

For the first risk measure τ_1 and its estimate in (4.4), an estimate of the variance is

$$\hat{\text{Var}}(\tau_1|f) = \sum_k I(f_k = 1)\exp(-\hat{\lambda}_k(1 - \pi_k))[1 - \exp(-\hat{\lambda}_k(1 - \pi_k))]. \tag{4.28}$$

For the second risk measures τ_2 and its estimate in (4.4), because of the complexity, we can compute a series approximation of $\text{Var}(1/F_k|f_k = 1)$. In this case, the variance would be approximated by

$$\sum_{r=1}^R \frac{1}{r^2}\Pr_{\lambda_k}(F_k = r|f_k = 1) - \left(\sum_{r=1}^R \frac{1}{r}\Pr_{\lambda_k}(F_k = r|f_k = 1)\right)^2$$

where R is a large number. We plug-in $\hat{\lambda}_k$ to obtain the estimate $\hat{\text{Var}}(\tau_2|f)$. Now the confidence intervals of (4.27) can be computed using $\hat{\tau}_1$ and $\hat{\tau}_2$ of (4.3) and the variance $\hat{\text{Var}}(\tau_1|f)$ of (4.28) and the corresponding $\hat{\text{Var}}(\tau_2|f)$.

Taking into account that the many different approximations, such as Taylor series and normal approximations, and used plug-in estimates, a rather imprecise coverage level can be obtained for the intervals. Rinott and Shlomo recommend in [22] that a larger coefficient be used, for example, $Z_{\alpha/2} = 3$ will provide good coverage in the types of data sets used for social surveys. Examples of confidence intervals for the global risk measures calculated from samples drawn from the extracts of the 2001 UK Census are presented in 6.3.

4.6 Examples of Applications

4.6.1 Estimating Disclosure Risk Measures Under No Misclassification

The authors of [26] provide empirical results of estimating disclosure risk measures under misclassification according to the methods described in Section 4.4.

Misclassification is purposely introduced into the microdata as an SDC technique in order to lower the probabilities of identifying individuals. Two specific perturbative SDC techniques are applied: record swapping and the post-randomization method (PRAM). Since the misclassification is under the control of the statistical agency, the misclassification matrix M is assumed known.

The key is defined by six traceable and visible key variables (the number of categories in each variable is in parenthesis): area (4.2), sex (4.2), age (101), marital status (4.6), ethnicity (4.17), and economic activity (4.10), giving $K = 412,080$ cells. To fit the log-linear models, iterative proportional fitting (IPF) [3] was used which directly generates the fitted values $\hat{\mu}_k = \pi_k \hat{\lambda}_k$ required for the risk estimates.

Table 4.1 presents true and estimated values of τ_1 and τ_2 for three of the samples that were drawn with 0.5, 1, and 2% sampling fractions and for three log-linear models: the independence model, the all 2-way interactions model, and the all 3-way interactions model, respectively.

In Table 4.1, we see a consistent pattern of estimates decreasing with increasing model complexity, with the independence model always leading to over-estimation, and the all 3-way interactions model always leading to under-estimation. The under-estimation (and over-fitting) of the all 3-way interactions model is consistently predicted by the negative signs of the test statistic but with some inconsistencies for the smaller sample size. This suggests that these tests should be used primarily to detect under-fitting.

The forward model search procedure presented in Section 4.2.3 is also demonstrated in [27]. For the 1% sample ($n = 9,448$), Table 4.1 suggests that the independence model under-fits and the all 2-way interactions model over-fits. We therefore start from the independence model and consider adding 2-way interaction terms until we find a model for which there is no evidence of lack of fit. Table 4.2 presents results of the best fitted models obtained for each round of a forward search, starting with the independence model, labeled as model I. Note that the 1-way (main effects) terms become obsolete when adding in 2-way interaction terms that contain them.

Table 4.1 Aggregated risk measures and test statistics for samples drawn from the 2001 UK Census

Sample size	Model[a]	True		Estimates		Minimum error test	
		τ_1^*	τ_2^*	$\hat{\tau}_1$	$\hat{\tau}_2$	$\hat{B}_1/\sqrt{v}$	$\hat{B}_2/\sqrt{v}$
4,724	I	80	183.9	197.4	385.1	16.76	53.14
	II			35.9	112.3	−0.52	−0.97
	III			0	11.0	0.01	−1.27
9,448	I	159	355.9	386.6	701.2	48.54	114.19
	II			104.9	280.1	−1.57	−2.65
	III			1.1	42.2	−0.26	−3.09
18,896	I	263	628.9	672.0	1, 170.5	105.24	226.1
	II			252.0	591.3	−1.10	−1.52
	III			11.3	150.2	−1.28	−6.95

[a]Model I – independence model, model II – all 2-way interactions model, model III – all 3 way interactions model

Table 4.2 Models selected by a forward search for 1% census sample under a simple random sampling design

Model	Estimates		Minimum error test	
	$\hat{\tau}_1$	$\hat{\tau}_2$	$\hat{B}_1/\sqrt{v}$	$\hat{B}_2/\sqrt{v}$
I	386.6	701.2	48.54	114.19
II	104.9	280.1	−1.57	−2.65
1: I + {a*ec}	243.4	494.3	54.75	59.22
2: 1 + {a*et}	180.1	411.6	3.07	9.82
3: 2 + {a*m}	152.3	343.3	0.88	1.73
4: 3 + {s*ec}	149.2	337.5	0.26	0.92
5a: 4 + {ar*a}	148.5	337.1	−0.01	0.84
5b: 4 + {s*m}	147.7	335.3	0.02	0.66

Area–ar, Sex–s, age–a, marital status–m, ethnicity–et, and economic activity–ec; true values are $\tau_1 = 159$, $\tau_2 = 355.9$

In Table 4.2, the first four rounds are clear-cut in the sense that, at each round, there is a clear choice of the set of 2-way interactions which best reduces all of the test criteria. The set of interaction terms between age and economic activity, denoted {a*ec}, is included in round 1 (leading to the model denoted 1). Three further rounds lead to the addition of the sets {a*et},{a*m}, and {s*ec} to give model 4. This model provides a good fit in the sense that the values of all the test statistics based on $\hat{B}_1$ and $\hat{B}_2$ are less than 2. At round 5, we select two models, 5a and 5b, each of which provides improvements over model 4 but neither appears to be uniformly better than the other in terms of all the criteria. In fact each of the latter models gives similar estimates $\hat{\tau}_1$ and $\hat{\tau}_2$ of around 149 and 337, respectively, implying a robustness of the search procedure to the choice of criterion.

Figure 4.1 presents a scatterplot (in log-scale) of the true risk $1/F_k$ against the estimated risk measure in (4.4): $h_2(\hat{\lambda}_k) = \{1 - \exp[-(1 - \pi_k)\hat{\lambda}_k]\}/[(1 - \pi_k)\hat{\lambda}_k]$ for 2,304 sample uniques under model 5a in Table 4.2 of the 1% census sample.

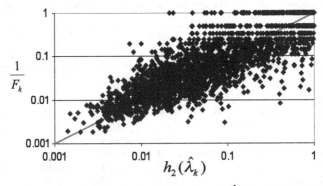

Fig. 4.1 Scatterplot (on logarithmic scales) of $1/F_k$ against $h_2(\hat{\lambda}_k)$ for 2,304 sample uniques for model 5a in Table 4.2 with 1% census sample

Table 4.3 Cross-classification of $1/F_k$ against $h_2(\hat{\lambda}_k)$ for sample uniques within bands for model 5a of 1% census sample

	$h_2(\hat{\lambda}_k)$			
$1/F_k$	$0-0.1$	$0.1-0.5$	$0.5-1$	Total
$0-0.1$	1,391	150	11	1,552
$0.1-0.5$	162	253	76	491
$0.5-1$	26	91	144	261
Total	1,579	494	231	2,304

Table 4.3 provides a corresponding cross-classification of these values within bands. We observe a strong positive relationship with a Spearman rank correlation of 0.80, i.e., the model is effective in using the key variable information to predict $1/F_k$. Nevertheless, it is good news from the point of view of disclosure protection that the prediction is far from perfect with, for example, many population unique cells not being picked up by high $h_2(\hat{\lambda}_k)$ values. The values of $1/F_k$ range above and below the diagonal line in Fig. 4.1, as anticipated if $h_2(\hat{\lambda}_k)$ is to be interpreted as an expected value of $1/F_k$.

Skinner and Shlomo [27] also demonstrate the application of the disclosure risk estimation and model selection criteria on a more demanding key by adding a nine category religion variable to the other key variables to produce $K=3,708,720$ cells. Taking a 1% sample, over 70% of the non-zero cells were sample unique. The number of population uniques in the sample rose to $\tau_1 = 311$ (compared to $\tau_1 = 159$ without the variable religion), representing over 3% of the 9,448 sample cases. Results are presented in Table 4.4. The all 2-way interactions model (II) provides a reasonable fit although, as before, there is some evidence of over-fitting. Forward selection from the independence model (I) works well, as in Table 4.3. The minimum error test criteria suggest the addition of five 2-way interaction terms and the resulting estimates of τ_1 and τ_2 are close to their true values.

The last example is the case when complex sampling is employed, typical of household survey designs implemented at Government Statistical Agencies. As

Table 4.4 Models selected by a forward search for 1% census sample with very large key ($K = 3,708,720$)

	Estimates		Minimum error test	
Model	$\hat{\tau}_1$	$\hat{\tau}_2$	$\hat{B}_1/\sqrt{v}$	$\hat{B}_2/\sqrt{v}$
I	962.7	1386.3	108.1	129.6
II	251.8	560.9	−0.9	−2.3
1: I + {a*ec}{ar*a}	716.0	1094.0	58.5	40.6
2: 1 + {s*a}{ar*ec}	715.2	1092.7	58.3	39.0
3: 2 + {et*r}{a*m}	419.0	777.3	16.7	30.2
4: 3 + {a*et}{s*ec}	356.3	687.4	1.1	1.6
5: 4 + {m*r}{ec*r}	320.9	662.4	0.5	0.4

Area–ar, Sex–s, age–a, marital status–m, ethnicity–et, economic activity–ec, religion–r; true values are $\tau_1 = 311$, $\tau_2 = 663.1$

described in [27], the samples are drawn randomly within two strata defined by the area key variable. Sampling fractions were 1:65 in the first area and 1:125 in the second area. In each stratum, a systematic sample of households was selected after sorting by finer geographical detail and all persons in the sampled households were included, so the sample of individuals is clustered by household. Differential non-response was generated at the household level based on household size: 20% non-response for small households, 10% for intermediate size households, and 5% for large households. The resulting number of responding individuals represented 1% of the population, enabling comparisons with the 1% sample in Section 4.6.2. Calibrated sample weights were also constructed based on 96 weighting classes defined by the two geographical areas, sex and 24 age groups. The weights were calculated to ensure that all individuals in the household receive the same weight and also that the weighted sample of individuals in each weighting class is equal to the known population total.

The key with six key variables was used. The values of the true risk measures are $\tau_1 = 136$, $\tau_2 = 331.8$ compared to the values $\tau_1 = 159$, $\tau_2 = 355.9$ for the 1% simple random sample. The differences arise from the sample dependence of the measures. The estimates obtained using the forward search algorithm described in Section 2.3 are given in Table 4.5.

From Table 4.5, a good fit is obtained in model 4 by the inclusion of four 2-way interactions as well as the main effects. This is similar to model 4 in Table 4.4 with three of the 2-way interactions the same. The estimates $\hat{\tau}_1 = 132$, $\hat{\tau}_2 = 334.1$ are even closer to the true values than for the simple random sample. Four other well-fitting models, 5a–5d, are also included in Table 4.5 and indicate as earlier that the risk estimates are fairly stable across these models. The observed robustness of the results to the complex design seems likely to arise here from the impact of household clustering being mitigated by the fact that the age and sex key variables cut across clusters and by the inclusion of the stratifying variable as a key variable.

Table 4.5 Models selected by a forward search for 1% census sample with complex survey design

	Estimates		Minimum error test	
Model	$\hat{\tau}_1$	$\hat{\tau}_2$	$\hat{B}_1/\sqrt{v}$	$\hat{B}_2/\sqrt{v}$
I	378.5	701.8	8.2	8.5
II	103.5	283.5	−1.5	−3.6
1: I + {a*m}	297.8	590.4	6.3	9.0
2: 1 + {a*et}	231.3	514.0	5.2	8.3
3: 2 + {a*ec}	153.8	357.0	2.5	3.1
4: 3 + {et*ec}	132.0	334.1	0.2	0.8
5a: 4 + {ar*a}	132.8	335.8	0.2	0.7
5b: 4 + {s*m}	129.0	331.3	0.0	0.8
5c: 4 + {ar*ec}	131.1	333.6	−0.1	0.5
5d: 4 + {m*ec}	128.3	327.4	−0.1	0.3

Area–ar, Sex–s, age–a, marital status–m, ethnicity–et, and economic activity–ec; true values are $\tau_1 = 136$, $\tau_2 = 331.8$

4.6.2 Estimating Disclosure Risk Measures Under Misclassification

The work in [26] provides empirical results of estimating disclosure risk measures under misclassification according to the methods described in Section 4.4. Misclassification is purposely introduced into the microdata as an SDC technique in order to lower the probabilities of identifying individuals. Two specific perturbative SDC techniques are applied: record swapping and the post-randomization method (PRAM). Since the misclassification is under the control of the statistical agency, the misclassification matrix M is assumed known.

For this empirical results study, the 2001 UK Census data set of size $N = 1,468,255$ individuals is used and 1% samples ($n = 14,683$) drawn. The six key variables are local authority (LAD) (4.11), sex (4.2), age groups (4.24), marital status (4.6), ethnicity (4.17), economic activity (4.10), where the numbers of categories of each variable are in parentheses so that $K = 538,560$.

First, a record swapping procedure was applied (see [4, 11]). The geographical variable LAD was swapped between pairs of individuals in the sample. This was carried out by first drawing a sub-sample of 20% of the individuals in each of the LADs. The remaining 80% of the individuals were not changed. On the 20% sub-sample, half of the individuals in each LAD were flagged. For each flagged record, an unflagged record was randomly chosen within the sub-sample to produce the pair for swapping, on condition that the record chosen was not previously selected for swapping and that the two individuals did not have the same LAD. For each randomly selected pair within the sub-sample, the LAD variables were swapped between them.

The misclassification matrix M for this simple record swapping design can be expressed simply in terms of the 11×11 misclassification matrix, denoted $M^g = \lfloor M^g_{kj} \rfloor$, for the geography variable g, since none of the other key variables are misclassified. The values M^g_{kj}, denoting the probability of being classified as LAD j given LAD k, are calculated as follows:

1. On the diagonal: $M^g_{kk} = 0.8$
2. Off the diagonal: $M^g_{kj} = 0.2 \times \frac{n_j}{\sum_{l \neq k} n_l}$, where n_j is the number of records in the sample from LAD j, $j = 1, \ldots, 11$.

A more direct method that is used for exchanging values of categorical variables is the post-randomization method (PRAM) (see [12]). For this method, values of categories in a given record are changed or not changed according to a misclassification matrix and a stochastic process based on the outcome of a random multinomial draw. The misclassification matrix can be developed in such a way as to preserve the expected marginal frequencies of the original variable. This is called invariant PRAM.

Using the same data, an invariant PRAM procedure was used to perturb the same geographical variable LAD. For the 11 categories of LAD, a new 11×11 misclassification matrix M^c was developed where the diagonal elements were 0.8 and the off-diagonal elements were all equal to a probability of 0.02 (i.e., 0.2/10). The invariant misclassification matrix was calculated from this matrix. For each record, a random uniform number between 0 and 1 was generated and the category of the LAD was changed (or not changed) if it was within the interval defined by the aggregated probabilities of the misclassification matrix.

Since the misclassification matrix M is known as well as the true population counts F_k in these experiments, the performance of expressions (4.17), (4.18), (4.19) as approximations to expression (4.16) can be assessed. We do this by summing all the expressions across sample unique records, as in the aggregate risk measure τ in (4.20) and comparing the resulting sums. In addition, the situation when neither the F_k nor the $\tilde{F}_k$ are known to the agency is considered and all that is observed is the misclassified sample. The matrix M is also assumed known. In this case, we carry out the risk estimation as described in Section 4.2.2 through the use of the Poisson log-linear model on the sample counts $\tilde{f}_k$. The log-linear model is chosen using a forward search algorithm and the minimum error test statistics as developed in Section 4.2.3. The naive estimated disclosure risk measure obtained from the log-linear model on the misclassified sample and the adjusted estimated risk measure taking into account the misclassification are calculated and compared. Table 4.6 presents results for both record swapping and the PRAM method of data masking, each for one simulation experiment.

The values in both columns of Table 4.6 are similar, which is not surprising since the misclassification matrices are similar. Misclassification reduces the risk in the file from about $\tau^* = 360$ to about $\tau^*_{CC} = 294$. The decrease in these experiments is modest since 80% of records remain unchanged.

The three approximations to the risk measure in (4.16) all provide good results although the approximation in (4.18) is slightly under-estimating. The measure in (4.20) relies on knowledge of both the full misclassification matrix M and the

Table 4.6 Aggregated risk estimates for samples generated from UK 2001 Census subject to two perturbative SDC methods

Identification risk measures	SDC method	
	Record swapping	PRAM
Identification Risk for unperturbed data		
Risk for original key variable values – τ^*	362.4	358.1
Identification risk measures for perturbed data with known population counts		
Risk measure τ based on (4.20)	298.9	299.7
Approximation based on (4.17)	298.4	299.3
Approximation based on (4.18)	280.4	283.5
Approximation based on (4.19)	298.9	299.8
Risk measure τ^*_{CC} given in (4.21)	292.6	294.2
Estimated risk measures based on sample data		
Naive risk measure from Poisson log-linear model on misclassified sample	358.6	345.3
Estimated risk measure based on Poisson log-linear model and adjusted for misclassification	286.8	280.1

population counts F_k. In contrast, the approximations (4.17), (4.18), (4.19) only require knowledge of the probability of not misclassifying a record, i.e., the probabilities on the diagonals. The alternative risk measure τ^*_{CC} in (4.21) also turns out to behave similarly to (4.20). In practice the population counts will generally be unknown to the statistical agency for survey data. We therefore consider the estimation method in Section 4.4 based on the Poisson log-linear model. The estimated aggregate risk measures is given in the last row of Table 4.6. The estimation methods appear to perform well with estimates for the risk measure under misclassification of about $\hat{\tau} = 284$.

To further explore the estimation method, Fig. 4.2 compares the individual record-level risk measures in (4.16) for the sample uniques with the estimated adjusted risk measures (as described in Section 4.4) based on the Poisson log-linear model on one sample under record swapping. In addition, the distribution of the sample uniques within bands of the individual record-level risk measures is presented in Table 4.7. From Fig. 4.2 and Table 4.7, we see a good fit between the risk measures in (4.16) to their estimated risk measures. The Spearman's rank correlation was 0.91.

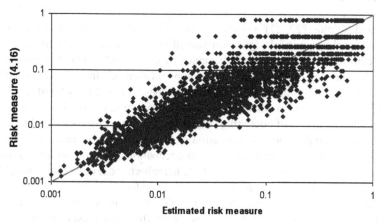

Fig. 4.2 Scatterplot of individual record-level risk measures in (4.16) against estimated risk measures based on Poisson log-linear model under record swapping

Table 4.7 Cross-classification of individual record-level risk measures in (4.16) against estimates based on Poisson log-linear model for sample uniques within bands under record swapping

Individual risk measures in (4.16)	Estimated risk measures from Poisson log-linear model			
	0.0 – 0.1	0.1 – 0.5	0.5 – 1.0	Total
0.0 – 0.1	1,961	133	4	2,098
0.1 – 0.5	180	325	76	581
0.5 – 1.0	8	69	75	152
Total	2,149	527	155	2,831

4.6.3 Variance Estimation and Confidence Intervals

Table 4.8 presents results of conditional confidence intervals for the global risk measures defined in (4.3) based on samples drawn from extracts of the 2001 UK Census as described in [22]. The population size N, the sample size n, the number of cells in the table K, and the key variables are given in each table with the number of categories in each attribute in parentheses. The table shows the resulting parameters τ_i and their estimates $\hat{\tau}_i$, the selection parameters $\hat{B}_i/\sqrt{\hat{v}_i}$, $i = 1, 2$, and the conditional confidence intervals with a coefficient of $Z_{\alpha/2} = 3$. The confidence intervals contain the true τ_1 in all the experiments using the coefficient $Z_{\alpha/2} = 3$ and indeed the same holds true for $Z_{\alpha/2} = 2$. The τ_2 is contained in about 80% of the experiments for $Z_{\alpha/2} = 3$ and in about 50% of the experiments for $Z_{\alpha/2} = 2$ (however, when it is outside the interval, it is very close and the approximation seems reasonable and useful).

4.7 Extensions to Probabilistic Modeling for Disclosure Risk Estimation

Rinott and Shlomo [20, 21] propose a method for estimating quantities τ_1 and τ_2 based on local polynomial regression smoothing techniques in neighborhoods of unique cells in the contingency table spanned by key variables. This method is based on the idea that one can learn about a given population cell from the density of the neighboring cells if a suitable definition of closeness is possible, without relying on complex modeling. The method works well for ordinal key variables (such as age, years of education, size of household) where the closer the categories the higher the correlation. A variable such as occupation is not ordinal but one can define reasonable notions of closeness between different occupations. For non-ordinal variables, the values can remain constant in the whole neighborhood. For example, neighborhoods always consist of individuals of the same gender.

The use of local neighborhoods assumes that if a sample unique is found in a part of the sample table where neighboring cells (by some reasonable metric) are small or empty, then it seems reasonable to believe that it is more likely to have arisen from a small population cell. Classical log-linear models do not take such closeness into account and, therefore, when such models are used for individual cell parameter estimation, the estimates involve data in cells which may be remote from the estimated cell.

The work in [21] proposes using the Poisson distribution assumption with local neighborhoods. Assuming that sample counts are realizations of the Poisson distribution: $f_k \sim P(\mu_k = \pi_k \lambda_k)$, apart from constants, the sample log-likelihood is $\sum_{k=1}^{K} [f_k \log \mu_k - \mu_k]$. However, if we use a model for μ_k that is valid only in some neighborhood M of a given cell, the log-likelihood of the data in this neighborhood is

$$\sum_{k \in M} [f_k \log \mu_k - \mu_k]. \qquad (4.29)$$

Table 4.8 Coverage rates for the estimated confidence intervals of the disclosure risk measures of samples from a UK Census population

Model	τ_1	$\hat{\tau}_1$	$\hat{B}_1/\sqrt{\hat{v}_1}$	$\hat{\tau}_1 \pm 3\sqrt{v(\hat{\tau}_1|f)}$	τ_2	$\hat{\tau}_2$	$\hat{B}_2/\sqrt{\hat{v}_2}$	$\hat{\tau}_2 \pm 3\sqrt{v(\hat{\tau}_2|f)}$
Example 1: $N = 1{,}468{,}255$, $K = 5{,}563{,}080$								
Area(4.3), sex(4.2), age(101), marital status(4.6), ethnicity(4.17), work status(4.10), religion(4.9)								
$n = 7{,}341$	212	195.7	1.31	$170.4 - 221.1$	444.3	421.4	0.80	$404.9 - 437.9$
$n = 14{,}683$	359	384.0	1.10	$348.9 - 419.1$	783.5	800.3	0.74	$777.2 - 823.4$
Example 2: $N = 1{,}468{,}255$, $K = 618{,}120$								
Area(4.3), sex(4.2), age(101), marital status(4.6), ethnicity(4.17), work status(4.10)								
$n = 7{,}341$	88	87.4	0.87	$69.3 - 105.6$	225.2	211.8	1.16	$200.0 - 223.7$
$n = 14{,}683$	167	167.5	-0.17	$141.9 - 193.2$	408.1	423.2	0.53	$406.3 - 439.9$
$n = 14{,}683$	147	171.5	0.60	$145.9 - 197.2$	403.6	413.3	0.57	$396.7 - 430.0$
$n = 14{,}683$	180	190.0	0.90	$164.4 - 215.7$	435.6	423.6	0.27	$407.1 - 440.1$
Example 3: $N = 1{,}468{,}255$, $K = 741{,}744$								
Area(4.36), sex(4.2), age(101), marital status(4.6), ethnicity(4.17)								
$n = 14{,}683$	142	142.2	0.09	$118.5 - 165.9$	379.0	376.2	1.51	$360.5 - 392.0$
$n = 14{,}683$	136	135.7	1.02	$112.3 - 159.1$	364.2	366.0	0.55	$350.4 - 381.6$
$n = 14{,}683$	152	146.5	-0.65	$122.8 - 170.2$	373.0	373.5	-0.03	$357.8 - 389.3$
Example 4: $N = 944{,}793$, $K = 412{,}080$								
Area(4.2), sex(4.2), age(101), marital status(4.6), ethnicity(4.17), work status(4.10)								
$n = 9{,}448$	159	152.2	0.88	$128.7 - 175.8$	355.9	343.3	1.73	$326.5 - 360.1$
$n = 18{,}896$	263	277.0	-0.27	$245.1 - 309.0$	628.9	638.1	0.92	$618.9 - 657.3$
Example 5: $N = 51{,}620{,}597$, $K = 443{,}520$[a]								
Region (4.11), age(101), sex (4.2), number of residents(4.7), marital status(4.6), number of cars(4.5)								
$n = 16{,}651$	18	18.6	-0.21	$10.2 - 27.0$	83.0	83.9	0.06	$77.9 - 89.8$
$n = 54{,}560$	24	33.8	1.24	$20.6 - 47.0$	220.3	211.0	0.54	$201.4 - 220.6$
$n = 119{,}618$	64	74.4	0.56	$55.2 - 93.6$	446.6	441.7	0.03	$427.8 - 455.7$
$n = 357{,}888$	211	189.5	-0.08	$157.9 - 221.2$	1193.8	1147.2	0.21	$1{,}123.8 - 1170.6$

[a]These samples are based on a complex survey design based on clustered samples.

For convenience of notation, assume that $m = 2$, a 2-way contingency table. The extension to m is straightforward. Following [23], a local smoothing polynomial model is defined.

For each fixed $k = (k_1, k_2)$ separately, the model below for μ_k can be written in terms of the parameters $\alpha = (\beta_0, \beta_1, \gamma_1, \ldots, \beta_t, \gamma_t)$ with $k' = (k_1', k_2')$ varying in some neighborhood of k:

$$\log \mu_{k'}(\alpha) \equiv \log \mu_{(k_1', k_2')}$$
$$= \beta_0 + \beta_1(k_1' - k_1) + \gamma_1(k_2' - k_2) + \cdots + \beta_t(k_1' - k_1)^t + \gamma_t(k_2' - k_2)^t$$
$$(4.30)$$

for some natural number t. The polynomial model is assumed valid with a suitable t for $k' = (k_1', k_2')$ in some neighborhood M of $k = (k_1, k_2)$. Substituting (4.30) into (4.29), the concave function is maximized:

$$L(\alpha) = L(\beta_0, \beta_1, \gamma_1, \ldots, \beta_t, \gamma_t) = \sum_{(k_1', k_2') \in M} [f_{(k_1', k_2')} \log \mu_{(k_1', k_2')} - \mu_{(k_1', k_2')}],$$
$$(4.31)$$

with respect to the coefficients in α of the regression model (4.30). With arg max $L(\alpha) = \hat{\alpha}$ and $\hat{\beta}_0$ denoting its first component, the estimate of $\mu_k = \mu_{(k_1, k_2)}$ is

$$\hat{\mu}_k \equiv \mu_k(\hat{\alpha}) = \exp(\hat{\beta}_0), \tag{4.32}$$

where the second inequality is explained by taking $k' = k = (k_1, k_2)$ in (4.30).

The maximization by the Newton–Raphson method is straightforward and fast. Each of the estimates $\hat{\mu}_k$ requires a separate maximization as above which leads to a value $\hat{\alpha}$ that depends on $k = (k_1, k_2)$ and a set of estimates $\mu_{k'}(\hat{\alpha})$ of which only $\hat{\mu}_k$ of (4.32) is used. For the risk measures presented in this chapter, it suffices to compute these estimates for cells k which are sample uniques, that is, $f_k = 1$.

With the estimate of (4.32) and recalling that $\mu_k = \pi_k \lambda_k$ and setting SU $= \{k : f_k = 1\}$, the set of sample uniques, the risk estimates of (4.3) can be applied under the Poisson formulae:

$$\hat{\tau}_1 = \sum_{k \in SU} \exp(-\mu_k(1 - \pi_k)/\pi_k), \quad \hat{\tau}_2 = [1 - \exp(-\hat{\mu}_k(1 - \pi_k)/\pi_k)]/[\hat{\mu}_k(1 - \pi_k)/\pi_k].$$
$$(4.33)$$

The work [20] generalizes the above approach using the negative binomial distribution (as briefly described in Section 2.2) under local neighborhoods. The sample counts are assumed to be distributed independently, negative binomial: $f_k \sim$ NB$(\alpha, p_k = \frac{1}{1 + N\pi_k\beta})$. Under this parameterization $\mu_k \equiv E f_k = N\pi_k\alpha\beta = \frac{\alpha(1 - p_k)}{p_k}$ and further calculations yield $F_k | f_k \sim f_k + NB(\alpha + f_k, \rho_k = \frac{N\pi_k + 1/\beta}{N + 1/\beta})$, $F_k \geq f_k$. Using this relation and setting $\rho_k = \frac{N\pi_k + \beta}{N + \beta}$, the individual risk measures for cell k are defined by

$$P(F_k = 1 | f_k = 1) = \rho_k^{1+\alpha}, \quad E\left[\frac{1}{F_k} | f_k = 1\right] = \frac{\rho_k(1 - \rho_k^\alpha)}{\alpha(1 - \rho_k)}. \tag{4.34}$$

The proposed estimation method is for the estimation of μ and α. These estimates are transformed to estimates of the parameters appearing in the individual risk measures (4.34), which in turn lead to estimates of the global risk measures under (4.3).

For each fixed cell k, define a neighborhood of cells $M = M_k$ and estimate the values of μ_k and α_k, using neighboring cells $k' \in M_k$ and the assumption:

$$f_{k'} \sim \mathrm{NB}\left(\alpha_k, \, p_{k'} = \frac{1}{1 + N\pi_{k'}\beta_k}\right), \tag{4.35}$$

so that α_k and β_k are fixed in the neighborhood and do not depend on k', while $p_{k'}$ actually also depends on k. Since k is now fixed, we suppress it as an index in α, β, or $p_{k'}$, and write $Ef_{k'} = \mu_{k'} = \frac{\alpha(1-p_{k'})}{p_{k'}}$. For the fixed k, set $\mu = \{\mu_{k'} : k' \in M\}$, so the index k is suppressed also in μ.

An expression for the likelihood of (4.35) under the parameters μ and $a = \frac{1}{\alpha}$, for each fixed k and observations $\{f_{k''} : k' \in M\}$ in a neighborhood $M = M_k$ of k:

$$L(a, \mu) \equiv L(a, \mu; \{f_{k'} : k' \in M\}) = \prod_{k' \in M} \frac{\Gamma(x + \alpha)}{\Gamma(x + 1)\Gamma(\alpha)} (1 - p_{k'})^{f_{k'}} p_{k'}^\alpha$$

$$= \prod_{k' \in M} \frac{\Gamma(x + \alpha)}{\Gamma(x + 1)\Gamma(\alpha)} \left[1 - \frac{\alpha}{\mu_{k'} + \alpha}\right]^{f_{k'}} \left[\frac{\alpha}{\mu_{k'} + \alpha}\right]^\alpha \tag{4.36}$$

For each k, estimate $\alpha = \alpha_k$ and $\mu_{k'}$ for $k' \in M = M_k$ using the likelihood (4.36) and the smoothing model below, and then use the estimates of α_k and μ_k (not using the $\mu_{k'}$ estimates for $k' \neq k$) for risk estimates in (4.34).

Again following [23], we use the local smoothing polynomial model. For convenience of notation assume $m = 2$ (a 2-way table); the extension to any m is straightforward. For each fixed $k = (k_1, k_2)$ separately, we write the model below for $u_{k'}$ in terms of the parameters $\theta = (\theta_0, \theta_1, \gamma_1, \ldots, \theta_t, \gamma_t)$, with $k' = (k'_1, k'_2)$ varying in the neighborhood $M = M_k$ of k:

$$\log \mu_{k'}(\theta) = \theta_0 + \theta_1(k'_1 - k_1) + \gamma_1(k'_2 - k_2) + \cdots + \theta_t(k'_1 - k_1)^t + \gamma_t(k'_2 - k_2)^t \tag{4.37}$$

for some natural number t. Substituting (4.37) into the likelihood function (4.36) using the relations between parameterizations as described above we obtain the likelihood function $L(a, \theta)$.

To maximize the likelihood function as a function of $a = \frac{1}{\alpha}$ and θ, the Fisher Scoring Algorithm which replaces the Hessian by its expectation should be used to ensure the convergence to the real MLE since it is possible that the Hessian is not positive definite for this likelihood function.

With $\arg\max L(a,\theta) = (\hat{a},\hat{\theta})$ and $\hat{\theta}_0$ denoting the first component of $\hat{\theta}$, the estimate of $\mu_k = \mu_{(k_1,k_2)}$ is obtained in the form:

$$\mu_k \equiv \mu_k(\hat{\theta}) = \exp(\hat{\theta}_0), \tag{4.38}$$

where the second equality is explained by taking $k' = k = (k_1, k_2)$ in (4.37).

To summarize, each of the estimates $\hat{a}_k$, $\hat{\mu}_k$ requires a separate maximization for each k, as explained above which leads to a value $\hat{\theta}$ and $\hat{a}_k$ both depending on k, and a set of estimates $\mu_{k'}(\hat{\theta})$ of which only $\hat{\mu}_k$ of (4.38) is used. For the risk measure in (4.34), it suffices to compute these estimates for cells k which are sample uniques, that is, $f_k = 1$.

Having estimated $\hat{a}_k$, $\hat{\mu}_k$ for each cell k separately on the basis of a neighborhood M_k, we use them to estimate the quantity ρ_k and α which are obtained by tracing back the re-parameterizations. Using the relations $\rho_k = \frac{N\pi_k\beta+1}{N\beta+1}$ and $\mu_k = N\pi_k\alpha_k\beta_k$, we obtain

$$\rho_k = \frac{\mu_k + \alpha_k}{\frac{\mu_k}{\pi_k} + \alpha_k}, \quad \alpha_k = \frac{1}{a_k}.$$

Plugging the estimates $\hat{a}_k$, $\hat{\mu}_k$ in the latter formula and then plugging the resulting estimates of α_k and ρ_k into (4.34), we obtain the individual risk estimates. The global risk measures are estimated as indicated in (4.3).

References

1. Benedetti R., Capobianchi A., and Franconi L. Individual risk of disclosure using sampling design. Contributi Istat, 1998.
2. Bethlehem J., Keller W., and Pannekoek J. Disclosure control of microdata. *Journal of the American Statistical Association*, 85:38–45.
3. Bishop Y., Fienberg S., and Holland P. *Discrete Multivariate Analysis: Theory and Practice.* MIT Press, Cambridge, MA, 1975.
4. Dalenius T. and Reiss S.P. Data swapping: A technique for disclosure control. *Journal of Statistical Planning and Inference*, 7:73–85.
5. Cameron A.C. and Trivedi P.K. *Regression Analysis of Count Data. Econometric Society Monographs*, Vol 30, Cambridge University Press, Cambridge, 1988.
6. Domingo-Ferrer J. and Torra V. Disclosure risk assessment in statistical microdata protection via advanced record linkage. *Statistics and Computing*, 13(4):343–354.
7. Duncan G. and Lambert D. The risk of disclosure for microdata. *Journal of Business and Economic Statistics*, 7:207–217, 1989.
8. Elamir E. and Skinner C.J. Record-level measures of disclosure risk for survey micro-data. *Journal of Official Statistics*, 22:525–539, 2006.
9. Elliot M., Manning A., Mayes K., Gurd J., and Bane M. SUDA: A program for detecting special uniques. In: *Proceedings of the Joint UNECE/Eurostat Work Session on Statistical Data Confidentiality*, Geneva, pp. 353–362, 2005.
10. Fienberg S.E. and Makov U.E. Confidentiality, uniqueness and disclosure limitation for categorical data. *Journal of Official Statistics*, 14:385–397, 1998.

11. Fienberg S.E. and McIntyre J. Data swapping: Variations on a theme by Dalenius and Reiss. *Journal of Official Statistics*, 9:383–406, 2005.
12. Gouweleeuw J., Kooiman P., Willenborg L.C.R.J., and De Wolf P.P. Post-randomisation for statistical disclosure control: Theory and implementation. *Journal of Official Statistics*, 14:463–478, 1998.
13. Kuha J. and Skinner C.J. Categorical Data Analysis and Misclassification. In: *Survey Measurement and Process Quality* (eds. L. Lyberg, P. Biemer, M. Collins, E. De Leeuw, C. Dippo, N. Schwarz, and D. Trewin),Wiley, New York, NY, 633–670, 1997.
14. Laird N.M., and Louis T.A. Empirical Bayes confidence intervals for a series of related experiments. *Biometrics*, 45:481–495, 1989.
15. Lambert D. Measures of disclosure risk and harm. *Journal of Official Statistics*, 9:313–331, 1993.
16. Paass G. Disclosure risk and disclosure avoidance for microdata. *Journal of Business and Economic Statistics*, 6:487–500, 1988.
17. Rao J.N.K. and Thomas D.R. Analysis of Categorical Response Data from Complex Surveys: An Appraisal and Update. In: *Analysis of Survey Data* (eds. R.L. Chambers and C.J. Skinner), Wiley, Chichester, pp. 85–108, 2003.
18. Reiter J.P. Estimating risks of identification disclosure in microdata. *Journal of the American Statistical Association*, 100:1103–1112, 2005.
19. Rinott Y. On models for statistical disclosure risk estimation. In: *Proceedings of the Joint ECE/Eurostat Work Session on Statistical Data Confidentiality*, Luxemburg, pp. 275–285, 2003.
20. Rinott Y. and Shlomo N. A Generalized Negative Binomial Smoothing Model for Sample Disclosure Risk Estimation. In: *PSD'2006 Privacy in Statistical Databases* (eds. J. Domingo-Ferrer and L. Franconi), vol. 4302, Springer LNCS, New York, NY, pp. 82–93, 2006.
21. Rinott Y. and Shlomo N. A smoothing model for sample disclosure risk estimation. In: *Complex Datasets and Inverse Problems: Tomography, Networks and Beyond*, IMS Lecture Notes Monograph Series, vol 54, Beachwood, OH, pp. 161–171, 2007.
22. Rinott Y. and Shlomo N. Variances and confidence intervals for sample disclosure risk measures. In: *56th Session of the International Statistical Institute Invited Paper*, Lisbon, 2007.
23. Simonoff S.J. Three sides of smoothing: Categorical data smoothing, nonparametric regression, and density estimation. *International Statistical Review*, 66:137–156, 1998.
24. Skinner C.J. and Holmes D. Estimating the re-identification risk per record in microdata. *Journal of Official Statistics*, 14:361–372, 1998.
25. Skinner C.J., and Elliot M.J. A measure of disclosure risk for microdata. *Journal of the Royal Statistical Society, Ser. B*, 64:855–867, 2002.
26. Skinner C.J. and Shlomo N. Assessing the disclosure protection provided by misclassification and record swapping. In: *56th Session of the International Statistical Institute Invited Paper*, Lisbon, 2007.
27. Skinner C.J. and Shlomo N. Assessing identification risk in survey microdata using log-linear models. *Journal of American Statistical Associations*, 103(483):989–1001, 2008.
28. Spruill, N.L. Measures of confidentiality. In: *Proceedings of the Survey Research Methods Section of the American Statistical Association*, Alexandria, Louisiana, USA, pp. 260–265, 1982.
29. Willenborg L. and DeWaal T. *Elements of Statistical Disclosure Control in Practice*. Lecture Notes in Statistics, vol. 155,Springer, New York, NY, 2001.
30. Yancey W.E., Winkler W.E., and Creecy R.H. Disclosure risk assessment in perturbative micro-data protection. In: *Inference Control in Statistical Databases* (ed. J. Domingo- Ferrer), Springer, New York, NY, pp. 135–151, 2002.
31. Zhang C.H. Estimation of sums of random variables: Examples and information. *Annals of Statistics*, 33:2022–2041, 2005.

Chapter 5
Exploiting Auxiliary Information in the Estimation of Per-Record Risk of Disclosure

Silvia Polettini and Loredana di Consiglio

Abstract Statistical Institutes as well as other data providers must comply with the obligation to preserve the privacy of respondents. Publication of files of microdata makes it possible for a malicious user to link one or more records in the released data to one or more records in the population, by combining information from external sources with the published data. Before publication, a careful risk assessment should be performed that allows to protect records through suitable utility preserving techniques. We define the disclosure risk as the probability of a correct record reidentification; for most population surveys, identification can be based on categorical variables such as place of residence, sex, age also known as key variables.

Rare traits in the population are the ones that could lead to disclosure, but to be actually exposed to risk, such rare records should also be included in the sample. As the population is almost invariably unknown, at least at the level of detail required for risk estimation, direct or indirect inference is required. A solution is to specify a model for the population group frequencies $F = (F_1, \ldots, F_k)$ in the contingency table defined by cross-classification of the key variables and derive suitable risk estimates. Typical applications consider very large and sparse contingency tables, often with logical constraints that induce structural zeroes; this makes inference particularly difficult, especially for high-risk traits.

Di Consiglio and Polettini [6, 7] derive disclosure risk estimates based on small area estimators that, besides borrowing strength from neighbouring groups, exploit auxiliary information obtained from external sources such as administrative registers or a census. In this contribution we review this approach to risk estimation and investigate whether the introduction of more sophisticated mixed effects models may account for unexplained variation thus leading to improved risk estimators. We analyse the performance over the sample space of some risk estimators based on models and auxiliary information. In particular, we compare simple SPREE-type estimators to the Skinner estimator considered in [21] and [11]; we also introduce a

S. Polettini (✉)
Dipartimento di Scienze Statistiche, Università degli Studi di Napoli Federico II, Napoli, Italy
e-mail: s.polettini@unina.it

J. Nin, J. Herranz (eds.), *Privacy and Anonymity in Information Management Systems*,
Advanced Information and Knowledge Processing,
DOI 10.1007/978-1-84996-238-4_5, © Springer-Verlag London Limited 2010

modified Skinner estimator that relies on a superpopulation model whose top level is informed by the SPREE.

5.1 Introduction

Statistical disclosure limitation addresses the problem of releasing analytically useful data while safeguarding confidentiality of respondents to statistical surveys. Whereas the general public might be satisfied with the analysis of a small set of two- or three-way tables, there is a growing demand from the research community for the release of files of microdata that may allow the estimation of complex statistical models.

A major concern in disclosure limitation is to avoid record reidentification. Even if data arise from a sample survey, it is always possible that an intruder, using information from other sources and the published data, might link one or more of the released records to one or more units in the population.

Before publication, a careful risk assessment should be performed that allows to protect records through suitable utility preserving techniques; assessment of the risk-utility trade-off [8] of the final data product is the last stage of the procedure. Proposals for data protection range from data masking methods such as suppression of values, microaggregation and top or bottom coding [25] to imputation based on suitable statistical models (a partial list of references includes [18, 1, 12, 13, 27] and references therein). This chapter focuses on the first task, that of quantifying the disclosure risk.

The definition of a disclosure risk measure relies on a disclosure scenario that specifies, besides the type of data release, how the disclosure experiment is performed, by what means, what is the information available for identification and finally what is the disclosure harm [9]. For microdata, disclosure harm is usually high as the survey variables most often include several sensitive variables that would be revealed upon record reidentification. Note also that disclosure may occur for a census as well as for sample survey data. In this chapter we focus on the latter type of data release. The disclosure scenario for record reidentification conceives the existence of external information, usually consisting of publicly available variables known for the population and also present in the file to be released, that enable a malicious user to match records in the population with records in the released data. For most population surveys, identification can be based on categorical variables such as place of residence, sex, age also known as key variables.

Intuitively, records in groups having the same key values are identical for reidentification and should receive the same risk of disclosure. Clearly, rare traits in the population are the ones that could lead to disclosure, but to be actually exposed to risk, such rare records should also be included in the sample. The problem is therefore discriminating between the groups that are structurally small in the population and those that are small in the microdata only due to sampling. Typical applications consider very large and sparse contingency tables, often with logical constraints that induce structural zeros. In addition, survey data often derive from complex sampling designs. In this framework, inference is particularly difficult, especially for high-risk traits having low sample and population sizes. Finite population theory cannot account for all the information about the population structure and would produce unreliable estimates for those unplanned domains, in particular, when the sampling fraction is small. In this respect, superpopulation models have been introduced (see, e.g., [3, 4, 14, 19, 21]); some of these approaches exploit the association structure among the key variables, which is estimated from the sample. Given the lack of sample information on small cells, models that allow "borrowing strength" from larger cells while avoiding excessive shrinkage of the estimates are the most appropriate ones. Besides borrowing strength from neighbouring cells, auxiliary information, derived from external sources such as administrative registers or a census, may be introduced in the estimation process. For population surveys, external information is often available for at least some margins of the contingency table induced by the disclosure scenario. For instance, current population counts for region, sex and age classes are available from public registers; for other classifications, it might be the case that design-based direct estimators at the national level give sufficiently accurate figures for the population. Calibration on some of these variables may increase further the precision of such direct estimates. For estimation of counts from a contingency table, the so-called structure preserving estimator (SPREE) makes precise use of the above-mentioned information [17, 26]. This approach has been investigated by [6, 7] in the context of risk estimation and is further pursued in this chapter to assess whether the introduction of more sophisticated mixed effects models may account for unexplained variation thus leading to improved risk estimators. We analyse the performance of risk estimators based on models and auxiliary information; in particular, we compare simple SPREE-type estimators to the Skinner estimator considered in [21] and [11]; we also introduce a modified Skinner estimator that relies on a superpopulation model whose first level is informed by the SPREE.

In the next section, we review models for risk estimation proposed in the literature, whereas in Sections 5.2.2, 5.3 and 5.4 we describe the SPREE-type approach along with the results of a simulation study performed to compare some risk estimators.

5.2 Risk Measures and Models for Risk Estimation

Consider a disclosure scenario defining q categorical identifying (key) variables, denoted by $Z_1, \ldots, Z_q$, having $C_1, \ldots, C_q$ categories, respectively. In this framework, records with the same key values are identical for reidentification and should have the same risk. Cross-classification of the key variables generates a contingency table with a total number of $K = \prod_k C_k$ cells at both the population and the sample level; cell frequencies in the population and sample table, respectively, are denoted by F_k and f_k. In Section 5.2.2, models for two-way and three-way contingency tables will be considered, in that case the cells will be indexed by a double or triple subscript (e.g. F_{dhi}) following the standard notation for log-linear models.

If the population contingency table were known, a simple risk measure for each record in cell k of the sample table could be defined using the corresponding population cell size, F_k: $r_k = 1/F_k$. As F_k is almost invariably unknown, at least at the level of detail required for risk estimation, direct or indirect inference is required. A solution is to specify a statistical model for $\mathbf{F} = (F_1, \ldots, F_k)$ and derive suitable risk estimates based on the sample frequencies $\mathbf{f} = (f_1, \ldots, f_k)$, such as $E(1/F_k|\mathbf{f})$; alternative per-record measures could be defined, such as those associated to sample uniques, e.g. $Pr(F_k = 1|f_k = 1)$, but we restrict our attention to the former quantity.

The next section reviews some superpopulation models proposed in the literature for risk estimation, whereas Section 5.2.2 considers the small area approach to estimation of counts in a contingency table based on auxiliary information.

5.2.1 Superpopulation Models for Risk Estimation with Survey Data

Part of the literature on disclosure risk assessment is related to the work of [3], which represents the first approach to defining a statistical model for samples where identifying variables form a contingency table. The model is a hierarchical Poisson–Gamma superpopulation model:

$$\pi_k \sim \text{gamma}(\alpha, K\alpha), \ k = 1, \ldots, K,$$
$$F_k|\pi_k \sim \text{Poisson}(N\pi_k),$$
$$f_k|F_k, \pi_k, p_k \sim \text{binomial}(F_k, p_k), \ \text{independently across cells,}$$

in which π_k is the probability that a unit of the population falls into cell k and p_k (assumed constant across cells) is the probability that an individual in cell k is sampled. The model was used to deduce the probability of population uniqueness given sample uniqueness. The constraints $\sum_k F_k = N$ and $\sum \pi_k = 1$ are not exactly satisfied under the model, which can be seen as an approximation to the more coherent Dirichlet-multinomial model analysed by [23]. The above-described Gamma–Poisson model was shown by [19] to have as limit when $\alpha \to 0$ the negative binomial model analysed in [2] and [15].

The model just outlined and its derivations are all based on an exchangeability assumption whereby all cells with the same sample frequency are assigned the same risk estimate. To gather information on small cells from larger ones, models can be introduced that use the structure of the table through a log-linear model which is fitted to the data. This is the approach pursued by [21], who focus on sample uniques and model the F_k, $k = 1, \ldots, K$, as Poisson with mean π_k. The mechanism generating $\mathbf{f}$ is assumed to be a Bernoulli sampling with known probability p, so that $f_k|\lambda_k \sim \text{Poisson}(p\pi_k)$; finally a log-linear model for the expected sample frequencies $p\pi_k$ (where p only produces an offset term) is defined, from which the π_ks are estimated. The superpopulation model implies that $F_k - f_k | f_k \sim$ Poisson$((1 - p)\pi_k)$ and this relation allows one to estimate the probability of population uniqueness given sample uniqueness

$$\Pr(F_k = 1 | f_k = 1) = \exp\{(1 - p)\hat{\pi}_k\}, \tag{5.1}$$

by plugging in the log-linear estimates. The model defined by [21] has greater generality, as it also accounts for overdispersion due to lack of fit by specifying a log-normal distribution for the log-linear parameters π_k, $\log(\pi_k) = \mu_k + \varepsilon_k$, $\varepsilon_k \sim N(0, \sigma^2)$, $\exp(\mu_k)$ being the expected frequencies in the log-linear model assumed for the population. An empirical Bayesian argument is used to determine a risk estimate analogous to (5.1). Practical application of the method, however, has dropped this assumption, partly because of possible negativity of empirical Bayes estimates of the log-normal variance. See also [20] for a related local smoothing approach.

A related model is considered by [14], who specify a multinomial$(N, \boldsymbol{\pi})$ distribution for **F** together with a decomposable graphical log-linear model for $\boldsymbol{\pi}$. The sample frequencies are finally assumed to be drawn by Binomial sampling, so that $\mathbf{f} \sim$ multinomial$(n, \boldsymbol{\pi})$, where $\boldsymbol{\pi}$ depends on $\boldsymbol{\beta}$ according to the same log-linear model as above. Given the log-linear parameters $\boldsymbol{\beta}$, $\mathbf{f}$ and $\mathbf{F} - \mathbf{f}$ are thus conditionally independent and $\mathbf{F} - \mathbf{f} | \boldsymbol{\beta}$ is multinomial$(N - n, \boldsymbol{\pi})$. Use of a convenient hyper-Dirichlet prior for the log-linear model parameters $\boldsymbol{\beta}$ allows a closed form expression for the posterior distribution to be deduced. Under this model and using the bracket notation to represent distributions, we have

$$[\mathbf{F} - \mathbf{f} | \mathbf{f}] \propto \int [\mathbf{F} - \mathbf{f} | \boldsymbol{\beta}][\mathbf{f} | \boldsymbol{\beta}][\boldsymbol{\beta}] \, d\boldsymbol{\beta}.$$

For disclosure risk estimation, one can refer to the marginal distribution $[F_k - f_k | \mathbf{f}]$ obtained by replacing the multinomial distribution $[\mathbf{F} - \mathbf{f} | \boldsymbol{\beta}]$ with the corresponding binomial marginal. A per-record risk estimate can be derived as

$$r_k = \mathrm{E}(1/F_k | \mathbf{f}) = \sum_{j=0}^{N-n} \frac{1}{f_k + j} \Pr(F_k - f_k = j | \mathbf{f}).$$

Monte Carlo Rao-Blackwellized risk estimates can be obtained by noting that

$$\Pr(F_k - f_k = j | \mathbf{f}) = \int [F_k - f_k = j | \mathbf{f}, \boldsymbol{\beta}][\boldsymbol{\beta} | \mathbf{f}] \, d\boldsymbol{\beta} = \mathrm{E}\{\Pr(F_k - f_k = j | \boldsymbol{\beta}) | \mathbf{f}\};$$

estimates of the probabilities $\Pr(F_k - f_k = j | \mathbf{f})$ can be obtained by averaging binomial $(N - n, \pi_k)$ probabilities evaluated on $F_k - f_k$ over samples from $[\boldsymbol{\beta} | \mathbf{f}]$.

In the above arguments, the issue of model misspecification is not considered. Rinott and Shlomo [20] note that in a disclosure context standard goodness-of-fit measure for log-linear models are not appropriate and propose a model selection strategy targeted to the accuracy of risk estimates. A different approach to allowing for model uncertainty, namely model averaging, has been proposed by [12] and pursued by [14] who introduce a potentially large number of competing models whose contribution to risk estimation is then weighted according to the support that they receive from the data. Compared to model averaging, restricting to a single good fitting model artificially reduces the uncertainty about the estimates; this uncertainty is fully accounted for under the former approach.

A potential drawback of the approach proposed in [14] is its complexity, with consequently increased computational times. For each of the model components considered in the model-averaging approach, approximate inference is proposed, based on a Poisson–Gamma model that is equivalent to the one proposed by [3], with the important difference that the Gamma distributions for the cell probabilities π_k match the corresponding marginal means and variances of $[\pi|\mathbf{f}]$. The Gamma distributions are derived as an approximation to the marginals of the Dirichlet posteriors. The risk estimates thus obtained generalize results of [19] and [16].

As a final comment, note that the approach outlined allows uncertainty about risk estimates to be reported in a straightforward manner, along with the estimates themselves.

5.2.2 SPREE-Type Estimators for Cross-Classifications

Small area methods exploit external information in the form of auxiliary variables with the aim to produce estimators with improved MSE properties. This is pursued by explicitly or implicitly modelling the relationship between the variable of interest and the auxiliary variables. The definition of disclosure risk that we have adopted is related to the cells of the contingency table built by cross-classifying the key variables. As already mentioned, for at least some margins of the contingency table induced by the disclosure scenario, external information at the population level is often available. For population surveys, the key variables typically comprise variables region, sex, age in classes, marital status, education. Current figures for cross-classification of region, sex and age classes are available from registers; for other classifications such as marital status by education, one can rely on design-based direct estimators at the national level as these may be considered sufficiently accurate.

The structure-preserving estimator (SPREE) makes precise use of the above-mentioned information [17, 26]. The SPREE is a simple estimation method that informs the population *association structure*, completely describing the relationship among key variables, through a supplementary table observed at a previous time. Most often, the full table observed at a previous census is available. To update the association structure derived from such a table, SPREE uses current information at time t on the (partial) association between the variables present in a table m defining the *allocation structure*. The *allocation structure* usually consists of margins of the current frequency table to be estimated; we consider counts on classes defined by region, sex and age, which can be obtained by administrative records, and finally reliable survey calibration estimates of counts obtained by aggregating over geography.

Since any multi-way table can be reduced to three-way by properly re-defining the classification, we consider a three-way table, where we let $d = 1, \ldots, D$ denote the geographical domain, $h = 1, \ldots, H$ the classification given by the auxiliary variables (sex and age in our application) and $i = 1, \ldots, I$ the classification given by the other survey key variables. As the auxiliary variables have known counts in the population, h can be considered to define strata.

Let X_{dhi} be the association structure, i.e. the table completely observed at previous time t_0. Finally, define by F_{dhi} the counts of the current contingency table to be estimated and by m the allocation structure, i.e. the updated margins.

In its original formulation, SPREE adjusts the X_{dhi} to agree with the updated information in m, while preserving the relationships among variables present in X_{dhi} as much as possible. The method is targeted to obtain estimates of the current population counts F_{dhi} that minimize the χ^2 distance between X_{dhi} and F_{dhi}, with constraints given by m. As mentioned in [17], explicit solutions only exist in trivial cases. In general, iterative proportional fitting (IPF), which consists of iteratively adjusting to marginal constraints until convergence, is applied to obtain an approximate solution, denoted by $\hat{F}_{dhi}^{\mathrm{SPREE}}$, to the above optimization problem.

The IPF on X_{dhi} may produce estimates of the current cell counts that are lower than the observed counts f_{dhi}; to overcome this inconsistency, we propose to apply the generalized iterative proportional fitting (GIPF, [10]) instead of IPF. In general, GIPF allows to obtain the solution of a minimization problem under convex constraints and can be easily applied with the constraints we have imposed. This strategy clearly differs from simply equating estimates and sample frequencies for the inconsistent cells.

Depending on the information available, SPREE allows different specifications of the allocation structure m. Here we consider the pair of two-way tables already illustrated and used in the simulation experiment (see Section 5.3), namely $m = (\{\hat{F}_{.hi}\}, \{F_{dh.}\})$, where $\hat{F}_{.hi}$ are design-based estimates and $F_{dh.}$ come from administrative registers.

The structure-preserving estimator is shown (see [17]) to preserve all the interactions of X_{dhi} but those redefined by the allocation structure, so that the higher order interactions of F_{dhi} are set equal to that of X_{dhi} (see formulas 5.5); the bias of $\hat{F}_{dhi}^{\mathrm{SPREE}}$ therefore depends on the extent to which the equality of the interactions holds for the data. For further details on SPREE, see [17] and [26]. Note that with respect to the Purcell and Kish estimator, the introduction of the additional constraints $\hat{F}_{dhi}^{\mathrm{SPREE}} > f_{dhi}, d = 1, \ldots, D, h = 1, \ldots, H, i = 1, \ldots, I$ in the allocation step is expected to induce slight modifications in the association structure.

Note that SPREE may exhibit large bias if the association structure was subjected to a significant alteration over time; in our application, by comparing the table structures at two consecutive censuses, we noticed a certain stability of the association structure over time, although with some exceptions, see Section 5.4.

To permit additional flexibility in the association structure, [26] introduces a class of log-linear structural models for the cross-classification which generalizes the SPREE by introducing linear models on the parameters defining the interactions among variables. Whereas the SPREE only uses the sample information to produce some of the margins present in the allocation structure m, the above-mentioned structural model is introduced to link the saturated association structure observed at a previous time to the corresponding current timetable, which is estimated from the sample.

In [26], the SPREE is shown to be a special case of a generalized linear structural model for the domain proportions. As before we consider the case that updated margins $m = (\{\hat{F}_{.hi}\}, \{F_{dh.}\})$ are available for the current population table.

Using the notation already introduced, consider the within-domain proportions θ_{dhi}^F and θ_{dhi}^X, relative to the target population table and the auxiliary table at time t_0, respectively:

$$\theta_{dhi}^F = \frac{F_{dhi}}{F_{dh.}}, \qquad \sum_i \theta_{dhi}^F = 1,$$

θ_{dhi}^X being defined similarly.

Define now the saturated log-linear representation of the population counts:

$$\log(F_{dhi}) = \log(\theta_{dhi}^F) + \log(F_{dh.}) = \alpha_0^F + \alpha_d^F + \alpha_h^F + \alpha_i^F + \alpha_{dh}^F + \alpha_{di}^F + \alpha_{hi}^F + \alpha_{dhi}^F$$

and of the auxiliary complete table:

$$\log(X_{dhi}) = \log(\theta_{dhi}^X) + \log(X_{dh.}) = \alpha_0^X + \alpha_d^X + \alpha_h^X + \alpha_i^X + \alpha_{dh}^X + \alpha_{di}^X + \alpha_{hi}^X + \alpha_{dhi}^X .$$

Let

$$\mu_{dhi}^F = \log(\theta_{dhi}^F) - \frac{1}{I} \sum_i \log(\theta_{dhi}^F) = \alpha_i^F + \alpha_{di}^F + \alpha_{hi}^F + \alpha_{dhi}^F , \qquad (5.2)$$

$$\mu_{dhi}^X = \log(\theta_{dhi}^X) - \frac{1}{I} \sum_i \log(\theta_{dhi}^X) = \alpha_i^X + \alpha_{di}^X + \alpha_{hi}^X + \alpha_{dhi}^X .$$

A generalized linear model is introduced to link the two structural models above to inform F_{dhi} through the known complete table X_{dhi}. With a three-way table, two different saturated models may be proposed. The first one assumes a linear structure with constant regression coefficient among strata:

$$\mu_{dhi}^F = \lambda_{hi} + \beta \mu_{dhi}^X \qquad (5.3)$$

where $\sum_i \lambda_{hi} = 0$. This model is a proportional interaction model, and SPREE is a special case of the latter for $\beta = 1$; see [26] for a more detailed description of the implications of the models.

If the regression coefficients are allowed to vary among strata the model is

$$\mu_{dhi}^F = \lambda_{hi} + \beta_h \, \mu_{dhi}^X \tag{5.4}$$

and is equivalent to a stratified proportional interaction model

$$\alpha_{i;h}^F = \lambda_{hi} + \beta_h \, \alpha_{i;h}^X, \tag{5.5}$$

$$\alpha_{di;h}^F = \beta_h \, \alpha_{di;h}^X . \tag{5.6}$$

In the practical application we discarded the estimator based on model (5.3); indeed the associated computational burden was heavy; moreover, a preliminary inspection of the population parameters (that are known in our simulation) revealed a certain variability of β_h across strata defined by age and by sex, so that model (5.4) was deemed more appropriate.

The GLSM (or Proportional Interaction Model) can be further generalized assuming a linear mixed relationship among the parameters of the current table $\{F_{dhi}\}$ and those of the association structure $\{X_{dhi}\}$. The introduction of random components is common in small area estimation to account for unexplained variation among areas that is not explained by covariates in the model.

Defining μ_{dhi}^F and μ_{dhi}^X as in formula (5.2), the generalized linear structural mixed model (GLSMM) is specified as

$$\mu_{dhi}^F = \lambda_{hi} + \beta_h \mu_{dhi}^X + \nu_{dhi}, \tag{5.7}$$

with $(\nu_{dh2}, \ldots, \nu_{dhI})$ distributed as $MN(0, \Sigma_h)$ and $\nu_{dh1} = -\sum_{i=2}^I \nu_{dhi}$. The above formulation in terms of stratum-specific parameters β_h and Σ_h leads to a stratified GLSMM and amounts to consider separate information layers; on the other hand, when these parameters are assumed constant across strata ($\beta_h = \beta$ and $\Sigma_h = \Sigma \; \forall h$), the model can be reformulated so that two different mixed models for higher order interaction are implicitly assumed, sharing the fixed parameter: up to $O_p(D^{-1/2})$, two different random effects, $\nu_{d.i}$ e $\nu_{dhi} - \nu_{d.i}$, affect second-order interactions α_{di}^F and third-order interactions α_{dhi}^F, respectively, see [26].

Note that the GLSMM differs from the usual mixed models in small area estimation, since, due to the constraints on the interactions, it cannot contain a unique area random effect (see [26]).

Due to the structure of the data we analysed, having a small number of regions (areas) compared to the number of age–sex classes (strata $h = 1, 2 \ldots H$), and recalling that the domain of interest for our estimation problem is given by the cross-classification of region by age and sex, in the application of the GLSMM we refer to a different representation of the population contingency table, namely a two-way representation where cell frequencies F_{li} are indexed by $l = 1, \ldots L$ and $i = 1, \ldots I, L = D * H$; here dimension indexed by l represents the domain of interest.

Defining μ_{li}^Y as

$$\mu_{li}^Y = \log(\theta_{li}^Y) - \frac{1}{I} \sum_i \log(\theta_{li}^Y) = \alpha_i^Y + \alpha_l^Y + \alpha_{li}^Y$$

and similarly for μ_{li}^X, the generalized linear structural mixed model (GLSMM) can be specified as

$$\mu_{li}^F = \lambda_i + \beta \mu_{li}^X + \nu_{li} \tag{5.8}$$

with $(\nu_{l2}, \ldots, \nu_{lI})$ distributed as $MN(0, \Sigma)$ and $\nu_{l1} = -\sum_{i=2}^I \nu_{li}$, model (5.8) can be equivalently written in terms of the α parameters as follows:

$$\alpha_i^F = \lambda_i + \beta \alpha_i^X + O_p(L^{-1/2}),$$
$$\alpha_{li}^F = \beta \alpha_{li}^X + \nu_{li} + O_p(L^{-1/2}),$$

note that, when L goes to ∞, random components affect second-order interactions of the log-linear model.

Models (5.4) and (5.8) represent examples of the so-called generalized linear structural model and generalized linear structural mixed model. Note that both refer to population quantities. For this reason unbiased estimates of cell proportions θ_{dhi}^F are introduced in (5.2). The presence of a complex sampling scheme is accounted for by selecting appropriate design-based estimators.

The model parameters are estimated by iterative weighted least squares, for both models, following standard techniques for generalized linear models, here the weighting matrix is designed to include the covariance matrix of the direct estimators of F_{dhi}. For GLSMM, the estimation of the mixed components relies on an approximate likelihood as well. See [26] for details.

The procedure outlined produces first-step estimates of the population counts, that we denote by $\tilde{F}_{dhi}^{GLSM}$ and $\tilde{F}_{dhi}^{GLSMM}$. Note that under SPREE the first-step estimate is just $\tilde{F}_{dhi} = X_{dhi}$, i.e. the previous table without adjusting for the observed data.

Recalling that updated margins $m = (\{\hat{F}_{.hi}\}, \{F_{dh.}\})$ are available, exactly as described for the SPREE methods, the first-step estimates can be adjusted by IPF to match margins in m, thus producing the final estimates $\hat{F}_{dhi}^{GLSM}$, $\hat{F}_{dhi}^{GLSMM}$. As before, IPF could produce estimated population cell counts that are lower than the observed sample counts; for this reason, we propose to modify the second estimating step by introducing the addition constraints $\hat{F}_{dhi}^{GLSM} > f_{dhi}, d = 1, \ldots, D, h = 1, \ldots, H, i = 1, \ldots, I, \hat{F}_{dhi}^{GLSMM} > f_{dhi}, d = 1, \ldots, D, h = 1, \ldots, H, i = 1, \ldots, I,$ respectively. The first-step estimates are therefore adjusted to auxiliary marginal tables by means of GIPF to ensure consistency with the sample frequencies.

5.3 Simulation Plan and Data

To assess the estimators, we ran a simulation study consisting of 1,000 synthetic samples drawn from a known real population, namely the population registered at the 2001 Italian Census for six Italian regions (Val d'Aosta, Piemonte, Toscana,

Umbria, Campania, Molise). Knowledge of the target population allows us to assess the performance of the estimators, as clearly the population contingency table is known and so is the associated target risk measure. Samples were drawn using the complex sampling design of Labour Force Survey (LFS), as detailed in [6]. Note that the LFS sampling design is used for most Italian social surveys. The LFS is based on a complex sample design with stratification of municipalities. In each sample municipality, a systematic sample of households is selected; all members of sampled households are included in the LFS sample.

The six regions above were selected in light of their different geographical position (North, Center and South), the differences they exhibit in the distribution of the key variables, their variability in the number of inhabitants (Val d'Aosta and Molise are small regions where we expect higher risks of disclosure) and finally the substantial variation of their sampling rates under the design used. The latter characteristic results from sample size being planned to guarantee a target precision level of LFS estimates.

In year 2001 the population of the six regions amounted to over 15 million; the effective sample size in terms of individuals results in over 80,000 records.

LFS estimates use sampling design weights obtained by a calibration process that controls over known totals of sex and age in 5-year classes (see [5]). Although the actual calibration process is more complex, for simplicity we have calibrated only on sex by age at regional level.

The key variables selected are region of residence (6 classes as described above), sex, age, marital status (in 4 classes), education (in 5 classes). In [6, 7] we considered a classification of age in 20 classes; here we also selected a finer classification (86 classes) that, excluding the extreme classes, corresponds to 1-year classification to study the performance of the estimators under a more challenging and realistic scenario. The resulting contingency table obtained by cross-classification of the key variables has 4,800 and 20,640 cells, respectively.

The estimators considered in this work exploit the association structure at a previous time; complete information on it is available from the census conducted in year 1991. The temporal lag is large, but we can study the performance of the method almost in its worst condition since we expect that the stability in the association structure decreases with time. The estimators also make use of available information on the margins of the above-mentioned contingency table at current time. In the terminology of Section 5.2.2, the allocation structure has been defined as $m = (\{\hat{F}_{.hi}\}, \{F_{dh.}\})$. In our application $F_{dh.}$ represents the 2001 census counts of the marginal table defined by sex by age by region; in the real practice, these counts would come from updated administrative sources. On the other hand, the counts $F_{.hi}$ of the marginal cross-table defined by education, by marital status (classes denoted with i), by sex and by age (classes denoted with h) are unknown; in our application we resort to calibration estimates $\hat{F}_{.hi}$. Increasing the number or detail of the key variables necessarily affects the precision of these estimators; variable age in previous work ([6, 7]) was indeed recoded to 5-year classes to limit the variability of direct estimators. The practical importance of this limitation is dictated by the data release strategy: indeed the key variables should be defined exactly as they appear in the released file. In fact, age is preferably released in 1-year classes, a classification that might be too fine to allow precise direct estimation of the $\{\hat{F}_{hi}\}$ margins, even at the national level, because these cells are not planned domains for the LFS. This aspect, together with the fact that the within-domain proportions in (5.2) are estimated using the sampling design weights, implies that increasing the number or detail of the key variables affects the precision of the risk estimators.

We also expect that especially the cells with smaller population counts, i.e. higher risk of identification if selected in the sample, will be present in a small subset of the universe of all samples. For the 1,000 simulated samples the average percentage of sample unique cells was about 9% (overall, between 8 and 10.2%) under the first classification of age and about 12% (overall, between 11.5 and 12.7%), under the second, finer classification. The average percentage of empty cells was over 45% (overall, ranging between 44.2 and 46.6%) under the first classification of age and about 59% (overall, ranging between 58.5 and 59.7%) under the second.

5.4 Risk Estimators and Simulation Results

We compare the Skinner estimator of risk described in Section 5.2.1 to risk estimators based on auxiliary information as described in Section 5.2.2. The formulation of estimator (5.1) assumes uniform selection probabilities within cells, an assumption that is not precisely met in the sampling design of the LFS (see also [22]). Indeed the level at which the sampling rate may be assumed constant is the province, which corresponds to a classification nested within the region. Although there is some variation of the rates within regions, to adjust to our framework, for each region d we specified in model (5.1) the mean sampling fraction p_d computed over the corresponding provinces. A simple analytic expression for the risk is available for sample uniques only; for simplicity the results presented are restricted to this case. The Skinner-type risk estimator that we consider, adapted to our framework, is therefore

$$\hat{r}_{dhi}^{SK} = \frac{1 - \exp\{-(1 - p_d)\hat{\pi}_{dhi}\}}{(1 - p_d)\hat{\pi}_{dhi}} . \tag{5.9}$$

We did not perform any model selection procedure as proposed in [22], but rather, to ensure comparability, we fitted to the sample data the log-linear model having as sufficient statistics the margins present in the allocation structure m used for the SPREE-type estimators.

We also introduce an intermediate estimator, referred to as modified Skinner estimator, that mixes the Poisson–Poisson superpopulation model used for the Skinner estimator and the SPREE. In this case the top-level population means π_k in the superpopulation model are the SPREE estimates of population cell counts, namely $\hat{F}_{dhi}^{SPREE}$, exploiting the auxiliary information, and no log-linear model for the sample expected frequencies is introduced:

$$F_{dhi}|\pi_{dhi} \sim \text{Poisson}(\pi_{dhi}),$$
$$f_{dhi}|F_{dhi}, \pi_{dhi}, p_d \sim \text{Poisson}(p_d\pi_{dhi}),$$

where $\pi_{dhi} = \hat{F}_{dhi}^{\text{SPREE}}$ and as for the estimator (5.9) above, p_d is the region-specific mean sampling rate, computed by averaging the original sampling fractions over the corresponding provinces. Unlike the Skinner estimator, the association structure is here introduced through the SPREE estimates; the modified Skinner estimator we propose is therefore

$$\hat{r}_{dhi}^{\text{MSK}} = \frac{1 - \exp\{-(1 - p_d)\hat{F}_{dhi}^{\text{SPREE}}\}}{(1 - p_d)\hat{F}_{dhi}^{\text{SPREE}}} . \tag{5.10}$$

Among the small area-type estimators, first we consider the SPREE-type estimator

$$\hat{r}_{dhi}^{\text{SPREE}} = 1/\hat{F}_{dhi}^{\text{SPREE}} . \tag{5.11}$$

Figure 5.1 shows the relationship among the second-order effects in the two-way tables $\{X_{di;h}\}$ and $\{F_{di;h}\}$, for selected values of h (a specific classification of age by sex). The selected strata are such that the second-order interactions in the $\{F_{di;h}\}$ table differ markedly from the corresponding second-order interactions in the auxiliary population table $\{X_{di;h}\}$. For these classifications of age by sex the graphs indicate that the assumption of constancy of $\alpha_{di;h}^F$ on which the SPREE-type risk estimator (5.11) is based is violated. In these cases, some improvement may be achieved by the stratified GLSM estimator, for which the corresponding risk estimator is

$$\hat{r}_{dhi}^{\text{GLSM}} = 1/\hat{F}_{dhi}^{\text{GLSM}} \tag{5.12}$$

and by a GLSMM-type estimator

$$\hat{r}_{dhi}^{\text{GLSMM}} = 1/\hat{F}_{dhi}^{\text{GLSMM}} . \tag{5.13}$$

Indeed the stratified GLSM-type estimator (5.12) may improve the SPREE estimator, for which a constant regression coefficient ($\beta = 1$) is assumed, by correcting for stratum-specific coefficient of regression. Furthermore, the presence of random effects in the GLSMM-type estimator (5.13) should improve the SPREE and stratified GLSM for strata such as those represented in Fig. 5.1 (e.g. $h = 9, h = 95$) where, although the relationship between interaction effect is close to identity, some outlying $\alpha_{di;h}^F$ deviate markedly from their corresponding $\alpha_{di;h}^X$. We notice that actually for these strata some of the cells of the cross-classification were empty in the previous census table X, but not in the current population table F.

As explained in Section 5.2.2, due to the small number of regions in this study, we do not exploit a three-way GLSMM stratified estimator, which would correspond

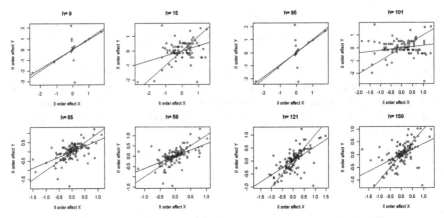

Fig. 5.1 Plot of log-linear second-order association effects $\alpha^X_{di;h}$ for the auxiliary population two-way table $\{X_{di;h}\}$ for selected h levels of sex–age classification vs corresponding effects $\alpha^F_{di;h}$ for the population table $\{F_{di;h}\}$. Tables refer to the finer classification of age

to the SPREE-type and the stratified GLSM-type estimators in terms of information used in the model. Instead, a two-way representation of the contingency table $\{F_{li}\}$ is used, in which the F_{ki} counts are indexed by $l = 1, \ldots, K$ and $i = 1, \ldots, I$, $L = D * H$; here dimension indexed by l represents the domain of interest, namely the cross-classification of region by sex by age.

In fact, the GLSMM-type estimator with a specific effect for the cell of such a table still allows a correction for wrong model specification for the above-mentioned strata; anyway, the resulting interaction model has a slight different use of association among variables. Indeed the structural mixed model does not exploit the main interaction effects of the classification variable for each sex by age class, so that the specification of the relationships among variables is less accurate than that used in SPREE and stratified GLSM-type estimator. This, together with a much higher difficulty in estimating the random effects, can be the reason why the GLSMM does not succeed in improving the other models even for those challenging strata as it will be shown below.

When assessing the risk estimators, there are two different sources of variation: the sample cell size and the population cell size. We consider a conditional assessment, by analysing the above measures for fixed sample frequency $f_k = 1$.

The assessment is clearly restricted to samples where the cell has been observed, as the risk is, of course, not defined (and not of interest) when sample cell is empty. By consequence, for the smallest cells, particularly for regions with lower sampling rates, the performance criteria have sometimes been evaluated on a very small number of samples. In this case, conclusions must be drawn with due care but can still be useful to outline the expected pattern.

Figure 5.2 reports the bias for the estimators considered, restricted to sample unique cells, vs the corresponding population cell frequencies under the two different classifications of the key variables. Whereas all the estimators tend to underesti-

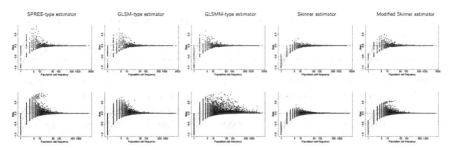

Fig. 5.2 Plot of bias vs population cell frequencies for sample unique cells under the two classification of the key variables. The first row contains the results for the coarser classification of age (20 classes), while the second contains the results for the finer classification of age (86 classes). *Broken lines* represent 25 and 75% percentiles of bias for given population cell size, *dots* joined by a *solid line* represent medians of the same quantities

mate very high-risk records, the Skinner estimator, not relying on detailed external information, shows a more evident tendency to a negative bias; the SPREE, GLSM, GLSMM and modified Skinner estimators benefit from external information, even though in the smallest regions, characterized by the highest sampling fractions, some cells are not well captured by the model. Note that the modified Skinner estimator benefits from a shrinkage effect induced by the superpopulation model that makes the latter issue less important if compared to the SPREE estimator, whose definition relies on the same quantities $\hat{F}_{dhi}^{SPREE}$.

The conclusions above do not change when refining the detail of key variable age, except for the risk estimator based on the GLSMM. This estimator indeed behaves poorly when the classification of the key variables is refined, showing substantial overestimation of risk for many cells.

The risk underestimation rapidly vanishes when the population cell size increases; when considering cells with sample frequency $f_k = 2$ (figure not shown here) the performance of the estimators improves, in particular bias is reduced for high-risk cells. The GLSMM again behaves poorly under the finer classification of age.

In [6, 7] evaluation of the performance of risk estimators relies on bias as above and relative root mean square error. Recall that the estimand is $r_{dhi} = 1/F_{dhi}$ for nonempty sample cells. Being the risk a bounded parameter ranging in [0, 1], use of the euclidean distance is not the best choice, other loss functions being perhaps more appropriate. In a disclosure limitation context, an underestimation of the true risk is more serious than is an overestimation. For these reasons to evaluate the estimation error we considered an asymmetric LINEX loss function (Varian, [24]) defined as

$$L(\Delta, a, b) = b[\exp(a\Delta) - a\Delta - 1]$$

where Δ is the estimation error and $a \neq 0$, $b > 0$ are parameters controlling asymmetry and shape of the loss function. To penalize underestimation more than overestimation of risk, we chose a negative value for a.

Table 5.1 Conditional assessment over sample unique cells of mean LINEX loss for the four estimators; classification of age in 20 classes

	Min.	First Qu.	Median	Mean	Third Qu.	Max.
rSPREE	0.000000	0.000002	0.000046	0.126900	0.001706	7.936000
rGLSM	0.000000	0.000003	0.000052	0.150700	0.001723	7.906000
rGLSMM	0.000000	0.000004	0.000053	0.156300	0.001584	7.928000
rSK	0.000000	0.000006	0.000085	0.186600	0.001159	7.813000
rMSK	0.000000	0.000003	0.000055	0.126000	0.001993	7.936000

Table 5.2 Conditional assessment over sample unique cells of mean LINEX loss for the four estimators; classification of age in 86 classes

	Min.	First Qu.	Median	Mean	Third Qu.	Max.
rSPREE	0.000000	0.000016	0.000314	0.170000	0.012750	7.975000
rGLSM	0.000000	0.000019	0.000348	0.203400	0.016650	7.930000
rGLSMM	0.000000	0.000091	0.001395	0.223100	0.036810	7.958000
rSK	0.000000	0.000035	0.000340	0.247500	0.007340	7.828000
rMSK	0.000000	0.000019	0.000358	0.167100	0.015180	7.975000

Table 5.1 contains a summary of the mean LINEX loss function ($a = -3$, $b = 0.5$) evaluated over sample unique cells for the first, coarser classification of the key variables, while Table 5.2 contains an analogous summary for the second, finer classification of the key variables.

These figures indicate that overall the SPREE and the modified Skinner estimator based on the SPREE have the best performance; however, such assessment refers to different cells in the cross-classification, having low as well as large frequencies in the population. Analysing population uniques, the SPREE appears to have lower mean LINEX loss than the other estimators; however, for population cell sizes ≥ 2, the modified Skinner estimator possesses the best mean LINEX loss.

Figure 5.3 reports a graphical assessment of the performance of the estimators over sample uniques for all the available samples, under the two classifications of variable age. To avoid plotting all the replications of sample uniques across all simulations, for each cell we plot a summary of the estimates over our 1,000 samples, showing the minimum and maximum (grey dots) and the median (black dots) of the estimates over the eligible samples. The x-axis reports the target risk that is known in the simulation. The red line represents a loess curve for the median estimated values, the broken lines are loess quantile curves of level 0.5 and 0.95, respectively, giving an idea of the variability of the estimates and finally the dotted lines are loess curves for minima and maxima. The first row shows the results for the coarser 5-year classification of age, whereas the second contains the same figures for the finer classification of age. Analogously, Fig. 5.4 reports a graphical assessment of the performance of the three SPREE-type estimators (excluding the modified Skinner estimator) over sample doubles. Figure 5.3 shows that in general all the estimators permit to distinguish sample uniques between risky and safe, the SPREE and stratified GLSM exhibiting a very similar behaviour and being apparently preferable

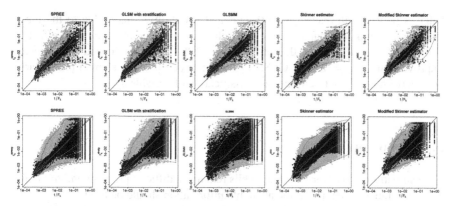

Fig. 5.3 Performance of the estimators for sample uniques under two age classifications

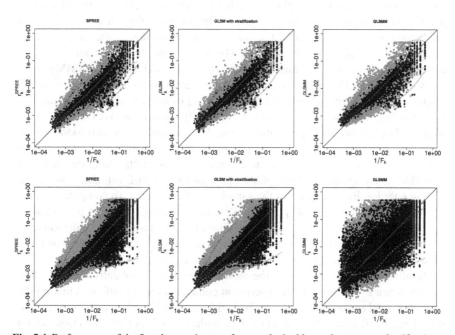

Fig. 5.4 Performance of the first three estimators for sample doubles under two age classifications

to the Skinner estimator. This is not surprising, as $\hat{r}^{SK}_{dhi}$ does not make use of auxiliary information. On the other hand, the modified, SPREE-based, Skinner estimator appears to improve both the SPREE and the Skinner estimators especially for the high-risk cells. The variability is also reduced due to the shrinkage effect.

Whereas the patterns remain unchanged when increasing the detail of age, as expected there is an increase in the variability, that is anyway not remarkable (see the broken loess curves), apart for the GLSMM estimator. The performance of such estimator is comparable to that of the other SPREE-based estimators for the first coarser classification of age, while under the second classification the estimator behaves poorly with respect to both bias and variability. This is due to the input table $\{F_{dhi}\}$ being too sparse to allow for reliable estimation of the random effects.

Figure 5.4 indicates that the performance of the estimators considered already improves when $f_k = 2$. The GLSMM estimator continues to show a particularly poor performance when refining the classification of variable age.

5.5 Comments

The estimation of risk for low count cells remains a difficult problem and to obtain more accurate estimators, all the available information should be used.

In this chapter we presented a comparative analysis of some simple risk estimators based on a linear structural method that is designed to estimate frequency in a population contingency table using auxiliary information. We considered the structure preserving estimator (SPREE) and two generalizations of the latter, namely the generalized linear structural model (GLSM) estimator and its mixed effects counterpart, namely the generalized linear structural mixed model (GLSMM). In all cases we have modified the estimation process so as to ensure that the observed cell frequency f_{dhi} does not exceed the corresponding estimated population frequency. Once the frequency has been estimated, we simply derived the risk estimate as the reciprocal of the estimated population count. We also considered two Skinner-type estimators, one based on a Poisson superpopulation model with log-linear modelling of the observed counts as proposed in [21] and a variation of the latter that relies on a similar superpopulation model, that is informed by SPREE estimates instead of relying on a log-linear model for the sample cell frequencies. To compare the estimators, a simulation plan was pursued following the sampling design of the Italian Labour Force Survey. We considered two different scenarios specifying the same set of key variable, though at two different levels of detail for variable age. The latter choice leads to a very large and sparse contingency table F to be estimated.

Results shown are restricted to the most challenging case of cells with low sample frequencies. The simulation experiment conducted clearly indicates that all the estimators tend to underestimate very high-risk records. The Skinner-type estimator, not relying on detailed information on the population table at a previous time nor on any other external information, shows a more evident tendency to a negative bias; note, however, that the underlying log-linear model is not saturated as in the models underlying the SPREE-type estimators. The latter estimators benefit from the introduction of external information, even though in the smallest regions, characterized by the highest sampling fractions, some cells are not well captured by the model. For the modified Skinner estimator based on the SPREE, this effect is mitigated by the shrinkage induced by the superpopulation model.

To assess the estimation error, instead of MSE we considered LINEX loss, an asymmetric loss function. Using this measure, the SPREE and the modified Skinner estimator based on the SPREE appear to be superior to the other estimators. In particular, the latter estimator exhibits better mean LINEX loss for low population frequencies. The introduction of mixed effects did not result in an improvement over the other estimators, especially when the detail of the key variables is such that the corresponding contingency table is very large and sparse.

Excluding the GLSMM whose overall performance deteriorates, the increase in variability of the estimators corresponding to an increase in the detail of key variables is moderate.

Whereas the estimator (5.9) only requires the observed data and information about the sampling fraction, the structural estimators (5.11), (5.12) and (5.13) come with some computational and administrative burden, as they require an estimation process (especially the GLSM and GLSMM estimators) and management of census data. The process of building the appropriate table is an important step that requires at least some insights about the available information and the classes in which estimates with sufficient precision can be obtained from the sample at hand. The population table from which the association structure is borrowed must be properly organized; besides that, margins must be computed from the available sources such as administrative archives and the sample on release. Finally, in order for the variables collected at a census to be compatible with the key variables available in the survey microdata, treatments, such as recoding, are usually necessary, as sometimes the definitions may vary. This process is nontrivial and might be computationally demanding, depending on the size of the population. An advantage is that the census table has to be collected and organized only once in several years. Indeed the same association structure is modelled at subsequent releases, the only change being the update of margins. Log-linear model estimation required for the estimator (5.9) relies on maximum likelihood; although the procedure is well known and readily available in standard software, when large tables are analysed, the associated computational costs may also be high.

Among the SPREE-type estimators, (5.11) is based on the simplest model; penalizing for underestimation, it emerges in our simulation study as a good performing estimator, even though the more flexible GLSM estimator has a very similar behaviour. The relative stability over time of many interaction effects in our data may be a reason for the good performance of the SPREE. The adoption of a superpopulation model that is informed by SPREE estimates, leading to the modified Skinner estimator, is a relatively simple procedure that leads to good performances, especially for high-risk cells, with no additional computational costs.

Acknowledgments The work was partially supported by the European Project ESSnet-SDC on statistical disclosure control. The simulation study was conducted under a joint research agreement between Istat and Università di Napoli Federico II (Protocollo di ricerca per la collaborazione alla ricerca e verifica sperimentale relativa ai metodi statistici utili per la valutazione del rischio di violazione della riservatezza).

References

1. An D. and Little R.J.A. Multiple imputation: an alternative to top coding for statistical disclosure control, *Journal of the Royal Statistical Society, Series A*, 170:923–940, 2007.
2. Benedetti R. and Franconi L. Statistical and technological solutions for controlled data dissemination. In: *Pre-proceedings of New Techniques and Technologies for Statistics Statistics – Sorrento, 4–6 November 1998*, vol. 1, 225–232, 1998.
3. Bethlehem J., Keller W. and Pannekoek J. Disclosure control of microdata. *Journal of the American Statistical Association*. 85:38–45, 1990.
4. Carlson M. Assessing microdata disclosure risk using the Poisson-inverse Gaussian distribution. *Statistics in Transition*, 5:901–925, 2002.
5. Deville J.C. and Särndal C.E. Calibration estimators in survey sampling. *Journal of the American Statistical Association*, 87:367–382, 1992.
6. Di Consiglio L. and Polettini S. Improving Individual Risk Estimators. In: Privacy in Statistical Databases 2006, Volume 4302 of Lecture Notes in Computer Science (eds. J. Domingo-Ferrer and L. Franconi), Springer, New York, NY, pp. 243–256, 2006.
7. Di Consiglio L. and Polettini S. Use of Auxiliary Information in Risk Estimation. In: *Privacy in Statistical Databases* (eds. J. Domingo-Ferrer and Y. Saygin) *UNESCO Chair in Data Privacy International Conference, PSD 2008, Istanbul, Turkey, September 24–26, 2008. Proceedings.*, volume 5262 of Lecture Notes in Computer Science Springer New York, NY, *Lecture Notes in Computer Science* pp. 213–226, 2008.
8. Duncan G.T., Keller-McNulty S. and Stokes S. L. Disclosure risk vs. data utility: The R-U confidentiality map, Technical Report LA-UR-01-6428, Los Alamos National Laboratory, Statistical Sciences Group, Los Alamos, N.M., 2001.
9. Duncan G.T. and Lambert D. Disclosure-Limited data dissemination (with comments). *Journal of the American Statistical Association*, 81:10–27, 1986.
10. Dykstra R.L. An iterative procedure for obtaining I-projections onto the intersection of convex sets. *The Annals of Probability*, 13:975–984, 1985.
11. Elamir E.A.H., Skinner C.J. Record level measures of disclosure risk for survey microdata. *Journal of Official Statistics*, 22(3):525–539, 2006.
12. Fienberg S.E. and Makov U.E. Confidentiality, uniqueness, and disclosure limitation for categorical data. *Journal of Official Statistics*, 14:385–397, 1998.
13. Fienberg S.E. and Makov U.E. Uniqueness and disclosure risk: Urn models and simulation, In: *Bayesian Methods With Applications to Science, Policy and Official Statistics*, Monographs in Official Statistics, Eurostat, Luxembourg, pp. 135–144, 2001.
14. Forster J. J. and Webb E. L. Bayesian disclosure risk assessment: Predicting small frequencies in contingency tables. *Journal of the Royal Statistical Society: Series C*, 56(5):551–570, 2007.
15. Franconi L. and Polettini S. Individual risk estimation in μ-Argus: A Review. In: *Privacy in Statistical Databases 2004* (eds. J. Domingo-Ferrer and V. Torra), Springer New York, NY, pp. 262–272, 2004.
16. Polettini S. Some remarks on the individual risk methodology. In: *Proceedings of the Joint ECE/Eurostat Work Session on Statistical Data Confidentiality, Luxembourg, 7–9 April 2003*, Eurostat, Luxembourg, pp. 299–311, 2004.
17. Purcell N.J. and Kish L. Postcensal estimates for local areas (small domains). *International Statistical Review*, 48:3–18, 1980.
18. Reiter J.P. Releasing multiply-imputed, synthetic public use microdata: an illustration and empirical study. *Journal of the Royal Statistical Society, A*, 168:185–205, 2005.
19. Rinott Y. On models for statistical disclosure risk estimation. In: *Proceedings of the Joint ECE/Eurostat Work Session on Statistical Data Confidentiality, Luxembourg, 7–9 April 2003*, Eurostat, Luxembourg, pp. 275–285, 2004.
20. Rinott Y. and Shlomo N. Variances and confidence intervals for sample disclosure risk measures. In: *Proceedings of the 56th Session of the ISI*, Lisbon, pp. 22–29 August, 2007.

21. Skinner C.J. and Holmes D.J. Estimating the re-identification risk per record in microdata. *Journal of Official Statistics*, 14:361–372, 1998.

22. Skinner C.J. and Shlomo N. Assessing identification risk in survey microdata using log-linear models. *Journal of the American Statistical Association*, 103:989–1001, 2008.

23. Takemura A. Some superpopulation models for estimating the number of population uniques. in: *Statistical Data Protection, Lisbon, 25–27 March 1998*. Eurostat, Luxembourg, pp. 45–58, 1999.

24. Varian, H.R. A Bayesian approach to real estate assessment In: *Studies in Honor of Leonard S. Savage* (eds. S.E. Fienberg and A. Zellner), North Holland, Amsterdam, pp. 195–208, 1975.

25. Willenborg L. and de Waal T.D. *Elements of Statistical Disclosure Control*. Springer, New York, 2000.

26. Zhang L. and Chambers R.L. Small area estimates for cross-classifications. *Journal of the Royal Statistical Society, Series B*, 66(2):479–496, 2004.

27. Zhou S., Lafferty J. and Wasserman L. Compressed regression, Technical report, available at http://arxiv.org/abs/0706.0534, 2009. Accessed date: 01/11/2008.

Chapter 6
Statistical Disclosure Control in Tabular Data

Jordi Castro

Abstract Data disseminated by National Statistical Agencies (NSAs) can be classified as either microdata or tabular data. Tabular data are obtained from microdata by crossing one or more categorical variables. Although cell tables provide aggregated information, they also need to be protected. This chapter is a short introduction to tabular data protection. It contains three main sections. The first one shows the different types of tables that can be obtained and how they are modeled. The second describes the practical rules for detection of sensitive cells that are used by NSAs. Finally, an overview of protection methods is provided, with a particular focus on two of them: "cell suppression problem" and "controlled tabular adjustment."

6.1 Introduction

National Statistical Agencies (NSAs) store information about individuals or *respondents* (persons, companies, etc.) in microdata files. A microdata file V of s individuals and t variables is a $s \times t$ matrix where V_{ij} is the value of variable j for individual i. Formally, it can be defined as a function

$$V : I \rightarrow D(V_1) \times D(V_2) \times \cdots \times D(V_t)$$

that maps individuals of set I to an array of t values for variables $V_1, \ldots, V_t$, $D()$ being the domain of those variables. According to this domain, variables can be classified as numerical (e.g., "age," "net profit") or categorical ("sex," "economy sector").

From those microdata files, tabular data are obtained by crossing one or more categorical variables. For instance, assuming a microdata file with information of inhabitants of some region and considering only the categorical variable "profession," we could get the one-dimensional table of Fig. 6.1. Crossing variables

J. Castro (✉)

Department of Statistics and Operations Research, Universitat Politècnica de Catalunya,
C. Jordi Girona 1–3, 08034 Barcelona, Catalonia
e-mail: jordi.castro@upc.edu

J. Nin, J. Herranz (eds.), *Privacy and Anonymity in Information Management Systems*,   113
Advanced Information and Knowledge Processing,
DOI 10.1007/978-1-84996-238-4_6, © Springer-Verlag London Limited 2010

P_1	P_2	P_3	P_4	P_5	TOTAL
130	73	46	90	31	370

Fig. 6.1 One-dimensional frequency table showing number of persons for each profession

	P_1	P_2	P_3	P_4	P_5	TOTAL
M_1	20	15	30	20	10	95
M_2	72	20	1	30	10	133
M_3	38	38	15	40	11	142
TOTAL	130	73	46	90	31	370

Fig. 6.2 Two-dimensional frequency table showing number of persons for each profession and municipality

"profession" and "municipality" we could get the two-dimensional table of Fig. 6.2. The above two tables count the number of inhabitants in each cell; these are named *frequency* tables. Instead, the table could provide information about a third variable. For instance, the table of Fig. 6.3 shows the overall salary for each profession and municipality; these are named *magnitude* tables. Formally, a table is a function

$$T: D(V_{i_1}) \times D(V_{i_2}) \times \cdots \times D(V_{i_l}) \to \mathbb{R} \text{ or } \mathbb{N},$$

l being the number of categorical variables that were crossed. The result of function T (cells' values) belongs to $\mathbb{N}$ for a frequency table and to $\mathbb{R}$ for a magnitude table.

Although tabular data show aggregated information, there is a risk of disclosing individual information. This can be easily seen from the tables of Figs. 6.2 and 6.3. Any attacker knows that the salary of the unique respondent of cell (M_2, P_3) is 22,000 €. This is named an *external attacker*. If there were two respondents in that cell, then any of them could deduce the other's salary, becoming an *internal attacker*. Even if there were a larger number of respondents, e.g., five, if one of them had a salary of, e.g., 18, there would be a disclosure risk. This scenario is named *internal attack with dominance*.

The number of registers in a microdata file r is in general much larger than the number of cells n in a table ($r \gg n \gg 0$). It could be thought that, therefore,

	P_1	P_2	P_3	P_4	P_5	TOTAL
M_1	360	450	720	400	360	2290
M_2	1440	540	22	570	320	2892
M_3	722	1178	375	800	363	3438
TOTAL	2522	2168	1117	1770	1043	8620

Fig. 6.3 Two-dimensional magnitude table showing overall salary (in 1,000 €) for each profession and municipality

the protection of microdata is more complex, since it involves a larger number of information. However, tabular data involve a number of linear constraints m; this linear constraints model the relations between inner and total cells, the most usual relation being that the sum of some inner cells is equal to some marginal cell. Microdata protection in general involves few (if not 0) linear constraints, and usually $m \gg 0$. For this reason, tabular data protection methods need linear programming (LP) and mixed integer linear programming (MILP) technology, making the protection of complex and large tables a difficult problem.

Although it contains some references to recent literature, this chapter cannot be considered a comprehensive survey on statistical disclosure control of tabular data. Additional information can be found, for instance, in the research monographs [20–22, 32] and in the recent survey [31]. Details about practical aspects of tabular data protection can be found in the handbook [27].

This chapter is made of three main sections associated with the three stages of the tabular data protection process. Section 6.2 shows the different types of tables that can be obtained and how they are modeled. Section 6.3 introduces some sensitivity rules for detection of sensitivity cells to be protected. Finally, Section 6.4 introduces some of the most widely used tabular data protection methods, mainly focusing on two of them, the *cell suppression problem* and the *controlled tabular adjustment*.

6.2 Tabular Data: Types and Modeling

The first stage of the tabular data protection process is to know the type of table to be protected and how to model it. It is an important stage, since some protection methods of Section 6.4 can be specialized (i.e., made more efficient) for some particular classes of tables.

6.2.1 Classification of Tables

Broadly, tables can be classified according to different criteria as follows:

6.2.1.1 According to the Cell Values

The two types of tables were already introduced in Section 8.1. They are as follows:

- **Frequency tables**: These are also named contingency tables. They count the number of respondents that belong to each cell. Cell values are in $\mathbb{N}$.
- **Magnitude tables**: They provide information about each cell respondents for another variable of the microfile. Cell values are in $\mathbb{R}$.

6.2.1.2 According to the Sign of Cell Values

Protection methods usually involve the solution of difficult LP or MILP problems. The lower bounds of the variables in those problems (either 0 or $-\infty$) are usually related to the sign of the cell values. We have two cases:

- **Positive tables:** Cell values are $\geq$ 0. It is the most usual situation. For instance, all frequency tables and most of the magnitude tables, like "salary" for "profession" $\times$ "municipality," are positive tables.
- **General tables:** Cell values can be either positive or negative. An example of general table would be "variation of gross domestic product" for "year" $\times$ "state."

6.2.1.3 According to Table Structure

This is likely the most important classification. Some protection methods can only be applied to some of the below classes of tables.

- **Single k-dimensional table:** Single table obtained by crossing k categorical variables. All the tables shown above are k-dimensional tables ($k = 1$ for the table of Fig. 6.1, $k = 2$ for the tables of Figs. 6.2 and 6.3). Note that the number of cells grows very quickly (exponentially) with k.
- **Hierarchical tables:** Set of tables obtained by crossing some variables, and a number of these variables have a hierarchical relation. For instance, consider the three tables of Fig. 6.4. The left subtable shows number of respondents for "region" $\times$ "profession"; the middle subtable, a "zoom in" of region R_2, provides the number of respondents for "municipality" (of region R_2) $\times$ "profession"; finally the right subtable, "zip code" $\times$ "profession," details municipality R_{21}. This table belongs to a particular class named 1H2D, two-dimensional tables with one hierarchical variable.
- **Linked tables:** It is the most general situation. Linked tables is a set of tables obtained from the same microdata file. In theory, the set of all tables obtained from a microdata file should be considered together as a (likely huge) linked table. Hierarchical and k-dimensional tables are particular cases of linked tables. Note that, in theory, the only safe way for protecting all the tables from a microfile is to jointly protect them as a single linked table. Unfortunately, in many cases the size of the resulting table would be excessive for current LP or MILP technology.

	C_1	C_2	C_3
R_1	5	6	11
R_2	10	15	25
R_3	15	21	36

T_1

	C_1	C_2	C_3
R_{21}	8	10	18
R_{22}	2	5	7
R_2	10	15	25

T_2

	C_1	C_2	C_3
R_{211}	6	6	12
R_{212}	2	4	6
R_{21}	8	10	18

T_3

Fig. 6.4 Hierarchical table made of three subtables: "region" $\times$ "profession," "municipality" $\times$ "profession," and "zip code" $\times$ "profession"

6.2.2 Modeling Tables

Since linked tables are the more general case, a model for them is valid for all types of tables. However, we will exploit the particular structure of two-dimensional, three-dimensional, and 1H2D tables.

6.2.2.1 Two-Dimensional Tables

A two-dimensional table of $r + 1$ rows and $c + 1$ columns as that of Fig. 6.5 is modeled by the following constraints.

$$\sum_{j=1}^{c} a_{ij} = a_{i(c+1)} \quad i = 1, \ldots, r,$$
$$\sum_{i=1}^{r} a_{ij} = a_{(r+1)j} \quad j = 1, \ldots, c. \tag{6.1}$$

Constraints (6.1) can be represented by the bipartite network of Fig. 6.6. This allows the application of efficient network optimization algorithms, such as those for minimum-cost network flows, or shortest paths [1]. This fact was originally noticed in [2], and it has been extensively used in other works [4–6, 9, 14, 23, 28].

a_{11}	$\cdots$	a_{1c}	$a_{1(c+1)}$
$\cdots$	$\cdots$	$\cdots$	$\cdots$
a_{r1}	$\cdots$	a_{rc}	$a_{r(c+1)}$
$a_{(r+1)1}$	$\cdots$	$a_{(r+1)c}$	$a_{(r+1)(c+1)}$

Fig. 6.5 General two-dimensional table

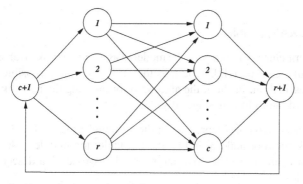

Fig. 6.6 Network representing constraints (6.1)

6.2.2.2 Three-Dimensional Tables

The linear constraints of a three-dimensional table of $r + 1$ rows, $c + 1$ columns, and $l + 1$ levels (levels refer to categories of third variable) are

$$
\begin{aligned}
\sum_{i=1}^{r} a_{ijk} &= a_{(r+1)jk} \quad j = 1, \ldots, c, \quad k = 1, \ldots, l, \\
\sum_{j=1}^{c} a_{ijk} &= a_{i(c+1)k} \quad i = 1, \ldots, r, \quad k = 1, \ldots, l, \\
\sum_{k=1}^{l} a_{ijk} &= a_{ij(l+1)} \quad i = 1, \ldots, r, \quad j = 1, \ldots, c.
\end{aligned}
\tag{6.2}
$$

Note the above constraints correspond to a *cube* of data. Rearranging (6.2), these constraints can be modeled as a multicommodity network [5]. Variables $x_{ijk}, i = 1, \ldots, r, j = 1, \ldots, c, k = 1, \ldots, l$ are ordered according to k, i.e., $x = (x_{ij1}^T, \ldots, x_{ijl}^T)^T$. Each group for a particular k contains rc variables, and it corresponds to a layer of the cube of data. Each layer is a two-dimensional table, which is modeled as the network of Fig. 6.6. Data for each particular layer (or level) correspond to a commodity. The l commodities are linked by capacity constraints, forcing that the sum for all the commodities (levels) is equal to the marginal level. The resulting constraint matrix structure is

$$
A =
\begin{array}{c}
\begin{array}{ccc} a_{ij1} & a_{ij2} & \cdots & a_{ijl} \end{array} \\
\left[
\begin{array}{cccc}
N & & & \\
 & N & & \\
 & & \ddots & \\
 & & & N \\
I & I & \cdots & I
\end{array}
\right]
\begin{array}{l}
\text{for } k = 1 \\
\text{for } k = 2 \\
\vdots \\
\text{for } k = l \\
\text{linking constraints,}
\end{array}
\end{array}
\tag{6.3}
$$

N being the node-arc incidence network matrix for the two-dimensional tables of each level, and $I \in \mathbb{R}^{rc \times rc}$ being the identity matrix. Exploiting this structure, significant computational savings can be obtained [7, 10].

6.2.2.3 Hierarchical Tables

In general, hierarchical tables have to be modeled as a general linked table. However, for the particular case of 1H2D tables, as that of Fig. 6.4, it is possible to obtain a network representation. In short, the algorithm for building the network of a 1H2D table consists of the following stages [9]:

1. Build a tree of subtables representing the structure of the 1H2D (i.e., for table of Fig. 6.4, the root node would be the left table; the middle table would be a descendant of the root table; and the right table would be a descendant of the middle table).
2. Search all the subtables of the tree using for instance a breadth-first-search and build the breadth-first-list.

3. Build the networks for each subtable.
4. For all the subtables in the breadth-first-list, embed the network of a table within the table of its parent table.

The above procedure is done in linear time. For instance, for the 1H2D table of Fig. 6.4 after the first iteration we would get the network of Fig. 6.7; after the second and last iteration the definitive network of Fig. 6.8 would be obtained. This network model was successfully used for a fast heuristic for protection of 1H2D tables in [9].

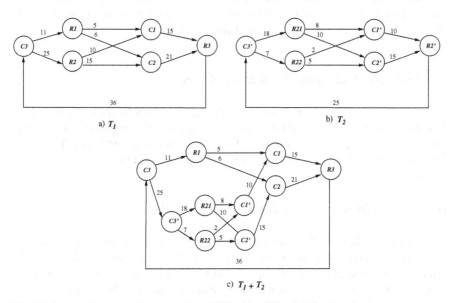

Fig. 6.7 Intermediate network representing 1H2D table of Fig. 6.4 (first iteration)

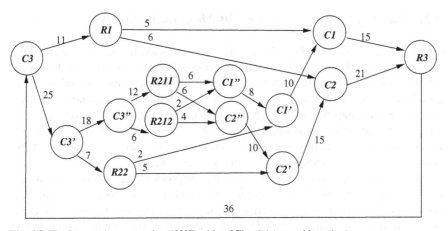

Fig. 6.8 Final network representing 1H2D table of Fig. 6.4 (second iteration)

6.2.2.4 Linked Tables

Any table can be modeled as a set of n cells $a_i, i = 1, \ldots, n$, which satisfy a set of m linear relations $Aa = b$, $A \in \mathbb{R}^{m \times n}$, $b \in \mathbb{R}^m$. If the table is positive, then we may add bounds $a_i \geq 0, i = 1, \ldots, n$. Each row of matrix $A = (a_{ij}), i = 1, \ldots, m$, $j = 1, \ldots, n$, is related to a table linear relation, and $a_{ij} \in \{1, 0, -1\}$. The value -1 of every equation is related to the marginal cell. The tables of the above sections are particular cases where A is either a node-arc incidence network flows matrix or a multicommodity network flows matrix. In real-world problems the dimension of n and m can be very large, up to millions of cells. Some huge instances can be found in http://www-eio.upc.es/~jcastro/data.html.

6.3 Sensitive Cells and Sensitivity Rules

Sensitivity rules are used for detection of the set of cells with disclosure risk. For frequency tables, the *threshold value* rule is mostly used. For magnitude tables, both the (n, k) and the $p\%$ can be used, the latter being in general preferred. The three rules are outlined below. More practical details can be found in [27].

6.3.1 The Threshold Rule for Frequency Tables

In a frequency table, a cell is considered sensitive (i.e., its value has to be protected) if less than t respondents contribute to this cell. An usual value could be $t = 3$. Although this rule could also be applied to magnitude tables, this is not a good practice, since it misses the contribution of each respondent to the cell value.

6.3.2 The (n, k) and $p\%$ Rules for Magnitude Tables

The (n, k) rule (also named *dominance rule*) considers a cell is sensitive if n or less respondents contribute to a $k\%$ (or more) of the cell value. For instance, for a cell $100 = 30 + 30 + 20 + 10 + 10$ (i.e., cell of value 100 and five respondents with contributions 30, 30, 20, 10, 10), if $n = 1$ and $k = 50$ then the cell is non-sensitive: any respondent contribution is less than a 50% of the cell value; however, if $n = 2$ and $k = 50$, then the cell is sensitive since $30 + 30 > 100 \cdot 0.5$. The (n, k) rule tries to avoid that a coalition of n respondents could obtain accurate estimates of the other respondents' contributions. Some usual values are, e.g., $(n = 3, k = 75)$.

For the $p\%$ rule a cell is sensitive if some respondent may obtain an estimate of other respondent contribution within a $p\%$ precision. The worse case – the one considered in practice – is obtained when the respondent with the second largest contribution tries to estimate the value of the respondent with the highest contribution. For instance, for the cell $100 = 55 + 30 + 10 + 3 + 2$ (i.e., cell of value 100 and five respondents with contributions 55, 30, 10, 3, 2), the second respondent knows that the value of the first respondent is at most $100 - 30 = 70$; the estimate of the first respondent done by the second is 70. If $p = 20\%$, since $70 > (1+20/100) \cdot 55 = 66$, then the cell in non-sensitive. If $p = 30$, since $70 < (1 + 30/100) \cdot 55 = 71.5$, the cell is considered sensitive. In general, for a cell $X = x_1 + x_2 + \cdots + x_t$ with t respondents and $x_1 \geq x_2 \geq \cdots \geq x_t$, the estimate of x_1 is $\hat{x}_1 = X - x_2$, and the cell is sensitive if

$$\hat{x}_1 - x_1 < p/100 x_1 \Leftrightarrow X - x_1 - x_2 < p/100 x_1. \qquad (6.4)$$

In general, the $p\%$ is preferred to the (n, k) rule. Indeed the (n, k) may wrongly consider as non-sensitive cells and vice versa. The following example, from [29], illustrates this situation. Consider the rule $(n = 1, k = 60)$. When applied to the cell $100 = 59 + 40 + 1$, this is considered non-sensitive, since $59 < 0.6 \cdot 100$. On the other hand, the cell $100 = 61 + 20 + 19$ is considered sensitive, since $61 > 0.6 \cdot 100$. However, for the cell declared non-sensitive, the second respondent gets a too tight estimation of the first one of value 60: $100 - 59 = 61$. Similarly, for the cell considered sensitive, the estimation by the second respondent would be $100 - 20 = 80$, far from the real value.

Situations as those of the above paragraph could be avoided by using a rule $(n = 2, k)$, but even in this case the $p\%$ rule is preferred. This is shown by noting that the $(n = 2, k)$ rule considers a cell as sensitive if

$$x_1 + x_2 > k/100 X \Leftrightarrow X - x_2 - x_1 < (1 - k/100) X. \qquad (6.5)$$

Comparing (6.4) and (6.5), it is seen that in both cases a cell is sensitive if $(X - x_2) - x_1$, i.e., the difference between the estimation of x_1 made by the second respondent and x_1 is less than a certain percentage of either the first respondent value x_1 in (6.4) or the cell value X in (6.5). Note that the $p\%$ rule is more natural, and that the $(n = 2, k)$ suffers from overprotection. Indeed, for some particular values of p and k, it can be proved that the set of sensitive cells provided by the rule $p\%$ is a subset of the set obtained with $(n = 2, k)$. This is clearly seen in the following result [27].

Proposition 6.1 *For p and k such that $k = 100 \frac{100}{100+p}$, every non-sensitive cell for the rule $(n = 2, k)$ is also a non-sensitive cell for the rule $p\%$; but the reverse implication does not hold.*

Proof First we prove the direct implication. If a cell $X = x_1 + x_2 + \cdots + x_t$ is non-sensitive for $(n = 2, k)$, then by (6.5)

$$x_1 + x_2 \leq \frac{k}{100} X = \frac{100}{100 + p} X \Rightarrow (X - x_2) - x_1 \geq \left(1 - \frac{100}{100 + p}\right) X = \frac{p}{100 + p} X \qquad (6.6)$$

and also

$$x_1 \leq \frac{k}{100} X = \frac{100}{100 + p} X \Rightarrow \frac{p}{100} x_1 \leq \frac{p}{100 + p} X. \qquad (6.7)$$

Connecting inequalities (6.6) and (6.7) we have

$$(X - x_2) - x_1 \geq \frac{p}{100 + p} X \geq \frac{p}{100} x_1,$$

thus the cell is non-sensitive for the rule $p\%$.

To show that the reverse implication is not true, we consider a counterexample. For $p = 10\%$ and $k = 100 \cdot 100/(100 + p)$, a cell $X = 110$ with $x_1 = 52$, $x_2 = 50$ is non-sensitive for the $p\%$ rule, since $\hat{x}_1 - x_1 = (110 - 50) - 52 = 60 - 52 > 52 \cdot p/100$. However, it is sensitive for the $(n = 2, k)$ rule, because $x_1 + x_2 = 102 > k/100 \cdot 110 = 100$.   □

6.4 Tabular Data Protection Methods

Tabular data protection methods can be classified as follows:

- *Non-perturbative*: They do not change the original data, instead they "hide" data or change the table structure. Among them we find *recoding* and *cell suppression*.
- *Perturbative*: They provide an alternative table with modified values. *Controlled rounding* and *controlled tabular adjustment* belong to this class.

The above four methods are introduced and outlined next. References for a full description of the solution approaches can be found within each section.

6.4.1 Recoding

This simple procedure consists in aggregating or changing some of the categorical variables that define the table, in order to satisfy sensitivity rules. This is shown in the example of Fig. 6.9, whose tables report the number of respondents for "profession" and "municipality." This method is implemented in the τ-Argus software [26]. The main advantages of this approach are its simplicity and that it works fine in practice. The main inconvenience is that it changes the table structure; an excessive aggregation may significantly reduce the utility of the resulting table.

| | Original table | | | | | | | Recoded table | | | | |
	P_1	P_2	P_3	P_4	P_5	TOTAL		P_1	$P_2 + P_3$	P_4	P_5	TOTAL
M_1	20	15	30	20	10	95	M_1	20	45	20	10	95
M_2	72	20	1	30	10	133	M_2	72	21	30	10	133
M_3	38	38	15	40	11	142	M_3	38	53	40	11	142
TOTAL	130	73	46	90	31	370	TOTAL	130	119	90	31	370

Fig. 6.9 Original and recoded table after aggregation of professions P_2 and P_3

6.4.2 Cell Suppression

Given a set of sensitive cells to be protected (named *primary* cells), the cell suppression method removes them, and an additional set of cells named *secondary* cells to guarantee the value of primary cells cannot be disclosed. The purpose of the *cell suppression problem* (CSP) is to find the set of secondary cells that minimize some information loss criteria. Figure 6.10 shows an example of a two-dimensional table with only one primary cell in boldface; removing this cell is not enough, since its value can be retrieved from marginals, thus forcing the suppression of three additional complementary cells.

From the protected table of Fig. 6.10, any attacker may deduce a lower and upper bound for the primary cell. Indeed, considering variables x_{11}, x_{13}, x_{21}, x_{23} for the primary and secondary cells, a lower bound $\underline{a_{23}}$ and an upper bound $\overline{a_{23}}$ for the primary cell can be obtained by solving

$$
\begin{aligned}
\underline{a_{23}} &= \min x_{23} \\
\text{subject to } & x_{11} + x_{13} = 72 - 24 \\
& x_{21} + x_{23} = 116 - 38 \\
& x_{11} + x_{21} = 98 - 40 \\
& x_{13} + x_{23} = 110 - 42 \\
& (x_{11}, x_{13}, x_{21}, x_{23}) \geq 0,
\end{aligned}
\quad \text{and} \quad
\begin{aligned}
\overline{a_{23}} &= \max x_{23} \\
\text{s.t } & x_{11} + x_{13} = 72 - 24 \\
& x_{21} + x_{23} = 116 - 38 \\
& x_{11} + x_{21} = 98 - 40 \\
& x_{13} + x_{23} = 110 - 42 \\
& (x_{11}, x_{13}, x_{21}, x_{23}) \geq 0.
\end{aligned}
$$
$$(6.8)$$

The solutions to (6.8) are $\underline{a_{23}} = 20$ and $\overline{a_{23}} = 68$. If, for instance, *lower* and *upper protection levels* of $lpl = upl = 10$ were imposed (i.e., the protection pattern must guarantee that no attacker can deduce a value of the sensitive cell within the range $[40-lpl, 40+upl] = [30, 50]$), then this cell would be protected by this suppression pattern since $\underline{a_{23}} = 20 < 30$ and $\overline{a_{23}} = 68 > 50$.

The above example illustrated the basics of CSP. A general formulation is now provided. Any instance of CSP is defined by the following parameters:

- A general table $a_i, i = 1, \ldots, n$, with m linear relations $Aa = b$, $a = (a_1, \ldots, a_n)^T$ being the vector of cell values.
- Upper and lower bounds u and l for the cell values, which are assumed to be known by any attacker: $l \leq a \leq u$ (e.g., $l = 0$, $u = +\infty$ for a positive table).

	Origina table					Protected table			
	P_1	P_2	P_3	TOTAL		P_1	P_2	P_3	TOTAL
M_1	20	24	28	72	M_1		24		72
M_2	38	38	**40**	116	M_2		38		116
M_3	40	39	42	121	M_3	40	39	42	121
TOTAL	98	101	110	309	TOTAL	98	101	110	309

Fig. 6.10 Original table with primary cell in *boldface* and protected table after suppression of three secondary cells

- Vector of non-negative weights associated with the cell suppressions $w_i, i = 1, \ldots, n$. If $w_i = 1$ the number of cells is minimized; if $w_i = a_i$ the value suppressed is minimized.
- Set $\mathcal{P} \subseteq \{1, \ldots, n\}$ of primary or sensitive cells.
- Lower and upper protection levels for each primary cell lpl_p and upl_p, $p \in \mathcal{P}$ (usually either a fraction of a_p or obtained from the sensitivity rules $p\%$ and (n, k)).

CSP looks for a set $\mathcal{S}$ of secondary cells to be removed such that for all $p \in \mathcal{P}$

$$\underline{a_p} \leq a_p - lpl_p \quad \text{and} \quad \overline{a_p} \geq a_p + upl_p, \tag{6.9}$$

$\underline{a_p}$ and $\overline{a_p}$ being defined as

$$
\begin{array}{ll}
\underline{a_p} = & \min \quad x_p \\
& \text{subject to } Ax = b \\
& \quad l_i \leq x_i \leq u_i \ \ i \in \mathcal{P} \cup \mathcal{S} \\
& \quad x_i = a_i \ \ i \notin \mathcal{P} \cup \mathcal{S},
\end{array}
\quad \text{and} \quad
\begin{array}{ll}
\overline{a_p} = & \max \quad x_p \\
& \text{subject to } Ax = b \\
& \quad l_i \leq x_i \leq u_i \ \ i \in \mathcal{P} \cup \mathcal{S} \\
& \quad x_i = a_i \ \ i \notin \mathcal{P} \cup \mathcal{S}.
\end{array}
\tag{6.10}
$$

The classical model for CSP was originally formulated in [28]. It considers two sets of variables:

- $y_i \in \{0, 1\}, i = 1, \ldots, n$ is 1 if cell has to be suppressed, 0 otherwise.
- For each primary cell $p \in \mathcal{P}$, two auxiliary vectors $x^{l,p} \in \mathbb{R}^n$ and $x^{u,p} \in \mathbb{R}^n$ represent cell deviations (positive or negative) from the original a_i values; they are needed to guarantee the protection levels.

The resulting model is

$$
\begin{aligned}
\min \quad & \sum_{i=1}^{n} w_i y_i \\
\text{subject to} \quad &
\left.
\begin{aligned}
Ax^{l,p} &= 0 \\
(l_i - a_i)y_i \leq \ x_i^{l,p} &\leq (u_i - a_i)y_i \quad i = 1, \ldots, n \\
x_p^{l,p} &\leq -lpl_p \\[6pt]
Ax^{u,p} &= 0 \\
(l_i - a_i)y_i \leq \ x_i^{u,p} &\leq (u_i - a_i)y_i \quad i = 1, \ldots, n \\
x_p^{u,p} &\geq upl_p
\end{aligned}
\right\} \quad \forall p \in \mathcal{P}. \\[6pt]
& y_i \in \{0, 1\} \quad i = 1, \ldots, n.
\end{aligned}
\tag{6.11}
$$

The inequality constraints of (6.11) with both right- and left-hand sides impose bounds on $x_i^{l,p}$ and $x_i^{u,p}$ when $y_i = 1$ and prevent deviations in non-suppressed cells (i.e., $y_i = 0$). Clearly, the constraints of (6.11) guarantee that the solutions of the linear programs (6.10) will satisfy (6.9).

Model (6.11) is the basis of several solution methods, either optimal or heuristic. Note, however, that it cannot be used directly as formulated here, because (6.11) gives rise to a MILP problem of n binary variables, $2n|\mathcal{P}|$ continuous variables, and $2(m + 2n)|\mathcal{P}|$ constraints. This problem is very large even for tables of moderate size and number of primary cells. For instance, for a table of 8,000 cells, 800 primaries, and 4,000 linear relations, we obtain a MILP with 8,000 binary variables, 12,800,000 continuous variables, and 32,000,000 constraints.

The unique currently optimal solution approach decomposes (6.11) by means of a Benders decomposition [3]. Initially applied to two-dimensional tables [23], it was later extended to general tables [24]. The main benefit of this approach is that it guarantees an optimal solution. The main drawback is that the number of cuts needed (i.e., iterations of Benders method) may be very large, resulting in a prohibitive computational time. This does not happen for two-dimensional tables (the approach is very fast for this kind of tables), but it becomes computationally very expensive for more complex tables, as it will be shown below in a numerical example. This method is implemented in the τ-Argus package [26].

Most heuristic approaches for (6.11) find a feasible, hopefully good point, by network optimization algorithms (in particular, minimum-cost network flows and shortest paths [1]). Unfortunately, those heuristics can only be used in tables that accept a network representation: two-dimensional and 1H2D hierarchical tables (the latter is, however, an interesting case for NSAs). Some attempts have been made for extending them to three-dimensional tables [18], but as mentioned in Section 6.2.2.2, three-dimensional tables correspond to multicommodity flows, and therefore "standard single-commodity" network optimization procedures are not valid (and rather unsuccessful). Among those heuristics we find the seminal paper [28] and [5, 14], which relies on minimum-network cost flows. For general tables Carvalho et al. [4] suggested an efficient procedure based on shortest paths. Some of those ideas were sensibly combined in the approach of Castro [9], based on shortest paths but valid for positive tables. This approach is very efficient, but it can only be applied to either two-dimensional or 1H2D hierarchical tables. This method is implemented in the τ-Argus package.

We finally mention two other heuristics, which are also available in the τ-Argus package. The *hypercube* [25], initially developed for k-dimensional tables, is a simple and fast procedure. For two-dimensional tables it can be seen as a network flows approach that only considers a subset of the flows (thus providing less quality solutions than heuristics based on network optimization). Although it is efficient, in practice it tends to oversuppress cells and, moreover, it does not guarantee a feasible solution (indeed, it finishes with some underprotected cells). Some of the above drawbacks are also shared by the other heuristic, named HiTaS [19]. That approach decomposes any table in a tree of smaller two-dimensional subtables and locally protects them by the previously cited optimal Benders decomposition approach. Since some linking constraints between subtables are removed, the final solution is not guaranteed to be feasible. However, the quality of the solutions is in general acceptable.

Table 6.1 Results for table "IndustryCode × Size → Var2" from microdata file of τ-Argus distribution

Method	#supp.	#val. supp.	CPU sec[a]
Hypercube	637	15494253	9
HiTas	528	9016562	15
Shortest paths	538	8795130	4
Benders decomposition	557	7830730	120[b]
Benders decomposition	483	7216286	622[b]

[a]Results on a PC with one AMD Athlon 44 00+ 64 bits dual core
[b] Time limit

It is not easy to compare the above procedures computationally, since the source code is not available. However, they can be run with the same table from the τ-Argus package, which implements four of them: the optimal approach of [24], the shortest paths heuristic of [9], and the two (infeasible) heuristics of [19] and [25]. To compare them, in a toy table 1H2D was generated with τ-Argus. This table was obtained from the microdata file accompanying the τ-Argus distribution, crossing categorical variables "industry code" and "size" and using "var2" as explanatory variable. The results are reported in Table 6.1. Columns "#supp." and "#val. supp." provide information about the solution reported (number of suppressions and total value suppressed, respectively). The total value suppressed is the objective function to be minimized. Column "CPU sec" provides the CPU time. Time limits of 2 and 10 min were set for the optimal procedure. Even such a small instance is very difficult for the Benders decomposition approach, but it provides a better objective. The shortest paths heuristic provides better results than the other heuristics (and it is guaranteed to provide a feasible solution). In addition it requires less than 1% of the CPU time of the optimal approach for a solution with an objective value only a 20% worse. However, if the table was more complex (instead of 1H2D) the shortest paths heuristic could not be used.

6.4.3 Controlled Rounding

The method of *rounding* achieves protection by rounding all cell tables to a multiple of a certain base number r. Figure 6.11 shows an example of a two-dimensional table using a base number $r = 5$. Note that the total cell could not be rounded

	Original table					Rounded table			
	P_1	P_2	P_3	TOTAL		P_1	P_2	P_3	TOTAL
M_1	20	24	28	72	M_1	20	25	30	75
M_2	38	38	40	116	M_2	40	40	40	120
M_3	40	39	42	121	M_3	40	40	40	120
TOTAL	98	101	110	**309**	TOTAL	100	105	110	**315**

Fig. 6.11 Original and rounded table using a base number $r = 5$

to the closest multiple of 5, otherwise the resulting table would not be additive. This variant that guarantees additivity is named *controlled rounding*, instead of rounding.

Although controlled rounding was already in use two decades ago [15], some recent extensions using lower and upper protection levels have been considered [30]. The complexity of the resulting model is similar to that of cell suppression, resulting in a large MILP which is solved by Benders decomposition [3]. This model is implemented in the τ-Argus package. One of the main drawbacks of controlled rounding is that it forces deviations for all the cells that are not originally a multiple of the base r, reducing the utility of the resulting table. In addition, to guarantee additivity, total cells have also to be rounded, likely to a multiple which can be far from the original value. The method of the next section, which also perturbs cell values, avoids some of these inconveniences of controlled rounding.

6.4.4 Controlled Tabular Adjustment

Given a table, a set of sensitive cells, and some lower and upper protection levels, the purpose of *controlled tabular adjustment* (also known as *minimum-distance controlled tabular adjustment* or simply *CTA*) is to find the closest safe table to the original one (i.e., the closest table that meets the protection levels). Figure 6.12 shows an example for a small two-dimensional table with one sensitive cell in boldface, with lower and upper protection levels equal to five (left table of the figure). If the protection sense is "lower," then the value published for the sensitive cell should be less than or equal to 35; the optimal adjusted table for this case is shown in the middle table of Fig. 6.12. If the protection sense is "upper," then the value must be greater than or equal to 45, as shown in the right table of Fig. 6.12.

CTA was introduced in the manuscript [17] and, independently and in an extended form, in [8] (in the latter they were named minimum-distance controlled perturbation methods). The parameters that define any CTA instance are the same than for the cell suppression problem (see Section 6.4.2), i.e.,

	Original table					Adjusted table, lower protection sense					Adjusted table, upper protection sense			
	P_1	P_2	P_3	TOTAL		P_1	P_2	P_3	TOTAL		P_1	P_2	P_3	TOTAL
M_1	20	24	28	72	M_1	15	24	33	72	M_1	25	24	23	72
M_2	38	38	**40**	116	M_2	43	38	**35**	116	M_2	33	38	**45**	116
M_3	40	39	42	121	M_3	40	39	42	121	M_3	40	39	42	121
TOTAL	98	101	110	309	TOTAL	98	101	110	309	TOTAL	98	101	110	309

Fig. 6.12 Original table with sensitive cell in *boldface* of lower and upper protection levels equal to five. Protected tables with "lower protection sense" and "upper protection sense" (i.e., value of sensitive is, respectively, reduced and increased by five units)

- A general table a_i, $i = 1, \ldots, n$, with m linear relations $Aa = b$.
- Upper and lower bounds u and l for the cell values, assumed to be known by any attacker: $l \leq a \leq u$.
- Vector of nonnegative weights associated with the cell perturbations w_i, $i = 1, \ldots, n$.
- Set $\mathcal{P} \subseteq \{1, \ldots, n\}$ of sensitive cells.
- Lower and upper protection levels for each primary cell lpl_p and upl_p $p \in \mathcal{P}$.

CTA finds the safe table x closest to a, using some distance L_w:

$$
\begin{aligned}
\min_x \ & \|x - a\|_{L(w)} \\
\text{subject to } & Ax = b \\
& l_x \leq x \leq u_x \\
& x_p \leq a_p - lpl_p \text{ or } x_p \geq a_p + upl_p \quad p \in \mathcal{P}.
\end{aligned}
\tag{6.12}
$$

Defining $z = x - a$, $l_z = l_x - a$, and $u_z = u_x - a$, (6.12) can be recast in terms of deviations:

$$
\begin{aligned}
\min_z \ & \|z\|_{L(w)} \\
\text{subject to } & Az = 0 \\
& l_z \leq z \leq u_z \\
& z_p \leq -lpl_p \text{ or } z_p \geq upl_p \quad p \in \mathcal{P}.
\end{aligned}
\tag{6.13}
$$

To model the "or" constraints it is necessary to consider binary variables $y_p \in \{0, 1\}$, $p \in \mathcal{P}$, such that $y_p = 1$ if cell is "upper protected" (i.e., $z_p \geq upl_p$) and $y_p = 0$ if it is "lower protected" ($z_p \leq -lpl_p$). For the particular case of distance L_1, a pair of variables z_i^+ and z_i^- is also needed such that $z_i = z_i^+ - z_i^-$ and $|z_i| = z_i^+ + z_i^-$. The resulting MILP model is

$$
\begin{aligned}
\min_{z^+, z^-} \ & \sum_{i=1}^{n} w_i(z_i^+ + z_i^-) \\
\text{subject to } & A(z^+ - z^-) = 0 \\
& 0 \leq z_i^+ \leq u_{z_i} \quad i \notin \mathcal{P} \\
& 0 \leq z_i^- \leq -l_{z_i} \quad i \notin \mathcal{P} \\
& upl_i \, y_i \leq z_i^+ \leq u_{z_i} y_i \quad i \in \mathcal{P} \\
& lpl_i (1 - y_i) \leq z_i^- \leq -l_{z_i}(1 - y_i) \quad i \in \mathcal{P} \\
& y_i \in \{0, 1\} \quad i \in \mathcal{P}.
\end{aligned}
\tag{6.14}
$$

Problem (6.14) has $|\mathcal{P}|$ binary variables, $2n$ continuous variables, and $m + 4|\mathcal{P}|$ constraints. The size of (6.14) is much less than that of the cell suppression formulation (6.11). For instance, for a table of 8,000 cells, 800 primaries, and 4,000 linear relations, CTA formulates a MILP of 800 binary variables, 16,000 continuous variables, and 7,200 constraints (these figures were 8,000, 12,800,000, and 32,000,000 for CSP, respectively).

Because of the smaller size of CTA compared to other approaches, it is possible to apply state-of-the-art MILP solvers. Such an implementation was developed using both CPLEX and XPRESS in a package to be used by Eurostat [13]. However, real-world large and complex instances are still difficult for such generic solvers, and some preliminary work has been started using optimal approaches based on Benders reformulation [11] and heuristics. The benefits of CTA are not limited to a smaller size of the resulting MILP problem. CTA can be easily extended with constraints to meet some data quality criteria [16]. It has also been experimentally observed that the quality of CTA solution is comparable (in some instances even better) than that of CSP [12]: indeed the number of cells with significantly large deviations is much smaller than the number of cells removed by CSP.

6.5 Conclusions

This chapter introduced some of the currently most used techniques for tabular data protection. All of them share, at different degrees, the same computational drawbacks: they result in large difficult MILP optimization problems. Current research for improving the solution of these MILP problems is being undertaken, mainly for the most recent method, controlled tabular adjustment. That research makes use of recent advances in mathematical optimization. There are alternative protection methods, like *interval protection* or *partial cell suppression*, which result in a very large, even massive, linear programming problem. Some approaches based on Benders decomposition were suggested in the literature. Being a continuous optimization problem, specialized interior-point methods for structured problems can also be a very efficient alternative. This is research to be conducted in the near future in this challenging field.

Acknowledgments This work has been supported by grant MTM2006-05550 of the Spanish Ministry of Science and Education.

References

1. Ahuja R.K., Magnanti T.L., and Orlin J.B. *Network Flows. Theory, Algorithms and Applications*, Prentice Hall, Upper Saddle River, NJ, 1993.
2. Bacharach M. Matrix rounding problems, *Management Science*, 9:732–742, 1966.
3. Benders J.F. Partitioning procedures for solving mixed-variables programming problems, *Computational Management Science*, 2:3–19, 2005. English translation of the original paper appeared in *Numerische Mathematik*, 4:238–252 (1962).
4. Carvalho F.D., Dellaert N.P., and Osório M.D. Statistical disclosure in two-dimensional tables: general tables. *Journal of the American Statistical Association*, 89:1547–1557, 1994.
5. Castro J. Network flows heuristics for complementary cell suppression: an empirical evaluation and extensions, *Lecture Notes in Computer Science*, 2316:59–73, 2002.
6. Castro J. A fast network flows heuristic for cell suppression in positive tables. *Lecture Notes in Computer Science*, 3050:136–148, 2004.
7. Castro J. Quadratic interior-point methods in statistical disclosure control. *Computational Management Science*, 2(2):107–121, 2005.

8. Castro J. Minimum-distance controlled perturbation methods for large-scale tabular data protection. *European Journal of Operational Research*, 171:39–52, 2006.
9. Castro J. A shortest-paths heuristic for statistical data protection in positive tables. *INFORMS Journal on Computing*, 19(4):520–533, 2007.
10. Castro J. An interior-point approach for primal block-angular problems. *Computational Optimization and Applications*, 36:195–219, 2007.
11. Castro J. and Baena D. Using a mathematical programming modeling language for optimal CTA. *Lecture Notes in Computer Science*, 5262:1–12, 2008.
12. Castro J. and Giessing S. Testing variants of minimum distance controlled tabular adjustment. In: *Monographs of Official Statistics. Work session on Statistical Data Confidentiality*, Eurostat-Office for Official Publications of the European Communities, Luxembourg, pp. 333–343, 2006. ISBN 92-79-01108-1.
13. Castro J., González A., and Baena D. User's and programmer's manual of the RCTA package, Technical Report DR 2009/01, Dept. of Statistics and Operations Research, Universitat Politècnica de Catalunya, 2009.
14. Cox L.H. Network models for complementary cell suppression. *Journal of the American Statistical Association*, 90:1453–1462, 1995.
15. Cox L.H. and George J.A. Controlled rounding for tables with subtotals. *Annals of Operations Research*, 20:141–157, 1989.
16. Cox L.H., Kelly J.P., and Patil R. Computational aspects of controlled tabular adjustment: algorithm and analysis. In: *The Next Wave in Computer, Optimization and Decision Technologies*, (eds. B. Golden, S. Raghavan, and E. Wassil), Kluwer, Boston, MA, pp. 45–59, 2002.
17. Dandekar R.A. and Cox L.H. Synthetic tabular data: An alternative to complementary cell suppression, manuscript, Energy Information Administration, US Department of Energy, Washington, DC, 2002.
18. Dellaert N.P. and Luijten W.A. Statistical disclosure in general three-dimensional tables. *Statistica Neerlandica*, 53:197–221, 1999.
19. de Wolf P.P. HiTaS: A heuristic approach to cell suppression in hierarchical tables. *Lecture Notes in Computer Science*, 2316:74–82, 2002.
20. Domingo-Ferrer J. and Franconi L. (eds.). *Privacy in Statistical Databases* Lecture Notes in Computer Science, vol. 4302, Springer, Berlin, 2006.
21. Domingo-Ferrer J. and Saigin Y. (eds.). *Privacy in Statistical Databases* Lecture Notes in Computer Science, vol. 5262, Springer, Berlin, 2008.
22. Domingo-Ferrer J. and Torra V. (eds.). *Privacy in Statistical Databases* Lecture Notes in Computer Science, vol. 3050, Springer, Berlin, 2004.
23. Fischetti M. and Salazar-González J.J. Models and algorithms for the 2-dimensional cell suppression problem in statistical disclosure control. *Mathematical Programming*, 84:283–312, 1999.
24. Fischetti M. and Salazar-González J.J. Solving the cell suppression problem on tabular data with linear constraints. *Management Science*, 47:1008–1026, 2001.
25. Giessing S. and Repsilber D. Tools and strategies to protect multiple tables with the GHQUAR cell suppression engine. *Lecture Notes in Computer Science*, 2316:181–192, 2002.
26. Hundepool A., van de Wetering A., Ramaswamy R., de Wolf P.P., Giessing S., Fischetti M., Salazar-González J.J., Castro J., and Lowthian P. τ-*Argus User's Manual*, Statistics Netherlands, The Netherlands 2007.
27. Hundepool A., Domingo-Ferrer J., Franconi L., Giessing S., Lenz R., Longhurst J., Schulte-Nordholt E., Giovanni Seri, and de Wolf P.P. *Handbook on Statistical Disclosure Control*, CENEX SDC. Available on-line at http://neon.vb.cbs.nl/casc/.\SDC_Handbook.pdf, 2007. Accessed date: 06/04/2010.
28. Kelly J.P., Golden B.L., and Assad A.A. Cell suppression: Disclosure protection for sensitive tabular data. *Networks*, 22:28–55, 1992.

29. Robertson D.A. and Ethier R. Cell suppression: Experience and theory. *Lecture Notes in Computer Science*, 2316:8–20, 2002.
30. Salazar-González J.J. Controlled rounding and cell perturbation: Statistical disclosure limitation methods for tabular data. *Mathematical Programming*, 105:583–603, 2006.
31. Salazar-González J.J. Statistical confidentiality: Optimization techniques to protect tables. *Computers and Operations Research*, 35:1638–1651, 2008.
32. Willenborg L. and de Waal T. (eds.). *Elements of Statistical Disclosure Control* Lecture Notes in Statistics, vol 155, Springer, New York, 2000.

Part III
Preserving Privacy in Distributed Applications

Chapter 7
From Collaborative to Privacy-Preserving Sequential Pattern Mining

Vishal Kapoor, Pascal Poncelet, Francois Trousset, and Maguelonne Teisseire

Abstract Research in the areas of privacy-preserving techniques in databases and subsequently in privacy enhancement technologies has witnessed an explosive growth spurt in recent years. This escalation has been fueled primarily by the growing mistrust of individuals toward organizations collecting and disbursing their personally identifiable information (PII). Digital repositories have become increasingly susceptible to intentional or unintentional abuse, resulting in organizations to be liable under the privacy legislations that are increasingly being adopted by governments the world over. These privacy concerns have necessitated new advancements in the field of distributed data mining, wherein collaborating parties may be legally bound not to reveal the private information of their customers. In this chapter, first we present the sequential pattern discovery problem in a collaborative framework and subsequently enhance the architecture by introducing the context of privacy. Thus we propose to extract sequential patterns from distributed databases while preserving privacy. A salient feature of the proposal is its flexibility and as a result is more pertinent to mining operations for real-world applications in terms of efficiency and functionality. Furthermore, under some reasonable assumptions, we prove that the architecture and protocol employed by our algorithm for multi-party computation is secure. Finally, we conclude with some trends of current research being conducted in the field.

7.1 Introduction

The increasing popularity of multi-database technology, such as communication networks and distributed, federated, and homogeneous multi-database systems, has led to the development of many large distributed transaction databases for real-world applications. However, for the purposes of decision making, large organizations would need to mine these distributed databases located at disparate locations. Moreover, the Web has rapidly transformed into an information flood, where individuals

V. Kapoor (✉)
Microsoft, One Microsoft Way, Redmond, WA - 98052, USA
e-mail: vishal.kapoor@microsoft.com

J. Nin, J. Herranz (eds.), *Privacy and Anonymity in Information Management Systems,*
Advanced Information and Knowledge Processing,
DOI 10.1007/978-1-84996-238-4_7, © Springer-Verlag London Limited 2010

and organizations can access free and accurate information and knowledge on the Internet while making decisions. Although this large data assists in improving the quality of decisions, it also results into a significant challenge of efficiently identifying quality knowledge from multi-databases [27, 33].

Therefore large corporations might have to confront the multiple data source problem. For example, a retail chain with numerous franchisees might wish to collaboratively mine the union of all the transactional data. The individual transactional databases contain information regarding the purchasing history of the same set of common customers transacting through e-commerce portals or brick and mortar stores. However, the bigger challenge of such computations is compliance to stringent privacy requirements laid down by the formulation of laws such as HIPAA [25]. These regulatory policies are the driving force behind the growing consciousness toward the protection of privacy of individuals and their data. Consequently, there has been a paradigm shift toward the creation of a privacy-aware infrastructure, which entails aspects ranging from data collection to analysis [4].

Conventionally, data mining has been applied to the traditional data warehouse model of a central data repository and conducting analysis on it. However, privacy considerations prevent this generic approach and hence privacy-preserving data mining has gained recognition among academia and organizations as an important and unalienable area, especially for highly sensitive data such as health records. Indeed, if data mining is to be performed on these sensitive data sets, due attention must be given to the privacy requirements. Recently there has been a spate of work addressing privacy-preserving data mining [6, 21]. This wide area of research includes classification techniques [8], association rule mining [9], and clustering [14] with privacy constraints. In early work on privacy-preserving data mining, Lindell and Pinkas [17] propose a solution to privacy-preserving classification problem using oblivious transfer protocol, a powerful tool developed by SMC research. The techniques based on SMC for efficiently dealing with large data sets have been addressed in [26], where a solution to the association rule mining problem for the case of two parties was proposed. In [15], a novel secure architecture has been proposed where the security and accuracy of the data mining results are guaranteed with improved efficiency.

Traditionally, secure multi-party protocols have been used for the secure computation for generic functions. A secure multi-party computation (SMC) problem deals with computing any function on any input, in a distributed network where each participant holds one of the inputs, while ensuring that no more information is revealed to a participant in the computation than can be inferred from that participants input and output. Secure two-party computation was first investigated by Yao [29, 30] and was later generalized to multi-party computation (e.g., [5, 7, 10]). It has been proved that for any polynomial function, there is a secure multi-party computation solution [5, 10]. The approach used is as follows: the function f to be computed is first represented as a combinatorial circuit and then the parties run a short protocol for every gate in the circuit. Every participant gets corresponding shares of the input wires and the output wires for every gate. While this approach is appealing in its generality and simplicity, the protocols it generates depend on the size of the circuit. This size depends on the size of the input (which might be huge as in a data mining application), and on the complexity of expressing f as a circuit (for example, a naive multiplication circuit is quadratic in the size of its inputs). However, the complexity of such a secure protocol is prohibitive for complex data mining tasks such as the discovery of sequential patterns.

In this chapter, we present an alternative privacy-preserving data mining approach (PRIPSEP), for discovering sequential patterns in the local databases of a large integrated organization. PRIPSEP is useful for mining sequential patterns via collaboration between disparate parties, employing secure architecture, operations, and underlying protocols. Hence, to counter the communication and bandwidth overhead of the oblivious transfer required between two parties in an SMC, this work proposes an alternate architecture consisting of "semi-honest" and "non-colluding" sites. This trade-off between security and efficiency is reasonable as none of the participating sites are privy to the intermediate or the final results of the calculus. Furthermore, due to the uniform random noise in the data sets, private information of any individual is also guarded from any possible leak.

Organization. The remainder of this chapter is organized as follows. Section 7.2 goes deeper into presenting the problem statement and provides an extensive description of the problem at hand. Section 7.3 describes our proposed solution with the description of the architecture and the algorithms for secure multi-party protocols. Finally, Section 7.4 concludes this chapter with a roadmap for future work as well as new trends on privacy-preserving sequential pattern mining approaches.

7.2 Problem Statement

In this section we give the formal definition of the problem of privacy-preserving collaborative sequential pattern mining. First, we give a brief overview of the traditional pattern mining problem by summarizing the formal description introduced in [2] and extended in [24]. Subsequently, we extend the problem by considering distributed databases. Finally, we formally define the problem of privacy-preserving sequential pattern mining.

7.2.1 Mining of Sequential Patterns

Let DB be a database containing a set of customer transactions where each transaction T consists of a customer-id, a transaction time, and a set of items involved in the transaction.

Let $I = \{i_1, i_2, \ldots, i_m\}$ be a set of literals called items. An itemset is a non-empty set of items. A sequence s is a set of itemsets ordered according to their timestamp. It is denoted by $< s_1, s_2, \ldots, s_n >$, where $s_j, j \in 1, \ldots, n$, is an itemset. In the rest of the chapter we will consider that itemsets are merely reduced to items. Nevertheless all the proposal could be easily extended to deal with itemsets. A k-sequence is a sequence of k items (or of length k). A sequence $S' = < s'_1, s'_2, \ldots, s'_n >$ is a subsequence of another sequence $S = < s_1, s_2, \ldots, s_m >$, denoted $S' \prec S$, if there exist integers $i_1 < i_2 < \cdots < i_j < \cdots < i_n$ such that $s'_1 \subseteq s_{i_1}, s'_2 \subseteq si_2, \ldots, s'_n \subseteq si_n$.

All transactions from the same customer are grouped together and sorted in increasing order and are called a data sequence. A support value (denoted $supp(S)$) for a sequence gives its number of actual occurrences in DB. Nevertheless, a sequence in a data sequence is taken into account only once to compute the support even if several occurrences are discovered. In other words, the support of a sequence is defined as the fraction of total distinct data sequences that contain S. A data sequence contains a sequence S if S is a subsequence of the data sequence. In order to decide whether a sequence is frequent or not, a minimum support value (denoted *minsupp*) is specified by the user, and the sequence is said to be *frequent* if the condition $supp(S) \geq minsupp$ holds. Given a database of customer transactions the problem of sequential pattern mining is to find all the sequences whose support is greater than a specified threshold (minimum support). Each of these represents a sequential pattern, also called a frequent sequence. The anti-monotonic Apriori property [1] holds for sequential patterns [20].

Since its introduction, more than a decade ago, the sequential pattern mining problem has received a great deal of attention and numerous algorithms have been defined to efficiently find such patterns (e.g., GSP [24], PSP [18], PrefixSpan [19], SPADE [31], FreeSpan[12], SPAM [3], CLOSPAN [28], PRISM [11], SAMPLING [22]).

In order to extract the set of frequent patterns, the various approaches have considered a "generating-pruning" approach and subsequently made multiple passes over the database. The first step aims at computing the support of each item in the database. After the completion of this step, all the frequent items (i.e., those that satisfy the minimum support) are computed. They are considered as frequent 1-sequences (sequences having a single itemset, itself a singleton). The set of candidate 2-sequences is built up according to the assumption that candidate 2-sequences could be any couple of frequent items, whether embedded in the same transaction or not. Frequent 2-sequences are determined by counting the support. Subsequently, candidate k-sequences are generated from frequent $(k - 1)$-sequences obtained in the prior pass-$(k - 1)$. The main idea of candidate generation is to retrieve pairs of sequences (s, s') from among $(k - 1)$-sequences, such that discarding the first element of the former and the last element of the latter results in two fully matching sequences. When such a condition holds for a pair (s, s'), a new candidate sequence is built by appending the last item of s' to s either as itemset extension (*I-extension*) or sequence extension (*S-extension*). The supports for these candidates are then computed and those with minimum support become frequent sequences. The process iterates until no more candidate sequences are formed. Moreover, to efficiently perform this operation, some approaches consider a new representation of the data. For example, in SPADE [31] the authors have proposed a vertical representation of the data and in SPAM [3], the authors propose a new data representation based on vertical bitmap. The originality of this approach lies in the fact that the generating and the pruning phase is done at the same time. Each customer transaction is mapped as a vector of bits in which a 1 is set at position *pos* if the item occurs at the time *pos* in the transaction. The *S-extension* is performed as follows: Let us consider that we would like to generate the candidate (1) (2). First the bitmap corresponding to the item 1 is transformed with the first occurrence of a 1 replaced by a zero and a 1 is set at the remaining position of the vector. Subsequently, the bitmap operator AND is applied between the transformed vector and the vector of 2. The main idea behind the transformation is since we know that the operator is AND, the value of the first occurrence is forced to 0, in order to find the position of the 2 after the first occurrence of 1. The *I-extension* is only performed with an AND between the two vectors (e.g., (1, 2)) since they must occur at the same date.

More recently, some approaches have been defined in order to avoid the generating step which could be very time consuming. For instance, in PrefixSpan [19], FreeSpan[12], and CLOSPAN [28], the authors have illustrated that due to the fact that the prefix is shared among sequences, sequences could be efficiently extracted by using projection and prefix-tree representations (as in PSP [18]).

7.2.2 From Collaborative to Privacy-Preserving Sequential Pattern Mining

Let DB be a database such as $DB = DB_1 \bigcup DB_2 \cdots \bigcup DB_D$. We consider that all databases $DB_1, DB_2, \ldots, DB_D$ share the same number of customers (CIDs), which is N. We also consider that for each customer in the databases, the number of transaction times (TIDs), K, is the same. Our data representation scheme considers that all transactions are depicted in the form of vertical bitmaps, which we denote as vectors for clarity in mathematical formulae.

Definition 7.1 Let V_i^j be a vector where j and i correspond, respectively, to the ith item and the jth database. V_j^i is defined as follows: $V_j^i = [C_1^{i,j}, \ldots, C_N^{i,j}]$ where for $u \in \{1..N\}$, $C_u^{i,j} = [T_1^{i,j,u}, \ldots, T_K^{i,j,u}]$. $T_{v=\{1,\ldots,K\}}^{i,j,u}$ corresponds to the transaction list of the customer u from the database DB_j and the item i. It is a K length bit string that has the vth bit as one if the customer has bought the item i from the database DB_j.

Given a set of databases $DB_1, DB_2, \ldots, DB_D$ containing customer transactions, the problem of collaborative sequential pattern mining is to find all the sequences whose support is greater than a specified threshold (minimum support). Furthermore, the problem of privacy-preserving collaborative sequential pattern mining is to find all the sequential patterns embedded in the set of databases by considering parties that do not want to share their private data sets with each other.

In order to illustrate this further, let us consider the following example.

Example 7.1 Let us consider an example of three retail franchisees Alice, Bob, and Carol wishing to extract securely the sequential patterns without disclosing the identities of any individual customers. Each item is provided with its timestamp (cf. Table 7.1).

Table 7.1 An example of
distributed databases

CID	Alice	Bob	Carol
1	$(1)_1$ $(3)_5$	$(2)_2$	$(7)_4$
2	$(2)_4$	$(1)_3$	$(3)_6$
3	$(2)_6$ $(3)_7$		$(1)_2$ $(7)_3$

Let us assume that the minimal support value is set to 50%. From the three distributed databases, we can infer that item (1) is not frequent in any one of the individual databases. However, by considering the union of all databases (cf. Table 7.2 where the superscript depicts the original database where the item is derived), we obtain the sequence of $< (1)(2)(3) >$. By considering privacy, this sequence has to be obtained by considering Alice, Bob, and Carol do not want to share their private data sets with each other.

Table 7.2 The union of all
databases

CID	Sequences
1	$(1)_1^A$ $(2)_2^B$ $(7)_4^C$ $(3)_5^A$
2	$(1)_3^B$ $(2)_4^A$ $(3)_6^C$
3	$(1)_2^C$ $(7)_3^C$ $(2)_6^A$ $(3)_7^A$

In [32], Zhan et al. have proposed a novel approach, which entails the transformation of the databases of each collaborating party, followed by a protocol, which results in the preservation of privacy, as well as the correct results. Theoretically, the approach is robust and secure, however, it has serious limitations relating to the initial constraints considered while developing the protocol. It has been assumed that each of the collaborating party carries a unique inventory. For instance, considering our previous example and our problem statement, and following the previous approach and not taking into account the possibility of items being shared among the distributed parties, we come up with erroneous results. An item such as (1) which is not supported by enough customers in one individual database might not appear in the final results. This assumption causes serious limitation for different real applications where items sharing between different databases is imperative and a fundamental requirement as proved earlier. Moreover, the same customer buying the same item twice from the same database but on different times is not permissible, employing their new data representation scheme for sequential data. The other drawback of mapping each item to a unique code is the additional overhead incurred while sorting the databases.

7.3 The PRIPSEP Approach

In this section, we propose our novel approach for privacy-preserving sequential pattern mining in distributed and collaborative databases. A preliminary version of this proposal has been published in [16]. First, we focus only on collaborative sequential pattern mining in order to clearly explain our methodology. This approach is extended in the next section in order to consider privacy requirements and finally we propose a new algorithm and underlying protocols within the secure architecture.

7.3.1 Collaborative Sequential Pattern Mining

7.3.1.1 An overview

As previously seen in Section 7.2, the main difficulty with collaborative mining is that we have to deal with different databases where the order of items is not known beforehand (e.g., consider the item (7) of the CID 1 in the Bob's database is before the item (3) of the Alice's database).

For brevity, we consider that we are provided with a Data Miner performing the generating and verifying phases of candidate sequences as Apriori-like algorithms. We assume that the candidate generation is performed conventionally by combining the $k - 1$ frequent sequences in order to generate k-candidate sequences (e.g., cf. GSP [24] generation phase). We extend the verification phase as follows. First, we consider that our data representation scheme has been extended from the SPAM algorithm [3], wherein for efficient counting, each customer's transactions are represented by a vertical bitmap. These bitmap or vectors are vertically aligned for various computations to calculate the support value for any sequence. As we have to deal with disparate distributed databases, we assume that the Miner could request the N original databases in order to obtain a vector corresponding to the specific item i, i.e., $V_i^{[1..D]}$ for any candidate sequence.

Let us consider that we are provided with two databases, namely DB_1 and DB_2. These databases contain three customers and each customer has five transaction times or CIDs. Let us consider that we are in the candidate step counting of an Apriori-like algorithm. Let us assume that we are currently finding how many times the sequence $< (1)(2) >$ appears in the set of all customers of the two databases. First, we extract from DB_1, the vector corresponding to the item (1), i.e., V_1^1, and from DB_2 the vector V_1^2 (left part of Fig. 7.1). From the given vectors, two key operations have to be performed: (i) merge the two vectors, and then (ii) transform the result in order to check if it could be followed by (2). These two vectors are merged together by applying a bitwise operator ($\vee$): $V_1^1 \vee V_1^2$. For the second operation, similar to the S-Step process of the SPAM algorithm, we consider a function that transforms the vector or bitmap. For each customer, following the occurrence of the first bit with value one, every subsequent bit in the vector is flagged as one. However, since we have to deal with different databases and due to efficiency considerations, we consider that these two operations are performed through the f function defined below and thus we obtain a new vector $Z_1 = f(V_1^1 \vee V_1^2)$.

Definition 7.2 Let us consider a vector V_i^j for a database j and an item i. V_i^j is defined as follows: $V_i^j = (C_1^{i,j}, \ldots, C_N^{i,j})$ where for $u \in \{1, \ldots, N\}$,

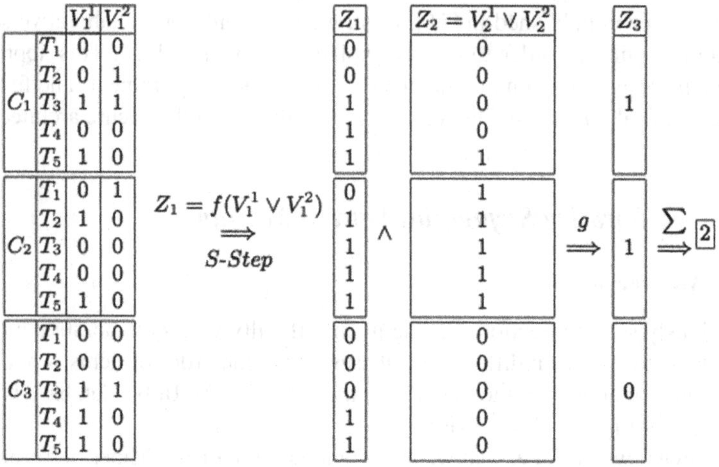

		V_1^1	V_1^2		Z_1	$Z_2 = V_2^1 \vee V_2^2$	Z_3
C_1	T_1	0	0		0	0	
	T_2	0	1		0	0	
	T_3	1	1		1	0	1
	T_4	0	0		1	0	
	T_5	1	0		1	1	
C_2	T_1	0	1		0	1	
	T_2	1	0		1	1	
	T_3	0	0		1	1	1
	T_4	0	0		1	1	
	T_5	1	0		1	1	
C_3	T_1	0	0		0	0	
	T_2	0	0		0	0	
	T_3	1	1		0	0	0
	T_4	1	0		1	0	
	T_5	1	0		1	0	

Transformations: $Z_1 = f(V_1^1 \vee V_1^2) \Rightarrow$ S-Step; $\wedge$; $g \Rightarrow$; $\Sigma \Rightarrow \boxed{2}$

Fig. 7.1 Processing of vectors for collaborative mining

$C_u^{i,j} = (T_1^{i,j,u}, \ldots, T_K^{i,j,u})$. K stands for the number of TIDs and N corresponds to the number of CIDs. For brevity, we denote this vector as V. Let $f: [0,1]^{N \times K} \rightarrow [0,1]^{N \times K}$ be a function such that $f(V) = f(C_1, \ldots, C_N) = [f_c(C_1) f_c(C_2), \ldots, f_c(C_N)]$. For each $u \in \{1, \ldots, N\}$, we have

$$f_c(C_u) = \begin{vmatrix} 0 \\ T_1^u \\ T_1^u \vee T_2^u \\ T_1^u \vee T_2^u \vee T_3^u \\ \ldots \\ T_1^u \vee \ldots \vee T_{k-1}^u \end{vmatrix}$$

where $\vee$ are bitwise operators. We can notice that $Card(V) = N \times K$, $Card(C_u) = K$, $Card(f(V)) = N \times K$.

Let $g: [0,1]^{N \times K} \rightarrow [0,1]^N$ be a function such that

$$g(V) = g(C_1, \ldots, C_N) = [g_c(C_1) g_c(C_2), \ldots, g_c(C_N)].$$

For each $u \in \{1..N\}$, we have: $g_c(C_u) = 1$ if it exists at least one 1 in the customer transactions, i.e. customer dates, or 0 otherwise. Note that $Card(g(V)) = N$.

In conjunction to the computation of the function f, the vectors corresponding to the item (2) are extracted from DB_1 and DB_2 (V_2^1 and V_2^2, respectively). Subsequently, similar to the previous step the vector ($Z_2 = V_2^1 \vee V_2^2$) is computed. Following that, the bitwise operator $\wedge$ is used to calculate $Z_1 \wedge Z_2$ and the count for each customer, for the sequence $< (1)(2) >$ has to be calculated. This is performed by the g function, i.e., $Z_3 = g(f(V_1^1 \vee V_1^2) \wedge (V_2^1 \vee V_2^2))$. As the resulting vector Z_3 has a cardinality corresponding to the number of customers, the last operation to be performed is a summation of the number of 1's in the vector Z_3. This is performed by the $\sum$ operation.

7.3.1.2 The Collaborative Support Counting Algorithm

The COLLABORATIVE FREQUENCY algorithm (see Algorithm 1) has been developed as follows. For each item i of the candidate sequence to be tested, a new vector X_i is generated by applying the $\vee$ bitwise operator on all vectors from the original databases. Then by considering the result of the previous operation, the f function is applied, followed by the bitwise operator $\wedge$ for each item. At the end of this iteration, a new vector Z of cardinality $N \times K$ is produced. Subsequently, the g function is applied to the intermediate result for generating a vector of cardinality N, i.e., Y. Finally, the number of bits which are 1 in Y are summated to compute the final value of support.

Algorithm 1: The COLLABORATIVE FREQUENCY algorithm

Data: $S = <it_1 \ldots it_q>$ a sequence to be tested; $DB = DB_1 \bigcup DB_2 \ldots \bigcup DB_D$ a set of databases; N the number of customers shared by all databases; K the number of date shared by all customers of all databases.

Result: The support of the sequence S in DB.

foreach $i \in 1..|S|$ **do**
$\quad \lfloor \; X_i \leftarrow V_{it_i}^1 \vee \ldots \vee V_{it_i}^D;$
$Z \leftarrow X_1;$
foreach $i \in 2..|S|$ **do**
$\quad \lfloor \; Z \leftarrow f(Z) \wedge X_i;$
$Y \leftarrow g(Z);$
$\text{return} \sum_{i=1}^{N} y_i; \qquad$ here $Y = (y_1, \ldots, y_N)$ is the bit-representation of Y.

Complexity: Let $V_s = N \times K$ be the size of the vectors which are sent and S be the candidate sequence to be verified. The main transfers that are performed by the algorithm are $(V_s \times D \times S)$ for $\vee$ and $(V_s \times S)$ for both the f function and $\wedge$ operation. There are $(N(K-2))$ $\vee$ computations performed by f. If f is already available, i.e., precomputed and stored, we have (N) $\vee$ operations otherwise $(N(K-1))$ $\vee$ operations are performed by g.

7.3.2 From Collaborative to Privacy-Preserving Sequential Pattern Mining

7.3.2.1 A Brief Overview of the Architecture

In this section we describe an architecture where secure multi-party techniques developed in the cryptographic domain can be easily extended for data mining purposes.

Previous work [10] has described that secure multi-party protocols can be used directly to solve with total security, any generic data mining task. However, the trade-off is the complexity of the protocol and the requirements that all parties need to be online during the entire duration of the lengthy process. Hence, it is potentially unviable for complex data mining tasks, particularly for cases with a large number of participants. The communication complexity prohibits efficient scalability and for situations that all parties cannot remain online for the entire process, the SMC protocols are rendered useless.

Evidently traditional approaches do not fulfill the requirements of a complex sequential mining algorithm. Hence, as proposed in [15], we deploy a safe architecture for performing the data mining task without leaking any useful or sensitive information to any of the intermediate parties. These independent sites collect, store, and evaluate information securely. PRIPSEP requires three *non-colluding* and *semi-honest* [10] sites which follow the protocol correctly but are free to utilize the information collected by them. They are also referred to as *honest but curious* sites. The detailed functions of each of these sites are described as follows:

- **Data Miner site** *DM*: The Data Miner is a randomly chosen collaborator between original databases. Its purpose is to interact with NC_1 and NC_2, and it receives the final result of the computation from the PS.
- **Non-colluding sites** NC_1 **and** NC_2: These symmetric sites collect the noisy data from each database including the Data Miner and perform secure operations without inferring any intermediate or final result.
- **Processing site** *PS*: This site is utilized by both NC_1 and NC_2 sites for computing securely the various functions and operations underlying PRIPSEP. Similar to NC_1 and NC_2, *PS* learns no actual results.

Let us consider Fig. 7.2 illustrating the sites. The operations are described as follows. Initially the following preprocessing steps are performed on the databases individually:

1. Each database $DB_1, DB_2, \ldots, DB_D$ adds ε customers with fake transactions and employ a non-secure counting strategy (this count could be performed by any conventional algorithm since this step is independent of the privacy) to note the number of customers, ε', that have to be pruned from the final result.
2. Let φ be a random number. Each database permutes individually their vector of transactions (V_i^j) according to the value of φ.
3. One of the collaborating parties is randomly elected to perform the data mining steps. This party is termed as the Data Miner (DM).

At the end of the preprocessing we are provided with databases having fake customer transactions and permuted list of vertically aligned vectors. Subsequently, the Data Miner can apply an Apriori-like algorithm as previously mentioned in Section 7.3.1. This step is immediately followed by the counting phase. For simplicity, let us consider that we are counting the value of support for the two length sequence $< (1)(2) >$. Now, each database DB_j sends its V_1^j vector to NC_1 and

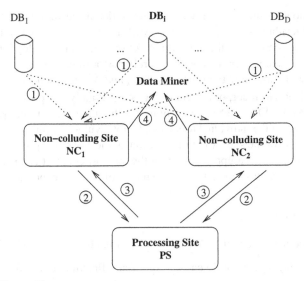

Fig. 7.2 PRIPSEP architecture

NC_2 (dashed arrows numbered 1 in Fig. 7.2). In order to minimize the risk of network transfers, we propose a hypothetical function $\text{SEND}^S \times DB_d(it)$ which securely transmits the item vector V_{it} from database DB_d to NC_1 and NC_2. Furthermore, in order to make sure that NC_1 and NC_2 receive minimal information, for each database DB_i, we calculate a vector: $Z_{DB_i} = V_{it} \oplus R_{DB_i}$ and send either Z_{DB_i} to NC_1 and R_{DB_i} to NC_2 or vice versa. It has been proved in [6], that any data mining task (h) defined on a vector $X = [x_1, x_2, \ldots, x_n]$, it suffices to evaluate $h(X \oplus R) = h(X)$ since $R = [r_1, r_2, \ldots, r_n]$ and $X \oplus R = [x_1 \oplus r_1, x_2 \oplus r_2, \ldots, x_n \oplus r_n]$. In this case, for NC_1 and NC_2 sites we have some R_{DB_i} vectors and since the other vectors are XOR-ed $\oplus$ with a random vector, they are indistinguishable from a uniform random distribution.

Similar to Algorithm 1, the bitwise operator $(\vee)$ has to be applied between every vector. As these vectors are shared by NC_1 and NC_2, we consider a new protocol $\bigvee^S$ (arrows numbered 2 in Fig. 7.2) aiming at computing a bitwise OR between the different vectors. This is performed by sending XOR-ed randomized values from NC_1 and NC_2 to PS. Then PS also garbles the resulting vectors in order to divide the result between NC_1 and NC_2. The calculation continues by computing the f and g functions (subsequently referred to as f^S and g^S) in a similar way and results are also stored between NC_1 and NC_2 (arrows numbered 3 in Fig. 7.2). Finally, in order to compute the number of bits which are in 1 ($\sum$ function, now termed as $\sum^S$), NC_1 and NC_2 collaborate to append their resultant vector with randomized values and then reorder the new vector. PS then calculates the summation of the number of bits and returns part of the result to NC_1 and NC_2. NC_1 removes the initial random noise and then return this final result to the Data Miner (arrows numbered 4 in Fig. 7.2). At this step, DM only has to combine the result from NC_1 and NC_2 and then remove the ε' value corresponding to random customers added in the preprocessing phase.

In the following sections, we will explain in detail the various protocols, functions, and algorithms necessary for PRIPSEP. First, we introduce some notations that are used for describing the algorithms. As our functions employ bitwise operators, we first present new protocols for securely performing bitwise operations. Continuing, we will show how the functions f, g, and $\sum$ are extended to f^S, g^S, and $\sum^S$, respectively, to incorporate security aspects. Finally, we present the SECURE COLLABORATIVE FREQUENCY algorithm. As the main goal of our approach is to preserve privacy of the individual users and do not divulge any information about the final result to any of the sites, we will show that at the end of the process, NC_1, NC_2, and PS will only learn a upper bound on the support count of sequences and will not have any information about the private inputs of any of the individual customers.

7.3.2.2 Notations

In the next sections, we will consider the following notations. Let $(\overset{+}{X} \mid \overset{-}{X}) \leftarrow h^S(\overset{+}{Y_1}$ $\dots \overset{+}{Y_n} \mid \overset{-}{Y_1} \dots \overset{-}{Y_n})$ be a tripartite calculation of any function h^S between NC_1, NC_2, and PS where NC_1 owns half of the input $\overset{+}{Y_1} \dots \overset{+}{Y_n}$ and gets half of the result $\overset{+}{X}$, and similarly NC_2 owns half of the inputs $\overset{-}{Y_1} \dots \overset{-}{Y_n}$ and gets half the result $\overset{-}{X}$ at the end of the process. The final result is the logical bitwise XOR ($\oplus$) of the $\overset{+}{X}$ and $\overset{-}{X}$. However, this does not imply that NC_1 directly sends $\overset{+}{Y_1} \dots \overset{+}{Y_n}$ to PS and receives the result $\overset{+}{X}$ from PS. Initially, NC_1 transforms its inputs $\overset{+}{Y_1} \dots \overset{+}{Y_n}$ to $\overset{+}{Y_1'} \dots \overset{+}{Y_n'}$ via the addition of uniform random noise and securely sends these transformed Y' to PS. Symmetrically, NC_2 also sends its garbled inputs to PS. At the end of the computation both the sites receive their share of the noisy result $\overset{+}{X'}$ and $\overset{-}{X'}$ from PS. Henceforth, this intermediate result can be used as the inputs for further computations.

7.3.2.3 The $\bigwedge^S$ and $\bigvee^S$ protocols

In this section, we define two basic algorithms $\bigwedge^S$ (see Algorithm 2) and $\neg^S$ (see Algorithm 3) providing the protocol which is used to compute securely the bitwise operators from two bits. The $\bigvee^S$ is obtained from the logical equation $A \bigvee B = \neg(\neg A \bigwedge \neg B)$ calculated by using the secure operators $\bigwedge^S$ and $\neg^S$. The fundamental principle that the algorithms operate upon is the addition of uniform random noise to the data which can be removed from the result by the data owners. The protocol initiates with both NC_1 and NC_2 perturbing their data by XOR-ing it with random values. Subsequently, the randomized data is sent (e.g., for NC_2, $X_2 = \overset{-}{X} \oplus R_2$, and $Y_2 = \overset{-}{Y} \oplus S_2$) to PS, which can calculate the $\bigwedge$ securely. It actually operates on the randomized inputs and calculates $C = (X_1 \oplus X_2) \bigwedge (Y_1 \oplus Y_2)$. It then also adds random noise to the intermediate results in order to avoid NC_1

Algorithm 2: The algorithm $\bigwedge^S$

Data: $(\overset{+}{X}, \overset{+}{Y} \mid \overset{-}{X}, \overset{-}{Y})$ bits are such as $\overset{+}{X}$ and $\overset{+}{Y}$ owned by NC_1, $\overset{-}{X}$ and $\overset{-}{Y}$ owned by NC_2

Result: $(A^R \mid B^R)$ are such that $A^R \oplus B^R = (\overset{+}{X} \oplus \overset{-}{X}) \bigwedge (\overset{+}{Y} \oplus \overset{-}{Y})$

1. NC_1 and NC_2 mutually generate and exchange four random bits R_1, R_2, S_1 and S_2 such that:

$X_1 = \overset{+}{X} \oplus R_1, Y_1 = \overset{+}{Y} \oplus S_1, X_2 = \overset{-}{X} \oplus R_2, Y_2 = \overset{-}{Y} \oplus S_2, R = R_1 \oplus R_2$ and $S = S_1 \oplus S_2$

2. NC_1 sends X_1 and Y_1 to PS.
3. NC_2 sends X_2 and Y_2 to PS.
4. PS calculates $C = (X_1 \oplus X_2) \bigwedge (Y_1 \oplus Y_2)$ and a random bit R_{PS}.
5. PS sends $A_{PS} = C \oplus R_{PS}$ to NC_1 and $B_{PS} = R_{PS}$ to NC_2 (or vice versa).
6. NC_1 calculates $A^R = A_{PS} \oplus (\overset{+}{X} \bigwedge S) \oplus (\overset{+}{Y} \bigwedge R) \oplus (R \bigwedge S)$.
7. NC_2 calculates $B^R = B_{PS} \oplus (\overset{-}{X} \bigwedge S) \oplus (\overset{-}{Y} \bigwedge R)$.

---

or NC_2 having the complete result. At the end of the protocol, non-colluding sites can then calculate the final result for their own part by removing the initial noise. For instance, for NC_1, the following operation: $A^R = A_{PS} \oplus (\overset{+}{X} \bigwedge S) \oplus (\overset{+}{Y} \bigwedge R)$ $\oplus (R \bigwedge S)$ could be done securely since it knows its own inputs $(\overset{+}{X}, \overset{+}{Y}, R_1,$ and $S_1)$ and random numbers from NC_2 $(R_2$ and $S_2)$. Hence, the final results $A^R \oplus B^R = A_{PS} \oplus (\overset{+}{X} \bigwedge S) \oplus (\overset{+}{Y} \bigwedge R) \oplus (R \bigwedge S) \oplus B_{PS} \oplus (\overset{-}{X} \bigwedge S) \oplus (\overset{-}{Y} \bigwedge R)$. Substituting the value of A_{PS} and B_{PS}, the initial and intermediate random numbers are removed due to the boolean property $R_{PS} \oplus R_{PS} = 0$. The desired result is $\overset{+}{X} \bigwedge \overset{+}{Y} \oplus \overset{+}{X} \bigwedge \overset{-}{Y} \oplus \overset{-}{X} \bigwedge \overset{+}{Y} \oplus \overset{-}{X} \bigwedge \overset{-}{Y}$. Although, this operation is never performed, the symmetrically divided result lies with both NC_1 and NC_2. More importantly, the Processing Site receives no information regarding to the private inputs of any individual. Due to the randomization performed during the initial step, it just sees a stream of uniformly distributed values and cannot distinguish between a genuine and a random value.

Algorithm 3: The $\neg^S$ protocol

Data: $(\overset{+}{X} \mid \overset{-}{X})$ bits are such as $\overset{+}{X}$ owned by NC_1, $\overset{-}{X}$ owned by NC_2

Result: $(A^R \mid B^R)$ are such that $A^R \oplus B^R = \neg(\overset{-}{X} \oplus \overset{+}{X}))$.

1. NC_1 calculates $A^R = \neg \overset{+}{X}$

2. NC_2 calculates $B^R = \overset{-}{X}$

   Remark: roles of NC_1 and NC_2 may be exchanged.

Theorem 7.1 *The operand $\bigwedge^S$ prohibits NC_1 from learning NC_2's private data and vice versa. Moreover, the third party PS learns none of their private inputs.*

Proof From the protocol, B_{PS} is all that NC_2 learns related to the private data of NC_1. Due to the randomness and secrecy of R_{PS}, NC_2 cannot find out the values of

$\overset{+}{X}$ or $\overset{+}{Y}$. As the roles of NC_1 and NC_2 are interchangeable, the same argument holds for NC_1 not learning the private inputs $\overset{-}{X}$ or $\overset{-}{Y}$ of NC_2. However, one key security aspect of not leaking any information to PS is achieved by randomizing the inputs before transmitting them to the Processing Site.

Remarks The privacy theorem is obvious for the $\neg^S$ operator as no data is exchanged.

Complexity: For the $\wedge^S$ operator, nine computations have to be performed ($6 \otimes$ and $3 \wedge$). As two more $\neg^S$ operations are needed by the $\vee^S$ protocol, we have in total 11 computations. For each $\wedge$, NC_1 and NC_2 exchange 2×2 bits among each other. From NC_1 or NC_2, 2×1 bits are sent to PS and 1 bit returned. Furthermore, both NC_1 and NC_2 calculate 2 random bits while 1 random bit is generated by PS.

7.3.2.4 The f^S, g^S, and $\sum^S$ Functions

Algorithm 4: The f^S function

Data: Vectors of bits $(\overset{+}{X} \mid \overset{-}{X})$. $\overset{+}{X}$ is coming from NC_1 and $\overset{-}{X}$ is coming from NC_2. K the number of dates shared by each customers of all databases.

Result: Vectors $(\overset{+}{Y} \mid \overset{-}{Y})$ such as $\overset{+}{Y}$ is the share of NC_1 and $\overset{-}{Y}$ the share of NC_2.

foreach $c \in 0..(|\overset{+}{X}|/K) - 1$ **do**
    // For each client c
    $(\overset{+}{Y_{Kxc+1}} \mid \overset{-}{Y_{Kxc+1}}) \leftarrow (0|0);$
    foreach $i \in 2..K$ **do**
        $(\overset{+}{Y_{Kxc+1}} \mid \overset{-}{Y_{Kxc+1}}) \leftarrow \vee^S(\overset{+}{Y_{Kxc+i-1}}, \overset{+}{X_{Kxc+i-1}} \mid \overset{-}{Y_{Kxc+i-1}}, \overset{-}{X_{Kxc+i-1}});$

return $(\overset{+}{Y} \mid \overset{-}{Y});$

Algorithm 5: The g^S function

Data: Vectors of bits $(\overset{+}{X} \mid \overset{-}{X})$. $\overset{+}{X}$ is coming from NC_1 and $\overset{-}{X}$ is coming from NC_2. K the number of dates shared by all customers of all databases.

Result: Vectors $(\overset{+}{Y} \mid \overset{-}{Y})$ such as $\overset{+}{Y}$ will be send to NC_1 and $\overset{-}{Y}$ will be send to NC_2.

foreach $c \in 0..(|\overset{+}{X}|/K) - 1$ **do**
    // For each client c
    $(\overset{+}{Y_c} \mid \overset{-}{Y_c}) \leftarrow (\overset{+}{X_{Kxc+1}} \mid \overset{-}{X_{Kxc+1}});$
    foreach $i \in 2..K$ **do**
        $(\overset{+}{Y_c} \mid \overset{-}{Y_c}) \leftarrow \vee^S(\overset{+}{Y_c}, \overset{+}{X_{Kxc+i}} \mid \overset{-}{Y_c}, \overset{-}{X_{Kxc+i}});$

return $(\overset{+}{Y} \mid \overset{-}{Y});$

In this section, we extend the f and g functions in order to incorporate security (see Algorithm 4). As previously mentioned, the SPAM algorithm's S-step Process requires that the vectors corresponding to every customer contain all 1's after the date of the first transaction for that customer. Hence, the f^S function recursively employs the $\bigvee^S$ function to securely compute the resultant vector. The inputs of the function are the randomly distorted customer data and the secure $\bigvee^S$ is used to find the boolean OR between the successive bits residing at the two sites NC_1 and NC_2. Similar to the previous algorithms, the final result of the operation is split into two parts with the Processing Site oblivious of the correct answer.

Similarly, the g^S function (see Algorithm 5) securely computes the existence of at least "1" in the vector of each customer transaction. It replaces the customer vector to either a "0" or a "1" depending on whether the sequence is supported at least once. This function is useful in calculating the support value at the penultimate step of the Algorithm 7.

Remarks In fact, calculating $g^S(\overset{+}{X}, \overset{-}{X}) \rightarrow (\overset{+}{Y}, \overset{-}{Y})$ can be returned while calculating $f^S(\overset{+}{X}, \overset{-}{X}) \rightarrow (\overset{+}{Z}, \overset{-}{Z})$ because $\overset{+}{Y_i}, \overset{-}{Y_i}$ can easily be obtained from $(Z_{i\times K+K}^{+}, Z_{i\times K+K}^{-})$ by using the following relation: $(\overset{+}{Y_i} \mid \overset{-}{Y_i}) = \bigvee^S(Z_{i\times K+K}^{+}, X_{i\times K+K}^{+} \mid Z_{i\times K+K}^{-}, X_{i\times K+K}^{-})$.

Algorithm 6: The $\sum^S$ protocol

Data: Vectors of bits $(X_1 \mid X_2)$. X_1 is coming from NC_1 and X_2 is coming from NC_2.

Result: A number which is shared in two parts: $(NB_1 \mid NB_2)$ corresponding to the number of bits at 1 in vectors $(X_1 \oplus X_2)$.

1. NC_1 and NC_2 generate and exchange two random vectors R_1 and R_2 of same cardinality such as $(Card(R_1) = Card(R_2) \geq 2N)$. They both calculate $R_1 \oplus R_2$ and calculate the number of 1s to be deleted, N_R, at the end of the computation from PS.;

2. NC_1 and NC_2 reorder respectively the vector (X_1, R_1) and (X_2, R_2) using a permutation value φ and get respectively Y_1 and Y_2.;

3. NC_1 sends Y_1 to PS and NC_2 sends Y_2 to PS.;

4. PS calculates $Y_1 \oplus Y2$ and count the number of bits at 1 and gets NB.;

5. PS gets a random number R_{PS} and returns $N_1 = NB + R_{PS}$ to NC_1 and $N_2 = NB - R_{PS}$ to NC_2.;

6. NC_1 computes $NB_1 = N_1 - N_R$, NC_2 keeps only $NB_2 = N_2$.;

Complexity: In Algorithm 6, the number of bits is increased by a value $\geq 2N$ for security reasons. Let us consider that we set this value as follows $t = \in [2 \dots K]$. For NC_1 and NC_2, $(2N(2t+1))$ operations are performed while $(2N(t+1))$ operations on PS. Furthermore, we have $N(t+1)$ operations for randomizing. The number of transfers between NC_1 and NC_2 is $(2tN)$. The $N(t+1)$ number of permutations could be neglected if NC_1 and NC_2 have their own generators. Finally between NC_1/NC_2 and PS, $N(t+1)$ bits are transferred.

7.3.2.5 The SECURE COLLABORATIVE FREQUENCY Algorithm

The SECURE COLLABORATIVE FREQUENCY algorithm (see Algorithm 7) extends the Algorithm 1 in order to perform all operations securely. It is applied after the preprocessing step and thus considers the original database having fake transactions.

Algorithm 7: The SECURE COLLABORATIVE FREQUENCY algorithm

Data: $S = < it_1 \ldots it_q >$ a sequence to be tested; $DB = DB_1 \bigcup DB_2 \ldots \bigcup DB_D$ a set of databases; N the number of customers shared by all databases; K the number of dates shared by all customers of all databases.

Result: The support of the sequence S in DB with random noise.

foreach $i \in 1..|S|$ **do**

$\quad (\overset{+}{X_i} \mid \overline{X_i}) \leftarrow \text{SEND}^S \times DB_1(i);$

$\quad$ **foreach** $j \in 2..D$ **do**

$\quad\quad (\overset{+}{V} \mid \overline{V}) \leftarrow \text{SEND}^S \times DB_j(it_i);$

$\quad\quad (\overset{+}{X_i} \mid \overline{X_i}) \leftarrow \bigvee^S(\overset{+}{C_i}, \overset{+}{V} \mid \overline{C_i}, \overline{V});$

$(\overset{+}{Z} \mid \overline{Z}) \leftarrow (\overset{+}{X_1} \mid \overline{X_1});$

foreach $i \in 2..|S|$ **do**

$\quad (\overset{+}{T} \mid \overline{T}) \leftarrow f^S(\overset{+}{Z} \mid \overline{Z});$

$\quad (\overset{+}{Z} \mid \overline{Z}) \leftarrow \bigwedge^S(\overset{+}{T}, \overset{+}{X_i} \mid \overline{T}, \overline{X_i});$

$(\overset{+}{Y} \mid \overline{Y}) \leftarrow g^S(\overset{+}{Z} \mid \overline{Z});$

$(\overset{+}{R} \mid \overline{R}) \leftarrow \sum^S(\overset{+}{Y} \mid \overline{Y});$

return $(\overset{+}{R} \mid \overline{R});$

For each item i of the sequence to be tested, all noisy vectors are sent by SEND^S to NC_1 and NC_2 in order to securely apply an OR between each vector $(\bigvee^S)$. The f^S function followed by the bitwise operator $\bigwedge^S$ is performed. At the end of this loop we are thus provided with a new vector $(\overset{+}{Z} \mid \overline{Z})$ where part of results are shared between NC_1 and NC_2. Then we apply the g^S function for generating $(\overset{+}{Y} \mid \overline{Y})$. Finally, we count the number of bits which are 1 in $(\overset{+}{Y} \mid \overline{Y})$ through the function $\sum^S$. At the end of the process, $\overset{+}{R}$ and $\overline{R}$ are sent by NC_1 and NC_2, respectively, to the Data Miner party. To get the real and final result, the miner has just to calculate $\overset{+}{R} + \overline{R}$ (integer summation) and has to remove the initial random noise, i.e., ε', they have added at the beginning of the process.

Theorem 7.2 *The randomization, performed at each level (original databases, NC_1, NC_2, and PS), does not affect the accuracy of the result.*

Proof The first randomization is performed by the original databases while inserting fake transactions, i.e., ε, and permuting the list of customers according to the value of φ. As DM is elected from the original databases, this information about the noise is available to DM and hence can easily be removed. The second randomization is performed by NC_1 and NC_2 while sending the transaction vectors to PS for the secure computation of $\bigvee^S$, $\bigwedge^S$, f^S, and g^S. This added noise is removed at the end of each computation from NC_1 and NC_2 when they receive results from PS by performing an XOR operation with the initial random values. Moreover, we have also proved that no private information about any individual could be learnt by any of the sites (cf. Theorem 7.1). Finally, for the computation of the $\sum^S$ function, NC_1 and NC_2 add random noise in their data, i.e., N_R, and also permutate their vector according to a φ value. PS also randomizes its integer value and this noise is removed by sending opposite parts to NC_1 and NC_2. The N_R value is removed by NC_1 and NC_2 when returning the result to DM. Finally, when combining results from NC_1 and NC_2, the only operation to be performed by DM to know the real result is to remove the ε' previously inserted.

Complexity: In the secure protocol, each database has to send $2NK$ data bits instead of NK. Subsequently, each DB has to calculate NK random bits and perform $(NK) \oplus$ operations. According to the previous results on the number of operations performed by the secure operators, the time complexity is $O(12NK)$ for binary operations and $O(7N)$ for randomizing operations. Hence, it could be bounded by $O(20N)$. Let us now consider the communication complexity of the protocol. Let $p = D \times S \times N \times K$. If the number of operations is at most $O(12p)$, then the number of transfers required is at most $O(4p)$ and for random values it is $O(3p)$. Hence, the whole algorithm has to send at most $O(20p)$.

Remarks The secure architecture could be further redefined in order to improve the communication cost between NC_1, NC_2, and PS. Furthermore, all the functions except f^S (it operates on individual customers) could be parallelized. The total overhead incurred by our secure protocol could be easily reduced by a factor of two. We notice that by considering SMC protocols, no such optimizations are possible, and hence for scalability issues, our alternative approach could be beneficial.

7.3.2.6 Security of the Protocol

For analyzing the security, let us examine the information divulged to each site participating in the protocol. Note that during the entire process, the random numbers are securely generated and the communication infrastructure is robust and intrusion free.

- NC_1 **and** NC_2 **View**: During the execution of the protocol, both sites only see a stream of random values with a uniform distribution. By the proposed protocol, they only receive noisy data and noisy shared results. Also NC_1 and NC_2 cannot share information as per the definition of semi-honest non-colluding sites. The value received from the DBs are XOR-ed with random numbers from a uniform distribution and indistinguishable from real values.
- **PS View**: It performs the computation of secure operations ($\bigwedge^S$, $\bigvee^S$, f^S, g^S, $\sum^S$) and provides the results to NC_1 and NC_2. As discussed earlier all of these operations reveal no private data of any individual customer from any of

the collaborating DBs. Even a succession or sequence of the secure operations remains secure.

- **Overall Security**: During the entire algorithm, no site obtains any additional information beyond of what they are already authorized to learn. Hence security and privacy of every customer is maintained during the computation of support in the architecture. The addition of fake transactions during the preprocessing steps and permutation of the lists enable that each site is ignorant of the correct intermediate results as well as the final result.

7.3.3 Improving the Robustness of the System

As described in the previous algorithms, all the data are stored in the two non-colluding sites NC_1 and NC_2. If a malicious party gains access to both sites, it will be trivial to obtain all the information and hence violate the tenets of privacy. Thus, in order to improve the robustness of the system, it would be interesting to have more than 2 NC_i (in fact an arbitrary number w) such that the knowledge of the data may only be obtained if one gains access to all the w NC_i and otherwise get no more than random numbers. Furthermore in order to be useful, the complexity must stay linear with w. In this section, we describe the secure operators generalized to w non-colluding sites NC_i and we focus on the most important protocols: $SEND^S$, $\bigwedge^S$, $\neg^S$, and $\sum^S$.

7.3.3.1 Sending Data to the w NC_i: $SEND^S$

In the original case, for sending a data D to NC_1, NC_2, sites must generate a random number R and send $D \oplus R$ to NC_1 and R to NC_2 (or vice versa). This method could be generalized to w sites NC_i by generating $w - 1$ random numbers, by calculating $V_1 = D \oplus R_1, V_2 = R_1 \oplus R_2, \ldots, V_i = R_{i-1} \oplus R_i, \ldots, V_w = R_w$ and then by sending one V_1 to each site NC_j in any order.

As in the original case, each NC_j obtains only random numbers such as $D = V_1 \oplus \cdots \oplus V_w$. The only way to obtain information on D is by gaining access to all the NC_j. If one has access to all but one, it is analogous to the NC_1 and NC_2 scenario, which has already been proven to be secure.

7.3.3.2 The $\neg^S$ operation

With w sites NC_i, this operation is still analogous and simple as the one when $w = 2$. In order to implement it, it is sufficient that an odd number of the sites (for example only one: NC_1) negate their part of the value and the other ones do nothing. There is still nothing exchanged and hence still no issues pertaining to privacy.

7.3.3.3 The $\bigwedge^S$ operation

Similar to the case $w = 2$ each site garbles its own part of the data (X_i and Y_i such that the real data is $X = X_1 \oplus \ldots \oplus X_w$ and $Y = Y_1 \oplus \ldots \oplus Y_w$) before sending it to PS. To do that they generate two random numbers R_i to encode X_i and S_i to encode Y_i and gets $X_i' = X_i \oplus R_i$ and $Y_i' = Y_i \oplus R_i$ which are sent to PS. They also exchange the value $R = R_1 \oplus \ldots \oplus R_w$ and $S = R_1 \oplus \ldots \oplus S_w$ between all NC_i. Then PS will calculate $P = (X_1' \oplus \ldots \oplus X_w') \bigwedge (Y_1' \oplus \ldots \oplus y_w')$ which could be written as $(X \oplus R) \bigwedge (Y \oplus S)$. PS sends its result P to all NC_i by using the $SEND^S$ protocol. Now all NC_i get a value P_i and they only need to remove garbled terms $(X \wedge S)$, $(Y \wedge R)$, and $(R \wedge S)$. To do that, it is sufficient that an odd number of NC_i (for example : NC_1) performs $Z_i = P_i \oplus (X_i \wedge S) \oplus (Y_i \wedge R) \oplus (S \wedge R)$ and all other ones perform $Z_i = P_i \oplus (X_i \wedge S) \oplus (Y_i \wedge R)$. We then obtain the expected results such that $Z = Z_1 \oplus \ldots \oplus Z_w = X \wedge Y$.

The number of operation performed by each site (real operations/random numbers generation/data sending and receiving) will increase linearly with the number of NC_i (w) and thus the full secure processing still remains linear compared to the unsecured one.

7.3.3.4 The $\sum^S$ operation

The generalization of the Sum^S algorithm is described in Algorithm 8. Its complexity increases linearly with the number w of NC_i and remains linear compared to the same unsecured process.

Algorithm 8: The $\sum^S$ protocol

Data: Vectors of bits $(X_1 | \ldots | X_w)$. X_i are coming from NC_i such that $X = X_1 \oplus \ldots \oplus X_w$

Result: A number which is shared in w parts: $(NB_1 | \ldots | NB_w)$ such that $NB = NB_1 + \ldots + NB_w$ corresponds to the number of bits at 1 in vectors X.

let $N = card(X) = card(X_i)$ be the number of bits in vector X. 1a. One of the sites (for example NC_1) will generate w random vectors of bits $(R_1 \ldots R_n)$ of same size such that $card(R_i) \geq 2 * N.$;

1b. It calculates $R = R_1 \oplus \ldots \oplus R_w$ and Nr the number of bits equal to 1 in $R.$;

1c. R and Nr are sent to all $NC_i.$;

2. A permutation φ is chosen to permute $card(R) + card(X)$ bits.;

3. Each NC_i reorder its vector (X_i, R_i) using the permutation φ and gets $Y_i.$;

4. Each NC_i sends its Y_i to $PS.$;

5. PS calculates $Y = Y_1 \oplus \ldots \oplus Y_w$ and counts the number of bits at 1 and gets $NB.$;

6. PS generates $w - 1$ random numbers RP_i and calculates $N_1 = NB + RP_1$, $N_2 = NB + RP_2 - RP_1 \ldots N_{w-1} = NB + RP_{w-1} - RP_{w-2}$ and $N_w = NB - RP_{w-1}.$;

7. PS sends one of the N_i to each NC_j in any order.;

8. NC_1 computes $NB_1 = N_1 - N_R$, all other NC_i keeps only $NB_i = N_i.$;

Remark: All additions and subtractions are done modulo $card(Y) = card(R) + card(X)$.

7.4 Conclusion

In this work we have addressed the problem of privacy-preserving sequential pattern mining in the context of distributed databases. We have presented a novel secure extension of the SPAM algorithm for mining patterns. We also prove that under reasonable assumptions, our algorithm and the underlying operations, protocols, and architecture for multiparty computation is secure.

There are various avenues for future work. First, here we have only focused on the S-step process of the SPAM algorithm, i.e., we only considered the problem of discovering sequences reduced to a list of items. The proposed secure functions can also be extended to the I-step process, i.e., a list of itemsets instead of items. Furthermore, in the current version of PRIPSEP, results are directly returned to the DM party. In order to improve the whole process, we plan to extend the role of DM wherein, it could store the lexicographic tree and could expand each node in the tree by considering that intermediate results could be stored in shared arrays between NC_1 and NC_2. Hence, incremental mining could be possible and unlike our current approach, previous results do not have to be recomputed. The storage of results would also be made secure by ensuring that each site has only noisy data or random values.

In addition, as the volume of data increases to a deluge, it becomes increasingly expensive (sometimes impossible) to store all available data before processing them and hence it is necessary to process it "on the fly" as streams of data. Several new applications directly generate streams of data produced by a large number of sensors (e.g., supermarket transactions, medical data). In order to address this increase of available data, for which the privacy issue could also be very important, new research work is being done to apply data mining methods such as sequential patterns mining directly on the streams without storing them [13]. Lastly, as network traffic data becomes more relevant in the context of detection of Internet worms and intrusions by discovering abnormal traffic patterns, recent research is trying to solve the problem while preserving privacy of customers [23].

In sum, research in privacy-preserving data mining, especially sequential patterns, is at an exciting stage, with new papers shaping the future for the field.

References

1. Agrawal R., Imielinski T., and Swami A. Mining association rules between sets of items in large database. In: *5th ACM SIGACT-SIGMOD Symposium on Principles of Database, SIGMOD 1993*, Washington, D.C., USA, pp. 207–216, 1993.
2. Agrawal R. and Srikant R. Mining sequential patterns. In: *21st International Conference on Data Engineering, ICDE 2005*, Tokyo, Japan, pp. 3–14, 1995.
3. Ayres J., Flannick J., Gehrke J., and Yiu T. Sequential pattern mining using bitmap representation. In: *8th ACM SIGKDD International Conference on Knowledge Discovery and Data Mining, KDD 2002*, Edmonton, Alberta, Canada, pp. 439–435, 2002.
4. Bhattacharya J., Gupta S., Kapoor V., and Dass R. Utilizing network features for privacy violation detection. In: *1st International Conference Communication System Software and Middleware, COMSWARE 2006*, Delhi, India, January 2006.
5. Chaum D., Crepeau C., and Damgard I. Multiparty unconditionally secure protocols. In *20th Annual Symposium on the Theory of Computing, STOC 1988*, Chicago, Illinois, USA, pp. 11–19, 1988.
6. Clifton C., Kantarcioglu M., Lin X., Vaidya J., and M. Zhu. Tools for privacy preserving distributed data mining. *SIGKDD Explorations*, 4(2):28–34, 2003.

7. Du W. and Atallah M.J. Secure multi-party computation problems and their applications: A review and open problems. In: *New Security Paradigms Workshop*, Cloudcroft, USA, pp. 11–20, 2001.

8. Du W., Han Y., and Chen S. Privacy-preserving multivariate statistical analysis: Linear regression and classification. In: *4th SIAM International Conference on Data Mining, SDM 2004*, pp. 222–233, 2004.

9. Evfimievski A., Srikant R., Agrawal R., and Gehrke J. Privacy-preserving mining of association rules. *Information Systems*, 29(4), pp. 343–364, June 2004.

10. Goldreich O. Secure multi-party computation. Working Draft, 2000.

11. Gouda K., Hassaan M., and Zaki M.J. Prism: A primal-encoding approach for frequent sequence mining. In: *7th IEEE International Conference on Data Mining, ICDM 2007*, Omaha NE, USA, pp. 487–492, 2007.

12. Han J., Pei J., Mortazavi-asl B., Chen Q., Dayal U., and M. Hsu. Freespan: Frequent pattern-projected sequential pattern mining. In *6th ACM SIGKDD International Conference on Knowledge Discovery and Data Mining, KDD 2000*, San Jose, California, USA, pp. 355–359, 2000.

13. Huang Q.-H. Privacy preserving sequential pattern mining in data stream. In *4th International Conference on Intelligent Computing, ICIC 2008*, Shanghai, China, 2008.

14. Jagannathan G. and Wright R. Privacy-preserving distributed k-means clustering over arbitrarily partitioned data. In: *11th ACM SIGKDD International Conference on Knowledge Discovery and Data Mining, KDD 2005*, Chicago, IL, USA, August 2005.

15. Kantarcioglu M. and Vaidya J. An architecture for privacy-preserving mining of client information. In *IEEE International Conference on Privacy, Security and Data Mining in Conjunction with the 2002 IEEE ICDM Conference, CRPIT 2002*, 2002.

16. Kapoor V., Poncelet P., Trousset F., and Teisseire M. Privacy preserving sequential pattern mining in distributed databases. In: *15th ACM International Conference on Information and Knowledge Management, CIKM 2006*, Arlington, USA, 2006.

17. Lindell Y. and Pinkas B. Privacy preserving data mining. *Journal of Cryptology*, 15(2), pp. 11–19, 2002.

18. Masseglia F., Cathala F., and Poncelet P. The PSP approach for mining sequential patterns. In: *2nd European Symposium of Principles of Data Mining and Knowledge Discovery, PKDD 1998*, Nantes, France, 1998.

19. Pei J., Han J., Pinto H., Chen Q., Dayal U., and Hsu M. Prefixspan: Mining sequential patterns efficiently by prefix projected pattern growth. In: *17th International Conference on Data Engineering, ICDE 2001*, Heidelberg, Germany, 2001.

20. Pei J., Han J., and Wang W. Mining sequential patterns with constraints in large databases. In: *ACM CIKM International Conference on Information and Knowledge Management, CIKM 2002*, MCLean, USA, pp. 18–25, 2002.

21. Pinkas B. Cryptographic techniques for privacy preserving data mining. *SIGKDD Explorations*, 4(2), pp. 18–25, Edmonton, Alberta, Canada, 2002.

22. Raissi C. and Poncelet P. Sampling for sequential pattern mining: From static databases to data streams. In: *7th IEEE International Conference on Data Mining, ICDM 2007*, Maebashi City, Japan, pp. 631–636, 2007.

23. Seung-Woo K., Sanghyun P., Jung-Im W., and Sang-Wook K. Privacy preserving data mining of sequential patterns for network traffic data. *Information Sciences: An International Journal*, 178(3):694–713, 2008.

24. Srikant R. and Agrawal R. Mining sequential patterns: Generalizations and performance improvements. In *5th International Conference on Extending Database Technology, EDBT 1996*, Avignon, France, pp. 3–17, 1996.

25. U. S. D. of Health & Human Services. Health insurance portability and accountability act of 1996. http://www.hipaa.org/, August 1996.

26. Vaidya J. and Clifton C. Privacy preserving association rule mining in vertically partitioned data. In: *8th ACM SIGKDD International Conference on Knowledge Discovery and Data Mining, KDD 2002*, Edmonton, Alberta, Canada, July 2002.

27. Wu X. and Zhang S. Synthesizing high-frequency rules from different data sources. *IEEE Transctions on Knowledge and Data Engineering*, 15(2):353–367, 2003.
28. Yan X., Han J., and Afshar R. Clospan: Mining closed sequential patterns in large datasets. In: *3rd SIAM International Conference on Data Mining, SDM 2004*, pp. 166–177, 2003.
29. Yao A.C. Protocols for secure computations. In: *23rd Annual IEEE Symposium on Foundations of Computer Science, SFCS 1982*, pp. 160–164, 1982.
30. Yao A.C. How to generate and exchange secrets. In: *27th Symposium on Foundations of Computer Science, FOCS 1986*, pp. 162–167, 1986.
31. Zaki M. SPADE: An efficient algorithm for mining frequent sequences. *Machine Learning Journal*, 42(1):31–60, February 2001.
32. Zhan J., Chang L., and Matwin S. Privacy-preserving collaborative sequential pattern mining. In: *Workshop on Link Analysis, Counter-terrorism, and Privacy in Conjunction with SIAM Interational Conference on Data Mining*, Lake Buena Vista, Florida, pp. 61–72, 2004.
33. Zhong N., Yao Y., and Ohsuga S. Peculiarity oriented multi-database mining. In: *3rd European Symposium of Principles of Data Mining and Knowledge Discovery, PKDD 1999*, pp. 136–146, 1999.

Chapter 8
Pseudonymized Data Sharing

David Galindo and Eric R. Verheul

Abstract In this chapter pseudonymization and pseudonym intersection algorithms are proposed and analyzed. These two procedures combined make pseudonymized data sharing possible. Pseudonymized data sharing is used by organizations, that typically do not share information, to build and provide pseudonymized copies of their private databases to third parties – called researchers. Some basic security properties are satisfied: pseudonymity, meaning that it is infeasible to relate a pseudonym to its identity; and unlinkability, meaning that it is infeasible to decide if pseudonyms belonging to different researchers correspond to the same identity. Computing the equijoin of pseudonymized databases held by researchers A and B is enabled provided that they are given proper cryptographic keys. The outcome of the equijoin protocol between A and B is that party A learns virtually nothing, while party B learns the equijoin of A and B's pseudonymized databases. We are able to prevent that malicious researchers abuse equijoin transitivity in the following sense: colluding researchers A, B, C cannot use equijoin keys for (A, B) and (B, C) to compute the equijoin of (A, C). As a prominent application of these algorithms we discuss the privacy-enhanced secondary usage of electronic health records.

8.1 Introduction

Let us consider databases containing sensitive and valuable data on individuals. Assume these data records consist of an identifier of the individual (e.g., name, social security number) and the data associated to the individual. This data originates from heterogenous mutually distrustful sources, which we name *suppliers*, such as statistical offices, hospitals, or insurance companies.

D. Galindo (✉)
University of Luxembourg, Luxembourg
e-mail: david.galindo@uni.lu

J. Nin, J. Herranz (eds.), *Privacy and Anonymity in Information Management Systems*,
Advanced Information and Knowledge Processing,
DOI 10.1007/978-1-84996-238-4_8, © Springer-Verlag London Limited 2010

Subjects' data records held by suppliers are the very primary ingredient for empirical research, but their release exposes the privacy of the individuals concerned. We name *researchers* the parties interested in getting access to this data for subsequent analysis. In health care, prominent scenarios include the secondary use of clinical data for research and confidential patient-safety reporting (e.g., adverse drug effects), to name but a few. The fact that statistical research is interested in collective features rather than individual distinctiveness makes it possible to reconcile data utility and individual privacy: identifiers can be removed or encoded into a pseudonym, and subjects' data can be de-identified by using statistical disclosure control methods. Ideally, the collective features of the resulting pseudonymized de-identified data are preserved.

In this chapter we study pseudonymity in the above context. We do so from a cryptographic point of view, namely by focusing on cryptographic techniques to transform personal identifiers into pseudonyms with several properties. Thus, our techniques are necessary but not sufficient to provide pseudonymity from a system-wide perspective. The reason is simple: even though the data is pseudonymized, there is the risk that the characteristics of the data singles out a person, e.g., by a combination of profession, age, and place of residence. The risk of *indirect identification*, cf. [5, 12], becomes even larger when linking several pseudonymized databases, which is our target. The issue of indirect identification, although far from trivial, is outside the scope of this chapter. The topic is covered by an abundant literature (the interested reader is referred to [12] for an introduction to this topic, to [13] for a grasp on the state of the art, to [16] for privacy risk assessment recommendations, and to [18] for an exemplification of the importance of de-identifying the individuals' private data). We briefly comment on some lines of defense against these problem. Keeping track and scrutinizing the queries by the parties as well as query restriction techniques from the statistical database literature can help. For instance, these techniques include restricting the size of query results and keeping audit trails of all answered queries to detect possible compromises.

8.1.1 Security Properties

To be more precise, let us consider *databases* consisting of entries of the form $(id, D(id))$, where id is a unique identifier field (called *identity*) and $D(id)$ is a private data field. A *pseudonymized database* is obtained by replacing the identity id in the database entries by a blind identifier called *pseudonym* and by modifying $D(id)$ into a pseudonymized data field $PD(id)$. Two basic security requirements apply to the pseudonymization of identities in the context of pseudonymization of databases. The first one, called *pseudonymity*, states that it should not be possible for any party to relate a given pseudonym with a given identity. That is, it should be infeasible to correctly answer whether a given pseudonym belongs to a given identity. The second basic security requirement is called *unlinkability*. This states that, unless explicitly warranted, it should not be possible for two researchers to relate their pseudonyms. Or alternatively put, two researchers should not be able to correctly answer whether two of their pseudonyms belong to the same individual.

This implies in particular that pseudonyms on the same identity must differ from one researcher to another. A pseudonym on identity id for researcher R_d is syntactically represented by $P(id, R_d)$. Clearly unlinkability is of paramount importance as a defense mechanism against indirect identification: it prevents researchers from correlating its databases without previous consent.

A third security requirement deals with the possibility of computing equijoins of pseudonymized databases. Let $\mathcal{I}_{R_s}, \mathcal{I}_{R_d}$ be the sets of unknown identities corresponding to the pseudonyms held by researchers R_s, R_d, respectively. Let

$$\left\{ \left(P(id, R_s), PD(id, R_s) \right) \right\}_{id \in \mathcal{I}_{R_s}} \text{ and } \left\{ \left(P(id, R_d), PD(id, R_d) \right) \right\}_{id \in \mathcal{I}_{R_d}}$$

be the pseudonymized databases held at a certain point in time by researchers R_s, R_d, respectively. Then we say that the equijoin between R_s and R_d pseudonymized databases, with R_s playing the role of *source researcher* and R_d playing the role of *destination researcher*, equals

$$\left\{ \left(P(id, R_d), PD(id, R_d) \right) \right\} \cup \left\{ \left(P(\overline{id}, R_d), PD(\overline{id}, R_d) \| PD(\overline{id}, R_s) \right) \right\},$$

where id's are such that $id \in \mathcal{I}_{R_d}$ and $id \notin \mathcal{I}_{R_s}$, while $\overline{id}$'s are such that $\overline{id} \in \mathcal{I}_{R_d} \cap \mathcal{I}_{R_s}$. This operation is possible only if explicitly warranted and it is under the control of secret cryptographic keys. Specifically, our equijoin protocols involve two researchers R_s and R_d, where researcher R_s learns virtually nothing while R_d learns the equijoin of their pseudonymized databases. The security property we consider, called *equijoin non-transitivity*, states that researchers cannot abuse equijoin transitivity in the following sense: colluding researchers R_s, R_d, R_o cannot use equijoin keys for (R_s, R_d) and (R_d, R_o) to compute the equijoin of (R_s, R_o).

For the sake of enabling flexible equijoins, our pseudonymizing systems make use of a Trusted Third Party (TTP). This trusted party can function either as a mighty partner involved in all the security-sensitive transactions in the system (i.e., pseudonymization, equijoin) or alternatively as a simple key distribution center, feeding interested parties with the cryptographic keys required for the operations. Apart from that, the existence of a TTP also reflects the fact that access to pseudonymized databases as well as the allowance of operations between different databases requires previous approval by a Regulatory Privacy Body (RPB). This privacy body has two main roles. On the one hand, it ensures that the exchange of information complies with data protection legislation. On the other hand, it minimizes the risk of indirect identification, for instance by implementing defense mechanisms against it. In this work we are primarily interested in the cryptographic aspects of the pseudonymization problem, and for this reason the functioning of the RPB is not described.

Overall the assumption on the existence of such a TTP is quite natural, even necessary, as the need to defend the system against indirect identification shows. In fact such a TTP is included in most of the pseudonymized data sharing platforms, either implemented (see [1]) or simply proposed, we are aware of, and it is explicitly considered in the only existing standard on pseudonymized databases [16].

8.1.2 Relevance

Pseudonymized data sharing is in use and has been discussed in multiple venues (see for instance [11, 23, 4, 17, 20]). More importantly, the ISO standard ISO/TS 25237:2008, *Health Informatics – Pseudonymization*, which has been recently released, contains principles and requirements for privacy protection in systems using pseudonymization services for the protection of personal health information. In this chapter we provide a cryptographic mechanism for building unlikeable pseudonym sets that can be made linkable if a Trusted Third Party decides so. In this sense, our work can be seen as a cryptographic implementation of a pseudonymization system satisfying the ISO/TS 25237:2008 requirements, yet with an enriching equijoin functionality not envisioned by the aforementioned standard.

8.1.3 Related Work

We are not aware of any previous proposal of a cryptographic technique for building pseudonymized databases containing unlinkable pseudonyms, yet allowing secure operations on different sets of pseudonyms. In any case, some of our techniques can be seen as an extension of the work by Agrawal et al. [2], in which protocols for secure equijoin among non-pseudonymized databases are proposed. The main tool used by Agrawal et al. is *commutative encryption* (see Section 8.3.4 for details) and a variant of Shamir's three-pass protocol [19, 21]. We stress that the problems addressed in [2] and our work, even if related, are orthogonal. Agrawal et al. intersect sets containing the same identifiers, while we intersect sects containing different identifiers (which are indeed unlinkable unless some cryptographic keys are known). We are able to extend Agrawal et al. techniques to build a basic pseudonymization scheme. The resulting system has, however, one drawback, namely colluding researchers R_s and R_d, who are allowed to compute an equijoin of their pseudonymized databases, can manage to translate pseudonyms $P(id, R_s)$ to $P(id, R_d)$, and vice versa, for individuals outside the intersection of the databases, and therefore can abuse equijoin transitivity (cf Theorem 5). In Section 8.6 we present a natural extension of our basic scheme using pairings, in which the above problem is avoided. As well as in [2], the security of our two last protocols is relative to the Random Oracle Model [7].

8.2 Description of a Pseudonymized Data Sharing System

In this section we shall describe the syntax and security properties of a pseudonymized data sharing system, which comprises (at least) a pseudonymization algorithm and an equijoin algorithm.

8.2.1 Syntax

Let us remind we are considering *databases* consisting of entries of the form $(id, D(id))$, where id is the identity field and $D(id)$ is the private data field. A *pseudonymized database* for a researcher R is obtained by replacing the identity id in the database entries by a blind identifier $P(id, R)$ called *pseudonym*. Each researcher has one, unique pseudonym set. That is, for the same identifier id and different researchers R and R', $P(id, R) \neq P(id, R')$ with overwhelming probability. However, those different pseudonyms sets can be synchronized under the control of secret cryptographic keys held by a trusted service provider. Thus our pseudonymized data sharing systems make use of a TTP that sets the system up, via a 'System Setup' algorithm. As part of this, the TTP generates on request a secret cryptographic key for each researcher through a 'Researcher Key Generation' algorithm, whose output is only known to the TTP. Additional keys are output by 'Supply Keys Generation' and 'Equijoin Keys Generation' algorithms. Later, these keys are distributed to the relevant suppliers and researchers, in the case where researchers and suppliers perform themselves the pseudonymization and equijoin operations; alternatively, these keys are kept secret in the case where the TTP is in charge of running those algorithms. These additional keys enable executing the two fundamental protocols in the scheme, namely "Researcher Supply" and "Researcher Equijoin".

> *Researcher supply* This protocol is run between a supplier S, a researcher R, and eventually the TTP. At the end of the protocol, the researcher R is supplied with a pseudonymized database that originates from the supplier's private database. When the TTP is involved, we denote this protocol as $S \xrightarrow{\text{TTP}}_P R$; otherwise, it is denoted $S \to_P R$. The result of the researcher supply protocol is that R possesses a pseudonymized database consisting of entries of the form $\big(P(id, R), PD(id, R)\big)$ where $PD(id)$ represents the de-identified data that the supplier is willing (or allowed) to share with the researcher on individual id. In particular, R can detect if a certain pseudonymized identity $P(id, R)$ was already present in its database and proceed to update the associated pseudonymized data.
>
> *Researcher equijoin* This protocol is run by a source researcher R_s and a destination researcher R_d and eventually the TTP. After the protocol is completed, R_d has an equijoin of R_s and R_d pseudonymized databases, while R_s learns at most the number of entries on R_d's database. This protocol does not provide R_d with any information on individuals that do not appear in both databases. When the TTP is involved, we denote this protocol as $R_s \xrightarrow{\text{TTP}}_{\bowtie} R_d$; otherwise, it is denoted $R_s \to_{\bowtie} R_d$.

A pseudonym scheme $\mathcal{P}$ thus consists on six algorithms "System Setup", "Researcher Key Generation", "Supply Keys Generation", "Equijoin Keys Generation", "Researcher Supply", and "Researcher Equijoin".

8.2.2 Security Requirements

We assume that suppliers are honest. That is, they will not deviate from protocols, they will not collude with any other party nor try to deduce secret information from the data flow they observe. In contrast, we assume that researchers are semi-honest, namely they will not deviate from the protocols but might try to deduce secret information they are not supposed to know. Moreover, researchers are willing to share cryptographic keys and pseudonyms sets with other researchers to deduce more information than what they are allowed to. In order to simplify security definitions and proofs, we do not consider researchers to be malicious in the traditional sense in multiparty computation [15]. That is, researchers will not abort nor use fake information as input to their protocols.

In the following we define the security requirements pseudonymity, unlinkability, and equijoin non-transitivity we mentioned in the introduction. We additionally define a secure equijoin property. We formalize them in what follows. Let us stress once again that our definitions imply that no vital information is leaking from our cryptographic protocols. However, we cannot guarantee anything regarding the safety of the data de-identification protocols nor of the multiple linkage of pseudonymized databases.

8.2.3 Notation

If x is a string then $|x|$ denotes its length, while if S is a set then $|S|$ denotes its size. If $k \in \mathbb{N}$ then 1^k denotes the string of k ones. If S is a set then $s_1, \ldots, s_n \xleftarrow{\$} S$ denotes the operation of picking n elements s_i of S independently and uniformly at random. Let us denote by $\mathcal{I}_{S_l}$ the set of identities held by supplier S_l. We denote by $\mathcal{P}_{R_d}$ the set of pseudonyms $P(id, R_d)$ held by researcher R_d; $\mathcal{I}_{R_d}$ the set of the corresponding unknown identities and $n_d = |\mathcal{P}_{R_d}|$ the cardinal of $\mathcal{P}_{R_d}$. We consider identities $id \in \{0, 1\}^*$ be finite binary strings. Let Pset be the set of all possible pseudonyms of a pseudonyms scheme $\mathcal{P}$.

Definition 8.1 (Pseudonymity) Let $\mathcal{A}$ be a probabilistic polynomial-time adversary (PPT) [15]. Consider the following situation:

1. S_l and $\mathcal{A}$ run the Researcher Supply protocol $S_l \to_P R_d$ (alternatively $S_l \xrightarrow{\text{TTP}}_P R_d$).
2. $\mathcal{A}$ has been able to break the pseudonymity for pseudonyms in the set $\mathcal{PI} = \{P(id_1, R_d), \ldots, P(id_t, R_d)\}$ corresponding to identities in the set $\mathcal{I} = \{id_1, \ldots, id_t\}$.

We say that a pseudonym scheme $\mathcal{P}$ provides *pseudonymity* if the distributions

$$\begin{pmatrix} id_1 & \cdots & id_{n_d} \\ P(id_1, R_d) & \cdots & P(id_{n_d}, R_d) \end{pmatrix} \text{ and } \begin{pmatrix} id_1 & \cdots & id_t & id_{t+1} \ldots id_{n_d} \\ P(id_1, R_d) & \cdots & P(id_t, R_d) & Z_{t+1} \ldots Z_{n_d} \end{pmatrix},$$

where $Z_j \overset{\$}{\leftarrow}$ Pset for $j = t + 1, \ldots, n_d$ are computationally indistinguishable in $\mathcal{A}$'s view.

Definition 8.1 asks that PPT adversaries $\mathcal{A}$ cannot distinguish between the distribution with real pseudonyms from a distribution with random values. Similarly to the definition of semantic security for encryption schemes (cf. [15] and Definition 8.5 in this chapter), the inability to distinguish captures the fact that pseudonyms do not reveal any information on their corresponding identities to PPT adversaries.

Definition 8.2 (Unlinkability) Let $\mathcal{A}$ be a PPT adversary. Consider the following situation:

1. S_l and $\mathcal{A}$ run the Researcher Supply protocol $S_l \rightarrow_P R_d$ (alternatively $S_l \overset{TTP}{\longrightarrow}_P R_d$).
2. $\mathcal{A}$ gets hold of $\mathcal{P}_{R_s}$, the pseudonyms' database of R_s.
3. $\mathcal{A}$ has been able to link polynomially many pseudonym pairs

$$\langle \big(P(id_1, R_s), P(id_1, R_d) \big), \ldots, \big(P(id_t, R_s), P(id_t, R_d) \big) \rangle,$$

corresponding to identities in a certain set $\mathcal{I} = \{id_1, \ldots, id_t\}$.

Let $\mathcal{I}_{R_s} \cap \mathcal{I}_{R_d} = \{id_1, \ldots, id_m\}$. We say that a pseudonym scheme $\mathcal{P}$ provides *unlinkability* if the distributions

$$\begin{pmatrix} id_{t+1} & \cdots & id_m \\ P(id_{t+1}, R_d) & \cdots & P(id_m, R_d) \\ P(id_{t+1}, R_s) & \cdots & P(id_m, R_s) \end{pmatrix} \quad \text{and} \quad \begin{pmatrix} id_{t+1} & \cdots & id_m \\ P(id_{t+1}, R_d) & \cdots & P(id_m, R_d) \\ Z_{t+1} & \cdots & Z_m \end{pmatrix},$$

where $Z_j \overset{\$}{\leftarrow}$ Pset for $j = t + 1, \ldots, m$ are computationally indistinguishable in $\mathcal{A}$'s view.

Definition 8.2 asks that PPT adversaries $\mathcal{A}$ cannot significantly better link $P(id, R_d)$ to $P(id, R_s)$ than they can link $P(id, R_d)$ to a random pseudonym. This inability ensures that pseudonyms are unlinkable by PPT adversaries.

Definition 8.3 (Secure equijoin) Let R_s, R_d be semi-honest researchers running the researcher equijoin protocol $R_s \rightarrow_{\bowtie} R_d$ (alternatively $R_s \overset{TTP}{\longrightarrow}_{\bowtie} R_d$). We say that a pseudonym scheme $\mathcal{P}$ provides *secure equijoin* if R_s learns nothing or alternatively the size of $\mathcal{P}_{R_d}$; R_d learns $(id, PD(id, R_s))$ for $id \in \mathcal{I}_{R_s} \cap \mathcal{I}_{R_d}$, and R_d is allowed to additionally learn the size of $\mathcal{P}_{R_s}$.

Definition 8.3 asks that PPT adversaries $\mathcal{A}$ only learn the minimal information that a secure equijoin protocol should disclose. We allow that the equijoin protocol might disclose the size of R_d's database to R_s, but this should be the only information R_s should apprehend. Analogously, we allow R_d to learn the size of R_s's database and obviously the de-identified data on the individuals belonging to both databases, but no more than that.

Definition 8.4 (Equijoin non-transitivity) Suppose that

1. R_s and R_d are allowed to compute the equijoin of their databases.
2. R_d and R_o are allowed to compute the equijoin of their databases.
3. R_s, R_d, R_o share their pseudonymized databases and cryptographic material.

Let $\mathcal{I}_{R_s} \cap \mathcal{I}_{R_o} = \{id_1, \ldots, id_m\}$ and $\mathcal{I}_{R_s} \cap \mathcal{I}_{R_d} \cap \mathcal{I}_{R_o} = \{id_1, \ldots, id_t\}$ with $t \le m$. We say that a pseudonym scheme $\mathcal{P}$ provides *equijoin non-transitivity* if the distributions

$$
\begin{pmatrix}
id_1 & \cdots & id_t & id_{t+1} & \cdots & id_m \\
P(id_1, R_s) & \cdots & P(id_t, R_s) & P(id_{t+1}, R_s) & \cdots & P(id_m, R_s) \\
P(id_1, R_o) & \cdots & P(id_t, R_o) & P(id_{t+1}, R_o) & \cdots & P(id_m, R_o)
\end{pmatrix} \quad \text{and}
$$

$$
\begin{pmatrix}
id_1 & \cdots & id_t & id_{t+1} & \cdots & id_m \\
P(id_1, R_s) & \cdots & P(id_t, R_s) & P(id_{t+1}, R_s) & \cdots & P(id_m, R_s) \\
P(id_1, R_o) & \cdots & P(id_t, R_o) & Z_{t+1} & \cdots & Z_m
\end{pmatrix},
$$

where $Z_j \xleftarrow{\$} \mathsf{Pset}$ for $j = t+1, \ldots, m$ are computationally indistinguishable in R_s, R_d, R_o's view.

Definition 8.4 captures the fact that R_s, R_d, R_o cannot meaningfully relate pairs $\big(P(id, R_s), P(id, R_o)\big)$ for any $id \in (\mathcal{I}_{R_s} \cap \mathcal{I}_{R_o}) - (\mathcal{I}_{R_s} \cap \mathcal{I}_{R_d} \cap \mathcal{I}_{R_o})$, and thus colluding researchers cannot abuse the transitivity property of equijoin. Notice that the intrinsic transitivity property of equijoin always allows R_s, R_d, R_o to compute $\mathcal{P}_{R_s} \cap \mathcal{P}_{R_d} \cap \mathcal{P}_{R_o}$.

8.3 Basic Tools

In this section we introduce some basic cryptographic tools that we will need in our algorithms. We start by defining semantically secure symmetric encryption.

8.3.1 Symmetric Encryption with Semantic Security

We adapt the classical definition of symmetric encryption [15] to what we actually need in our protocols.

Definition 8.5 (Semantically secure encryption) Let $\mathcal{E} = \big(\mathrm{Enc}_K(\cdot), \mathrm{Dec}_K(\cdot)\big)$ be a symmetric encryption scheme with secret keys belonging to a certain set $\mathcal{K}$. More precisely, let $\mathrm{Enc}_K \colon \{0, 1\}^M \to \{0, 1\}^{M'}$ with $M \le M'$ being integers, and let $\mathrm{Dec}_K \colon \{0, 1\}^{M'} \to \{0, 1\}^M$ be such that $\mathrm{Dec}_K\big(\mathrm{Enc}_K(m)\big) = m$ for any $m \in \{0, 1\}^M$. Let $\mathcal{O}_K(\cdot)$ be an encryption oracle, which when queried on $m \in \{0, 1\}^M$ outputs $\mathrm{Enc}_K(m)$. We say that $\mathcal{E}$ is a *symmetric encryption scheme with semantic security* if no PPT algorithm $\mathcal{A}$ can meaningfully distinguish between the distributions $\big(m, \mathrm{Enc}_K(m)\big)$ and $\big(m, Z\big)$, where $K \xleftarrow{\$} \mathcal{K}$, $m \in \{0, 1\}^M$ is a message of $\mathcal{A}$'s choosing and $Z \xleftarrow{\$} \{0, 1\}^{M'}$. $\mathcal{A}$ is allowed to arbitrarily query the encryption oracle $\mathcal{O}_K(\cdot)$, except for the chosen message m.

Definition 8.5 requires that for any message of the adversary's choice, it is infeasible to distinguish the encryption of this message from a random ciphertext. The importance of this definition stems from the fact that the security level it provides is the computational analogue of Shannon's perfect secrecy (see [15]): a ciphertext $\text{Enc}_K(m)$ reveals 'no information' on the underlying plaintext m to an attacker which does not know the secret encryption key K.

Next we informally describe the computational assumptions we use in the sections that follow.

8.3.2 Decisional Diffie–Hellman Assumption

Let $\mathcal{G}$ be a (cyclic) group of order q prime. The decisional Diffie–Hellman (DDH) problem consists on distinguishing the probability distributions (u, v, u^a, v^a) and (u, v, u^a, v^r) in polynomial time, where $u, v \xleftarrow{\$} \mathcal{G}$ and $a, r \xleftarrow{\$} \mathbb{Z}_q$.

Definition 8.6 (Decisional Diffie–Hellman assumption) Let $\mathcal{G}$ be a group of order q prime. We say that $\mathcal{G}$ satisfies the *Decisional Diffie–Hellman assumption* if no PPT algorithm $\mathcal{A}$ can meaningfully distinguish the probability distributions (u, v, u^a, v^a) and (u, v, u^a, v^r), where $u, v \xleftarrow{\$} \mathcal{G}$ and $a, r \xleftarrow{\$} \mathbb{Z}_q$.

8.3.3 Pairings

Let $\mathbb{G}_1 = \langle g \rangle$, $\mathbb{G}_2 = \langle h \rangle$ and $\mathbb{G}_3 = \langle G \rangle$ be efficiently samplable cyclic groups of order q prime. A map $e : \mathbb{G}_1 \times \mathbb{G}_2 \to \mathbb{G}_3$ to a group $\mathbb{G}_3$ is called a *pairing* (or bilinear map), if it satisfies the following two properties:

Bilinearity: $e(g^a, h^b) = e(g, h)^{ab}$ for all integers a, b
Non-Degenerate: $e(g, h)$ has order q in $\mathbb{G}_3$.

Moreover, we assume there exists no efficiently computable homomorphism $\psi : \mathbb{G}_1 \to \mathbb{G}_2$, while an efficient homomorphism $\phi : \mathbb{G}_2 \to \mathbb{G}_1$ does exist. Such a pairing is called a Type 2 pairing [14]. We set $g = \phi(h)$.

Since $\mathbb{G}_1$ is a prime order group, we can define the DDH problem in $\mathbb{G}_1$. Thorough this chapter we assume that the DDH assumption holds in $\mathbb{G}_1$. A prominent type of groups of which it is widely believed that they satisfy the explained assumptions is presented in [9]. These groups are also used in [3, 6, 8, 10]. It is easy to see that the DDH assumption in $\mathbb{G}_1$ implies the DDH assumption in $\mathbb{G}_3$.

We need an extra final assumption. This assumption states that a variant of the decisional Diffie–Hellman problem in Type 2 pairing groups is infeasible to solve for PPT adversaries. The problem consists on distinguishing the distributions $(g, g^a, g^b, h^b, g^{ab})$ and (g, g^a, g^b, h^b, g^r), where $g = \phi(h)$ generate $\mathbb{G}_1, \mathbb{G}_2$, respectively, and $a, b, r \overset{\$}{\leftarrow} \mathbb{Z}_q$. Notice that the problem statement does not give h out, since otherwise the problem would be trivially solvable: to distinguish whether $v = g^{ab}$ or $v = g^r$ it suffices to check whether $e(v, h) = e(g^a, h^b)$. An adversary cannot compute h from g since, by assumption, there does not exist any computable isomorphism $\psi : \mathbb{G}_1 \rightarrow \mathbb{G}_2$.

Definition 8.7 (Asymmetric DDH assumption) Let $\langle \mathbb{G}_1, \mathbb{G}_2, \mathbb{G}_3, e, \phi, g, h, q \rangle$ be a Type 2 pairing group. We say that such a pairing group satisfies the *asymmetric decisional Diffie–Hellman assumption* if no PPT algorithm $\mathcal{A}$ can distinguish the probability distributions $(g, g^a, g^b, h^b, g^{ab})$ and (g, g^a, g^b, h^b, g^r) where $g = \phi(h), h$ generate $\mathbb{G}_1, \mathbb{G}_2$, respectively, and $a, b, r \overset{\$}{\leftarrow} \mathbb{Z}_q$.

The asymmetric DDH assumption trivially implies the DDH assumption in $\mathbb{G}_1$.

8.3.4 Commutative Encryption

The next primitive plays a fundamental role in two of our protocols.

Definition 8.8 (Commutative encryption) A *commutative encryption* function $\mathcal{F} = \{F_k\}_{k \in \text{Keys } \mathcal{F}}$ is a family of computable functions $f \colon \text{Keys } \mathcal{F} \times \text{Dom } \mathcal{F} \rightarrow \text{Dom } \mathcal{F}$, defined on finite computable domains, that satisfies the properties listed below. We denote $f_a(x) := f(a, x)$.

1. Commutativity: for all $a, a' \in \text{Keys } \mathcal{F}$ we have $f_a \circ f_{a'} = f_{a'} \circ f_a$.
2. Each $f_a \colon \text{Dom } \mathcal{F} \rightarrow \text{Dom } \mathcal{F}$ is a bijection.
3. The inverse f_a^{-1} is computable in polynomial time given a.
4. The distribution of $\big(u, f_a(u), v, f_a(v)\big)$ is indistinguishable from the distribution of $\big(u, f_a(u), v, z\big)$, where $u, v, z \overset{\$}{\leftarrow} \text{Dom } \mathcal{F}$ and $a \overset{\$}{\leftarrow} \text{Keys } \mathcal{F}$.

Example 8.1 Let $\mathcal{G}$ be a group of prime order q. Let $\text{Dom } \mathcal{F} := \mathcal{G}$ and let $\text{Keys } \mathcal{F} := \mathbb{Z}_q$. Then if $\mathcal{G}$ satisfies the DDH assumption, the power function $f_a(x) = x^a \in \mathcal{G}$ is a commutative encryption function. Properties 1, 2, and 3 are trivially satisfied since $\mathcal{F}$ is the exponentiation function. Property 4 is implied by the DDH assumption. In effect, the distributions $\big(u, f_a(u), v, f_a(v)\big)$ and $\big(u, f_a(u), v, z\big)$ are precisely the distributions in the DDH assumption, since z and v^r follow the uniform distribution for $z \overset{\$}{\leftarrow} \mathcal{G}$ and $r \overset{\$}{\leftarrow} \mathbb{Z}_q$. Let us note a further property satisfied by the exponentiation function: $f_a \circ f_b = f_{ab}$ and $f_a^{-1} = f_{a^{-1}}$. We refer to this as the Property 5 of the exponentiation function. Actually, this property is exploited in our protocols, in contrast to [4], where properties 1–4 suffice for their protocols.

8.3.5 Intersection Protocol

Before giving out our protocols, it is helpful to recall the basic intersection protocol by Agrawal et al. ([2], Section 4). In this protocol there are two parties, a sender S and a receiver R, who hold private databases of the form $(id, D(id))$. Let $\mathcal{I}_S$, $\mathcal{I}_R$ be the set of identifiers in S and R's databases, respectively. At the end of the protocol S only learns $|\mathcal{I}_R|$, while R only learns $|\mathcal{I}_S|$ and $\mathcal{I}_R \cap \mathcal{I}_S$. It can later be extended to an equijoin protocol, which is slightly more technically involved. The basic ideas are the same, though.

In order to use the properties of the commutative encryption primitive, we need to map identities id to uniformly distributed random values. This is the reason why we need a *random oracle* [7] in these protocols. A random oracle is an artifice used in security proofs. It idealizes (in our case) a hash $H : \{0, 1\}^* \rightarrow \mathrm{Dom}\,\mathcal{F}$ function, which means that $H(id)$ can be considered computed by a random oracle: every time $H(\cdot)$ is evaluated for a new identity id, the output $H(id)$ is distributed uniformly at random and independently from the previous output values.

In the following, if $\mathcal{I}$ is a set (list), then we denote by $H(\mathcal{I})$ the set (list) $\{H(id)\}_{id \in \mathcal{I}}$.

8.3.5.1 Intersection Protocol

Input: S inputs $H(\mathcal{I}_S)$; R inputs $H(\mathcal{I}_R)$.

1. R generates a random $\kappa_R \xleftarrow{\$} \mathbb{Z}_q$ and computes the list $L_R = \langle\, \mathcal{I}_R,\, f_{\kappa_R}(H(\mathcal{I}_R))\,\rangle$. Next, it sends S the list L_0 given by

$$L_0 = \langle\, f_{\kappa_R}(H(\mathcal{I}_R))\,\rangle.$$

2. S generates a random $\kappa_S \xleftarrow{\$} \mathbb{Z}_q$ and send R two lists L_0', L_1. First, it sends the list L_0' based on L_0 given by

$$L_0' = \langle\, f_{\kappa_R}(H(\mathcal{I}_R)),\, f_{\kappa_S}(f_{\kappa_R}(H(\mathcal{I}_R)))\,\rangle.$$

Second, it sends R the list L_1 given by

$$L_1 = \langle\, f_{\kappa_S}(H(\mathcal{I}_S))\,\rangle.$$

3. R transforms the list L_1 into the list

$$L_1' = \langle\, f_{\kappa_R}(f_{\kappa_S}(H(\mathcal{I}_S)))\,\rangle.$$

4. R selects, with the help of L_R, all $id \in \mathcal{I}_R$ such that $f_{\kappa_R}(f_{\kappa_S}(H(id)))$ appears both in L_0' and L_1'.

Output: S outputs $|\mathcal{I}_R|$; R outputs $|\mathcal{I}_S|$ and $\mathcal{I}_S \cap \mathcal{I}_R$.

The protocol is correct since, assuming there are no hash collisions and the commutativity property of the family $\mathcal{F}$, $id \in \mathcal{I}_S \cap \mathcal{I}_R$ iff $id \in \mathcal{I}_R$, and $f_{\kappa_R}\big(f_{\kappa_S}(H(id))\big)$ $= f_{\kappa_S}\big(f_{\kappa_R}(H(id))\big)$ appears in L_0' and L_1'. Since H is modeled as a random oracle, the probability that n hash values have at least one collision equals [22]:

$$\Pr[\text{collision}] = 1 - \prod_{i=1}^{n-1} \frac{|\mathcal{G}| - i}{|\mathcal{G}|} \approx 1 - \exp\left(\frac{-n(n-1)}{2|\mathcal{G}|}\right).$$

In our protocols we use $|\mathcal{G}| \geq 2^{160}$, which renders $\Pr[\text{collision}]$ negligible. Therefore, with very high probability, the intersection protocol is correct.

8.4 A Pseudonym Scheme with Ubiquitous TTP

In this section we present a pseudonym scheme $\mathcal{P}^{\text{TTP}}$ and state its security properties. The description of the scheme starts by defining the system setup and key generation by the TTP and follows with the two fundamental protocols in the scheme: researcher supply and researcher equijoin. We assume that any two parties in the protocol communicate via a confidential channel. Our protocols distinguish between a sending and a receiving party which execute the protocols with the active help of the TTP. The sending and receiving parties send their inputs to the TTP. Finally the sending and receiving parties obtain their outputs from the TTP. This is why this scheme is called *ubiquitous TTP*, since the TTP is involved in all the exchanges between the parties, be it supply-to-researcher or researcher-to-researcher.

This scheme uses a semantically secure symmetric encryption scheme (cf. Definition 8.5). The pseudonym of individual id in researcher R_s's pseudonymized database has the form $P(id, R_s) := \text{Enc}_{K_s}(id)$, where $K_s \xleftarrow{\$} \mathcal{K}$ is a random key that the TTP secretly assigns to researcher R_s, but which is never revealed.

We next describe the scheme $\mathcal{P}^{\text{TTP}}$. The TTP is in charge of performing the following operations:

System setup. The TTP also selects a semantically secure symmetric encryption algorithm $\big(\text{Enc}_K(\cdot), \text{Dec}_K(\cdot)\big)$, with $\text{Enc}: \mathcal{K} \times \{0,1\}^M \to \{0,1\}^{M'}$ for some integers M, M' such that $M \leq M'$. Individuals, suppliers, and researchers identifiers are binary strings of length M. The TTP publishes $\langle (\text{Enc}, \text{Dec}) \rangle$.

Researcher key generation. For each researcher R_j in the system, the TTP generates a secure key as $K_j \xleftarrow{\$} \mathcal{K}$. These keys are *secret* and only known to the TTP.

Supply keys generation. This algorithm is void.

Equijoin keys generation. This algorithm is void.

Researcher supply. The operation $S_l \xrightarrow{\text{TTP}}_P R_d$ is performed as follows:

1. S_l sends to the TTP the list $\mathcal{I}_{S_l}$ of individuals in its database.

2. The TTP computes the list of pseudonyms as $\text{Enc}_{K_d}(\mathcal{I}_{S_l})$. The TTP sends back to S_l the list $\langle id, P(id, R_d) \rangle$, where $P(id, R_d) = \text{Enc}_{K_d}(id)$.
3. S_l sends to R_d the pseudonymized database $\langle P(id, R_d), PD(id, S_l) \rangle$.
4. R_d joins the data with already existing pseudonyms and new rows for new pseudonyms.

Researcher equijoin. The protocol $R_s \xrightarrow[\bowtie]{\text{TTP}} R_d$ is performed as follows:

1. R_s sends its pseudonymized database $\langle P(id, R_s), PD(id, R_s) \rangle$ to the TTP.
2. R_d sends its pseudonymized database $\langle P(id, R_d), PD(id, R_d) \rangle$ to the TTP.
3. The TTP recovers $\mathcal{I}_{R_s}$ by decrypting the pseudonyms in R_s's list. The TTP recovers $\mathcal{I}_{R_d}$ similarly.
4. For every $id \in \mathcal{I}_{R_s} \cap \mathcal{I}_{R_d}$, the TTP computes the pseudonyms $P(id, R_d) := \text{Enc}_{K_d}(id)$ and sends $\langle P(id, R_d), PD(id, R_s) \rangle$ to R_d.
5. R_d joins the data with already existing pseudonyms and new rows for new pseudonyms.

Result 1 ($\mathcal{P}^{\text{TTP}}$ is secure) *The pseudonyms' scheme $\mathcal{P}^{\text{TTP}}$ satisfies pseudonymity, unlinkability, secure equijoin, and equijoin non-transitivity provided that $\mathcal{E}$ is a semantically secure symmetric encryption scheme.*

Sketch of the proof. These properties are proven in a straightforward manner given the fact that the TTP is invoked in every algorithm, and that suppliers and researchers are given no cryptographic material.

For instance, regarding pseudonymity, one needs to prove that the distributions

$$\begin{pmatrix} id_1 & \ldots & id_{n_d} \\ \text{Enc}_{K_d}(id_1) & \ldots & \text{Enc}_{K_d}(id_{n_d}) \end{pmatrix} \text{ and } \begin{pmatrix} id_1 & \ldots & id_t & id_{t+1} \ldots id_{n_d} \\ \text{Enc}_{K_d}(id_1) & \ldots & \text{Enc}_{K_d}(id_t) & Z_{t+1} \ldots Z_{n_d} \end{pmatrix}$$

are indistinguishable, where $Z_{t+1}, \ldots, Z_{n_d} \xleftarrow{\$} \{0, 1\}^{M'}$. Given that $\mathcal{E}$ is semantically secure, we know that $(id, \text{Enc}_{K_S}(id))$ is indistinguishable from (id, Z), for any $id \in \{0, 1\}^*$ and $Z \xleftarrow{\$} \{0, 1\}^{M'}$. The result then follows by applying a standard hybrid argument [15].

Regarding unlinkability, we need to prove that the distributions

$$\begin{pmatrix} id_{t+1} & \ldots & id_m \\ \text{Enc}_{K_d}(id_{t+1}) & \ldots & \text{Enc}_{K_d}(id_m) \\ \text{Enc}_{K_s}(id_{t+1}) & \ldots & \text{Enc}_{K_s}(id_m) \end{pmatrix} \text{ and } \begin{pmatrix} id_{t+1} & \ldots & id_m \\ \text{Enc}_{K_d}(id_{t+1}) & \ldots & \text{Enc}_{K_d}(id_m) \\ Z_{t+1} & \ldots & Z_m \end{pmatrix}$$

are indistinguishable. Since $\mathcal{E}$ is semantically secure, we know that

$$\begin{pmatrix} id_{t+1} & \ldots & id_m \\ \text{Enc}_{K_d}(id_{t+1}) & \ldots & \text{Enc}_{K_d}(id_m) \end{pmatrix} \text{ and } \begin{pmatrix} id_{t+1} \ldots id_m \\ Z_{t+1} \ldots Z_m \end{pmatrix}$$

are indistinguishable, and that

$$\begin{pmatrix} id_{t+1} & \cdots & id_m \\ \mathrm{Enc}_{K_s}(id_{t+1}) & \cdots & \mathrm{Enc}_{K_s}(id_m) \end{pmatrix} \quad \text{and} \quad \begin{pmatrix} id_{t+1} \cdots id_m \\ Z_{t+1} \cdots Z_m \end{pmatrix}$$

are indistinguishable. These two facts imply that the distributions involved in the unlinkability definition are also indistinguishable.

Finally, secure equijoin and equijoin non-transitivity are implied by the fact that the operation "equijoin" is performed by the trusted third party.   □

The scheme $\mathcal{P}^{\mathrm{TTP}}$ with ubiquitous TTP reaches all the requested security properties at the expense of the TTP being involved in every single transaction in the system. This is something that could be undesirable in certain settings. For instance, if the number of transactions is high, then the TTP becomes a potential bottleneck in the system.

In the next section we propose protocols where the TTP is only required to hand on certain cryptographic keys to the parties. Apart from that, the TTP is not involved in any transaction, be it supplier-to-researcher or researcher-to-researcher.

8.5 A Basic Pseudonym Scheme with Light TTP

In this section we present a basic pseudonym scheme $\mathcal{P}^{\mathrm{basic}}$ and state its security properties. This scheme fulfills all the security properties we have identified, except for equijoin non-transitivity. It is included here as a first step toward a scheme satisfying all four security properties, to be presented in Section 8.6.

The description of the scheme starts with the system setup and key generation/distribution by the TTP and follows with the two fundamental protocols in the scheme: Researcher Supply and Researcher Equijoin. These protocols distinguish between a sending and a receiving party which are both provided with the necessary cryptographic keys by the TTP. The sending party (supplier or researcher) sends a chunk of data and possibly some temporary cryptographic keys to the receiver (researcher).

In this scheme we use commutative encryption both for creating pseudonyms and implementing the protocols. Researcher R_j's pseudonyms will depend on integers x_j. These quantities are secret and only known to the TTP. Researcher R_j's pseudonyms are elements in $\mathcal{G}$ and take the form $P(id, R_j) = f_{x_j}(H(id))$, where $\mathcal{G}$ and f_{x_j} are defined as in Example 8.1, and $H: \{0, 1\}^* \to \mathcal{G}$ is hash function. Our equijoin protocol heavily relies in the equijoin protocol of Agrawal et al. [2]. To give the basic idea behind our protocol, we illustrate it by extending the intersection algorithm described in Section 8.3.5 to a pseudonyms intersection algorithm between R_s and R_d.

Recall that in the intersection algorithm from Section 8.3.5, the inputs of the *Sender S* and *Receiver R* parties are $H(\mathcal{I}_S)$ and $H(\mathcal{I}_R)$, respectively, where $\mathcal{I}_R, \mathcal{I}_S$ are the sets of identities held by each party. In our case, we have that R_s does not hold a set of identities but a set of pseudonyms of the form $P(id, R_s) = H(id)^{x_s}$, and similarly, R_d holds a set of pseudonyms $P(id, R_d) = H(id)^{x_d}$, where

$x_s, x_d \in \mathbb{Z}_q$ are unknown to R_s, R_d, respectively. The idea is that the TTP feeds R_s (respectively R_d) with a pseudonyms' intersection key $\beta \cdot x_s^{-1}$ (respectively $\beta \cdot x_d^{-1}$) for $\beta \xleftarrow{\$} \mathbb{Z}_q$. This allows researchers R_s, R_d to respectively compute the commutative encryptions $f_{\beta \cdot x_s^{-1}}$ and $f_{\beta \cdot x_d^{-1}}$ of their respective pseudonyms' sets $\mathcal{P}_{R_s}$ and $\mathcal{P}_{R_d}$. That is, in the case of researcher R_s, it computes

$$f_{\beta \cdot x_s^{-1}}\big(P(id, R_s)\big) = f_{\beta \cdot x_s^{-1}}\big(f_{x_s}(H(id))\big) = f_\beta\big(H(id)\big),$$

where the last equality is due to the property $f_a \circ f_b = f_{ab}$ of the exponentiation function family $\mathcal{F}$. This property is not used in [2], and this is one of the technical novelties with respect to the protocol in Section 8.3.5. Therefore, researchers end up with a *common representation* of their pseudonyms, namely researcher R_s obtains the set $\{H(\mathcal{I}_s)^\beta\}$, while researcher R_d obtains the set $\{H(\mathcal{I}_d)^\beta\}$. At this point, R_s and R_d can run the intersection protocol from Section 8.3.5, with inputs $\{H(\mathcal{I}_s)^\beta\}$ and $\{H(\mathcal{I}_d)^\beta\}$, respectively. As a result, R_s gets as output $|\mathcal{P}_{\mathcal{I}_s}|$, while R_d gets as output $|\mathcal{P}_{\mathcal{I}_d}|$ and $\mathcal{P}_{\mathcal{I}_s} \cap \mathcal{P}_{\mathcal{I}_d}$.

Here follows the description of the pseudonyms scheme $\mathcal{P}^{\text{basic}}$. The TTP is in charge of performing the following operations:

System setup. The TTP chooses a cyclic group $\langle \mathcal{G}, p \rangle$ where the decisional Diffie–Hellman assumption is believed to hold. It next picks a hash function $H : \{0, 1\}^\ell \to \mathcal{G}$ for integer ℓ. The TTP also selects a semantically secure symmetric encryption algorithm $\big(\text{Enc}_K(\cdot), \text{Dec}_K(\cdot)\big)$, with $\text{Enc} : \mathcal{G} \times \{0, 1\}^M \to \{0, 1\}^{M'}$ for integers M, M' with $M \leq M'$. The TTP publishes $\langle \mathcal{G}, p, H, (\text{Enc}, \text{Dec}) \rangle$.

Researcher key generation. For each researcher R_j in the system, the TTP generates a secure key as $x_j \xleftarrow{\$} \mathbb{Z}_q$. These keys are *never delivered* to the researcher.

Supply key generation. For each pair supplier/researcher (S_l, R_j), the TTP recovers the researcher's assigned key $x_j \in \mathbb{Z}_q$ and hands it to the supplier through a secure channel. These keys are *never delivered* to any researcher.

Equijoin keys generation. For each pair (R_s, R_d) of researchers that is allowed to perform the protocol $R_s \longrightarrow_{\bowtie} R_d$ (or $R_d \longrightarrow_{\bowtie} R_s$), the TTP generates a random $\beta_{s,d} \in \mathbb{Z}_q$ and sends $\beta_{s,d} \cdot x_s^{-1}$ (respectively $\beta_{s,d} \cdot x_d^{-1}$) to R_s (respectively R_d).

Researcher supply. The operation $S_l \to_P R_d$ is performed as follows:

1. S_l computes $P(id, R_d) = f_{x_j}(H(id))$ for $id \in \mathcal{I}_{S_l}$ and sends to R_d the pseudonymized list $\langle P(id, R_d), PD(id, S_l) \rangle$.
2. R_d joins the data with already existing pseudonyms and new rows for new pseudonyms.

Researcher equijoin. The protocol $R_s \to_{\bowtie} R_d$ is performed as follows:

1. R_s computes $f_{\beta_{s,d} \cdot x_s^{-1}}\big(\mathcal{P}_{R_s}\big)$ and obtains the set $\{H(\mathcal{I}_s)^{\beta_{s,d}}\}$.

2. R_d computes $f_{\beta_{s,d}\cdot x_d^{-1}}(\mathcal{P}_{R_d})$ and obtains the set $\{H(\mathcal{I}_d)^{\beta_{s,d}}\}$.
3. R_s and R_d run the Agrawal et al.'s equijoin protocol ([2], Section 4) with
   inputs $\{(H(id)^{\beta_{s,d}}, PD(id, R_s))\}_{\mathcal{I}_s}$ and $\{(H(id)^{\beta_{s,d}}, PD(id, R_d))\}_{\mathcal{I}_d}$,
   respectively. That is,

   a. R_d generates a random $\kappa_d \xleftarrow{\$} \mathbb{Z}_q$ and sends R_s the list L_0 given by

   $$L_0 = \langle\ f_{\kappa_d}(H(id)^{\beta_{s,d}})\ \rangle_{\mathcal{I}_d}.$$

   b. R_s generates random $\kappa_s, \kappa_s' \xleftarrow{\$} \mathbb{Z}_q$ and sends R_d two lists L_0', L_1. First,
   it creates the list L_0' based on L_0 given by

   $$L_0' = \langle f_{\kappa_d}(H(id)^{\beta_{s,d}}),\ f_{\kappa_s}\left(f_{\kappa_d}(H(id)^{\beta_{s,d}})\right),\ f_{\kappa_s'}\left(f_{\kappa_d}(H(id)^{\beta_{s,d}})\right)\rangle_{\mathcal{I}_d}.$$

   Second, it creates the list L_1 given by

   $$L_1 = \left\langle\ f_{\kappa_s}(H(\overline{id})^{\beta_{s,d}}),\ \mathrm{Enc}_{K_s(\overline{id})}(PD(\overline{id}, R_s))\ \right\rangle_{\mathcal{I}_s},$$

   where $K_s(\overline{id}) = f_{\kappa_s'}(H(\overline{id})^{\beta_{s,d}})$ for $\overline{id} \in \mathcal{I}_s$.
   c. Based on L_0' the researcher R_d calculates, by applying $f_{\kappa_d}^{-1}$, the list

   $$L_2 = \langle\ H(id)^{\beta_{s,d}},\ f_{\kappa_s}(H(id)^{\beta_{s,d}}),\ f_{\kappa_s'}(H(id)^{\beta_{s,d}})\rangle_{\mathcal{I}_d}.$$

   d. Then R_d determines the elements in the list L_1, L_2 such that
   $f_{\kappa_s}(H(\overline{id})^{\beta_{s,d}}) = f_{\kappa_s}(H(id)^{\beta_{s,d}})$. For those elements, which single
   out the pseudonyms such that $id \in \mathcal{I}_s \cap \mathcal{I}_d$, researcher R_d uses the
   corresponding values $f_{\kappa_s'}(H(id)^{\beta_{s,d}}) = K_s(id)$ in L_2 to decrypt

   $$PD(id, R_s) = \mathrm{Dec}_{K_s(\overline{id})}\left(\mathrm{Enc}_{K_s(\overline{id})}(PD(id, R_s))\right).$$

   e. Finally, R_d joins the new data $PD(id, R_s)$ with its already existing
   data on $P(id, R_d)$.

Researcher equijoin correctness. It is easy to see that the intersection algorithm
is correct, i.e., at the end of the protocol R_d learns $\left(P(id, R_d), PD(id, R_s)\right)$
for $id \in \mathcal{I}_{R_s} \cap \mathcal{I}_{R_d}$, as long as the hash function $H : \{0, 1\}^\ell \to \mathcal{G}$ does not
present collisions.

Next we show that the scheme $\mathcal{P}^{\mathrm{basic}}$ satisfies pseudonymity, unlinkability, and
secure equijoin.

Result 2 *The pseudonym scheme* $\mathcal{P}^{\mathrm{basic}}$ *has pseudonymity provided that* $\mathcal{F}$ *is a
commutative encryption family.*

Proof We want to show that the distributions

$$\begin{pmatrix} id_1 & \cdots & id_{n_d} \\ f_{x_d}\big(H(id_1)\big) & \cdots & f_{x_d}\big(H(id_{n_d})\big) \end{pmatrix} \text{ and } \begin{pmatrix} id_1 & \cdots & id_t & id_{t+1} & \cdots & id_{n_d} \\ f_{x_d}\big(H(id_1)\big) & \cdots & f_{x_d}\big(H(id_t)\big) & Z_{t+1} & \cdots & Z_{n_d} \end{pmatrix}$$

are indistinguishable, where $Z_{t+1}, \ldots, Z_{n_d} \xleftarrow{\$} \mathcal{G}$. Given that $\mathcal{F}$ is a commutative encryption family, we know that the distributions

$$\big(H(id), f_{x_d}\big(H(id)\big), H(id'), f_{x_d}\big(H(id')\big)\big) \text{ and } \big(H(id), f_{x_d}\big(H(id)\big), H(id'), Z\big),$$

where $id, id' \in \{0, 1\}^l$, $Z \xleftarrow{\$} \mathcal{G}$, and $x_d \xleftarrow{\$} \text{Dom } \mathcal{F}$ are indistinguishable, since for a random oracle H the values $H(id)$, $H(id')$ follow a uniformly random distribution. The result then follows by applying a standard hybrid argument [2, 15]. □

Result 3 *The pseudonym scheme* $\mathcal{P}^{\text{basic}}$ *has unlinkability provided that* $\mathcal{F}$ *is a commutative encryption family.*

Proof We want to show that the distributions

$$\begin{pmatrix} id_t & \cdots & id_m \\ f_{x_d}\big(H(id_t)\big) & \cdots & f_{x_d}\big(H(id_m)\big) \\ f_{x_s}\big(H(id_t)\big) & \cdots & f_{x_s}\big(H(id_m)\big) \end{pmatrix} \text{ and } \begin{pmatrix} id_{t+1} & \cdots & id_m \\ f_{x_d}\big(H(id_t)\big) & \cdots & f_{x_d}\big(H(id_m)\big) \\ Z_{t+1} & \cdots & Z_m \end{pmatrix}$$

are indistinguishable, where $Z_{t+1}, \ldots, Z_m \xleftarrow{\$} \mathcal{G}$, $x_d, x_s \xleftarrow{\$} \text{Keys } \mathcal{F}$. Given that $\mathcal{F}$ is a commutative encryption family, we use the following lemma.

Lemma 8.1 (Agrawal et al. [2]) *For any integer n, the distributions of the tuples*

$$\begin{pmatrix} s_1 & \cdots & s_n \\ f_{x_e}(s_1) & \cdots & f_{x_e}(s_n) \\ f_{x_d}(s_1) & \cdots & f_{x_d}(s_n) \end{pmatrix} \text{ and } \begin{pmatrix} s_1 & \cdots & s_n \\ y_1 & \cdots & y_n \\ z_1 & \cdots & z_n \end{pmatrix}$$

are computationally indistinguishable, where $0 \le n$, $\forall i : s_i, y_i, z_i \xleftarrow{\$} \text{Dom } \mathcal{F}$, *and* $x_d, x_s \xleftarrow{\$} \text{Keys } \mathcal{F}$, *provided that* $\mathcal{F}$ *is a commutative encryption family.*

Now, if we identify $s_i := H(id_i)$, the result holds due to the fact that H is a random oracle. □

Result 4 *The pseudonym scheme* $\mathcal{P}^{\text{basic}}$ *provides secure equijoin provided that* $\mathcal{F}$ *is a commutative encryption family.*

Proof This result follows from the fact that our equijoin protocol is an extension of the equijoin protocol by Agrawal et al. The only change is on the inputs to the protocol. Let us see that. In ([2], Section 4) the parties R and S input the sets

$\{(H(id), D(id))\}_{id \in \mathcal{I}_R}$ and $\{(H(id), D(id))\}_{id \in \mathcal{I}_S}$, respectively. The output they obtain is $|\mathcal{I}_R|$, $|\mathcal{I}_S|$, and the equijoin of their databases.

In our protocol, parties R_s and R_d input the sets $\{(P(id, R_s), PD(id, R_s))\}_{id \in \mathcal{I}_{R_s}}$ and $\{(P(id, R_d), PD(id, R_d))\}_{id \in \mathcal{I}_{R_d}}$, respectively. The output they obtain is $|\mathcal{I}_{R_s}|$, $|\mathcal{I}_{R_d}|$, and the equijoin of their pseudonymized databases.

Now, from the discussion in Section 8.3.5, we know (and this can also be straight-forwardly checked by looking at the protocol in ([2], Section 4.3)) that our equijoin protocol is obtained by changing the inputs to the Agrawal *et al.* equijoin protocol. More precisely, we replace $\{(H(id), D(id))\}_{id \in \mathcal{I}_R}$ and $\{(H(id), D(id))\}_{id \in \mathcal{I}_S}$ by $\{(H(id)^{\beta_{s,d}}, PD(id, R_s))\}_{id \in \mathcal{I}_{R_s}}$ and $\{(H(id)^{\beta_{s,d}}, PD(id, R_d))\}_{id \in \mathcal{I}_{R_d}}$, respectively. As a consequence, the output is as expected, and the secure equijoin property is preserved, since both $H(id)$ and $H(id)^{\beta_{s,d}}$ follow the uniform distribution for any id.   □

Alas, the scheme $\mathcal{P}^{\text{basic}}$ does not satisfy the equijoin non-transitivity property. Indeed,

Result 5 (Security breach with colluding researchers) *The scheme $\mathcal{P}^{\text{basic}}$ does not provide equijoin non-transitivity.*

Proof Let us assume the pairs of researchers R_s, R_d and R_d, R_o are allowed to compute the equijoin of the corresponding databases. If these researchers collude, they can compute cryptographic keys enabling translation of $P(id, R_s)$ into $P(id, R_d)$, and the translation of pseudonyms $P(id, R_d)$ into $P(id, R_o)$ as follows. Remember the intersection key for R_s is $\beta_{s,d} \cdot x_s^{-1}$, while for R_d is $\beta_{s,d} \cdot x_d^{-1}$. Then $\beta_{s,d} \cdot x_s^{-1}/(\beta_{s,d} \cdot x_d^{-1}) = x_s^{-1}x_d$ and $f_{x_s^{-1}x_d}(P(id, R_s)) = P(id, R_d)$. And similarly for researchers R_d, R_o. Therefore a transformation $P(id, R_s) \mapsto P(id, R_d) \mapsto P(id, R_o)$ can be computed for any pseudonym $P(id, R_s)$ in possession of R_s, which allows R_s, R_d, R_o to compute the equijoin $\mathcal{P}_{R_s} \cap \mathcal{P}_{R_o}$. As a result, equijoin non-transitivity is broken and the scheme is not fully secure.   □

In the next section we propose a fully secure protocol using pairings.

8.6 A Fully Secure Pseudonym Scheme with Light TTP

The problem with the previous solution lied on the fact that malicious researchers could translate pseudonyms from researcher R_s to researcher R_o by operating with the equijoin keys. This was possible because the equijoin keys were elements in $\mathbb{Z}_q$ that could be manipulated to produce keys enabling translation of pseudonyms. The proposal in this section seeks to solve the problem by giving out keys as elements in a finite group instead of integers in a modular ring. We accomplish that by using pairing groups and by making equijoin keys elements in $\mathbb{G}_2 = \langle h \rangle$. In short, the equijoin protocol remains essentially the same, but the researchers' equijoin keys will be $h^{\beta_{s,d} \cdot x_s^{-1}}$ for R_s (in contrast to $\beta_{s,d} \cdot x_s^{-1}$ for the basic protocol) and $h^{\beta_{s,d} \cdot x_d^{-1}}$ for R_d (in contrast to $\beta_{s,d} \cdot x_d^{-1}$ for the basic protocol). Informally, when R_s and

R_d collude to break equijoin non-transitivity in this new situation, they will need to compute $h^{x_s^{-1} x_d}$ from the elements $h^{\beta_{s,d} \cdot x_s^{-1}}$ and $h^{\beta_{s,d} \cdot x_d^{-1}}$, which would amount to solving the computational Diffie–Hellman problem in $\mathbb{G}_2$. However, the latter is assumed to be infeasible.

An important change to be noticed is that now R_s, R_d do not input $\{H(\mathcal{I}_s)^{\beta_{s,d}}\}$ and $\{H(\mathcal{I}_d)^{\beta_{s,d}}\}$, respectively, to the equijoin protocol, but $\{e(H(\mathcal{I}_s), h)^{\beta_{s,d}}\}$ and $\{e(H(\mathcal{I}_d), h)^{\beta_{s,d}}\}$. In the case of R_s, the new set is computed as

$$e\left(P(id, R_s), h^{\beta_{s,d} \cdot x_s^{-1}}\right) = e\left(H(id)^{x_s}, h^{\beta_{s,d} \cdot x_s^{-1}}\right)$$
$$= e\left(H(id)^{x_s \cdot x_s^{-1}}, h\right)^{\beta_{s,d}} = e\left(H(id), h\right)^{\beta_{s,d}},$$

thanks to bilinearity of the pairing $e(\cdot, \cdot)$. To be more precise, the new equijoin protocol works with elements $U \in \mathbb{G}_3$ and uses the commutative encryption function family $\mathcal{F}' := \{F_a \colon U \mapsto U^a\}_{a \in \mathbb{Z}_q}$.

We proceed to describe the pseudonyms scheme $\mathcal{P}^{\mathrm{advanced}}$ that provides equijoin non-transitivity against colluding researchers.

System setup. The TTP chooses a pairing group $\langle \mathbb{G}_1, \mathbb{G}_2, \mathbb{G}_3, e, g, q \rangle$. It next picks a hash function $H \colon \{0, 1\}^\ell \to \mathbb{G}_1$. Individuals' identifiers are binary strings of length ℓ. The TTP also selects a semantically secure symmetric encryption algorithm $\left(\mathrm{Enc}_K(\cdot), \mathrm{Dec}_K(\cdot)\right)$, where K denotes the encryption key. The TTP publishes $\langle \mathbb{G}_1, \mathbb{G}_2, \mathbb{G}_3, e, \phi, g, q, H, (\mathrm{Enc}, \mathrm{Dec}) \rangle$.

All operations are as in the basic scheme with the only exception of the equijoin keys generation and equijoin algorithms. For the comprehension of the new protocols, let us note the following equivalences

$$F_a\left(e(u, h)\right) = e(u, h)^a = e(u, h^a) = e(u^a, h) = e(f_a(u), h) \qquad (8.1)$$

for any $a \in \mathbb{Z}_q$, $u \in \mathbb{G}_1$, $h \in \mathbb{G}_2$.

Equijoin keys generation. For each pair (R_s, R_d) of researchers that is allowed to perform the protocol $R_s \longrightarrow_{\bowtie} R_d$, the TTP generates a random $\beta_{s,d} \in \mathbb{Z}_q$ and sends $h^{\beta_{s,d} \cdot x_s^{-1}}$ to R_s and $h^{\beta_{s,d} \cdot x_d^{-1}}$ to R_d through a secure channel.

Researchers equijoin The protocol $R_s \to_{\bowtie} R_d$ is performed as follows:

1. R_s computes $e\left(\mathcal{P}_{R_s}, h^{\beta_{s,d} \cdot x_s^{-1}}\right)$ and obtains the set $\left\{e\left(H(\mathcal{I}_s)^{\beta_{s,d}}, h\right)\right\}$.
2. R_d computes $e\left(\mathcal{P}_{R_d}, h^{\beta_{s,d} \cdot x_d^{-1}}\right)$ and obtains the set $\left\{e\left(H(\mathcal{I}_d)^{\beta_{s,d}}, h\right)\right\}$.
3. R_s and R_d run Agrawal et al.'s equijoin protocol ([2], Section 4) but with the commutative encryption family $\{F_a \colon U \mapsto U^a\}_{a \in \mathbb{Z}_q}$ and inputs $\{(e\left(H(id), h\right)^{\beta_{s,d}}, PD(id, R_s))\}_{\mathcal{I}_{R_s}}$ and $\{(e(H(id), h)^{\beta_{s,d}}, PD(id, R_d))\}_{\mathcal{I}_{R_d}}$, respectively. That is,

   a. R_d generates a random $\kappa_d \xleftarrow{\$} \mathbb{Z}_q$ and sends R_s the list L_0 given by

$$L_0 = \langle\, F_{\kappa_d}\left(e(H(id), h)^{\beta_{s,d}}\right) \,\rangle_{\mathcal{I}_d}.$$

b. R_s generates random $\kappa_s, \kappa'_s \xleftarrow{\$} \mathbb{Z}_q$ and sends R_d two lists L'_0, L_1. First, it creates the list L'_0 based on L_0 given by

$$L'_0 = \left\langle F_{\kappa_d}\left(e(H(id), h)^{\beta_{s,d}}\right), \; F_{\kappa_s}\left(F_{\kappa_d}\left(e(H(id), h)^{\beta_{s,d}}\right)\right), \right.$$
$$\left. F_{\kappa'_s}\left(F_{\kappa_d}\left(e(H(id), h)^{\beta_{s,d}}\right)\right) \right\rangle_{\mathcal{I}_d}.$$

Second, it creates the list L_1 given by

$$L_1 = \left\langle F_{\kappa_s}\left(e(H(\overline{id}), h)^{\beta_{s,d}}\right), \; \mathrm{Enc}_{K_s(\overline{id})}\left(PD(\overline{id}, R_s)\right) \right\rangle_{\mathcal{I}_s},$$

where $K_s(\overline{id}) = F_{\kappa'_s}\left(e(H(\overline{id}), h)^{\beta_{s,d}}\right)$ for $\overline{id} \in \mathcal{I}_s$.

c. Based on L'_0 the researcher R_d calculates, by applying $F_{\kappa_d}^{-1}$, the list

$$L_2 = \left\langle e(H(id), h)^{\beta_{s,d}}, \; F_{\kappa_s}\left(e(H(id), h)^{\beta_{s,d}}\right), \; F_{\kappa'_s}\left(e(H(id), h)^{\beta_{s,d}}\right) \right\rangle_{\mathcal{I}_d}.$$

d. Then R_d determines the elements in the list L_1, L_2, such that $F_{\kappa_s}\left(e(H(\overline{id}), h)^{\beta_{s,d}}\right) = F_{\kappa_s}\left(e(H(id), h)^{\beta_{s,d}}\right)$. For those elements, which single out the pseudonyms such that $id \in \mathcal{I}_s \cap \mathcal{I}_d$, researcher R_d uses the corresponding values

$$F_{\kappa'_s}\left(e(H(id), h)^{\beta_{s,d}}\right) = K_s(id)$$

in L_2 to decrypt

$$PD(id, R_s) = \mathrm{Dec}_{K_s(\overline{id})}\left(\mathrm{Enc}_{K_s(\overline{id})}\left(PD(id, R_s)\right)\right).$$

e. Finally, R_d joins the new data $PD(id, R_s)$ with its already existing data on $P(id, R_d)$.

Researcher equijoin correctness. It is easy to see that the equijoin algorithm is correct, i.e., at the end of the protocol R_d learns $\left(P(id, R_d), PD(id, R_s)\right)$ for $id \in \mathcal{I}_{R_s} \cap \mathcal{I}_{R_d}$, as long as the hash function $H : \{0, 1\}^\ell \to \mathbb{G}_1$ does not present collisions.

The following results follow directly by extending the corresponding results from Section 8.5.

Result 6 *The pseudonym scheme $\mathcal{P}^{\mathrm{advanced}}$ has pseudonymity provided that $\mathcal{F}'$ is a commutative encryption family.*

Result 7 *The pseudonym scheme $\mathcal{P}^{\mathrm{advanced}}$ has unlinkability provided that $\mathcal{F}'$ is a commutative encryption family.*

Result 8 *The pseudonym scheme* $\mathcal{P}^{\text{advanced}}$ *has secure equijoin provided that* $\mathcal{F}'$ *is a commutative encryption family.*

Next, we show that $\mathcal{P}^{\text{advanced}}$ satisfies the equijoin non-transitivity property.

Result 9 *The pseudonym scheme* $\mathcal{P}^{\text{advanced}}$ *has secure equijoin transitivity provided that the asymmetric DDH assumption holds.*

Proof Let us first recall that the asymmetric DDH assumption states the indistinguishability of the probability distributions $(g, g^a, g^b, h^b, g^{ab})$ and (g, g^a, g^b, h^b, g^r), where $g = \phi(h)$, h generate $\mathbb{G}_1$, $\mathbb{G}_2$, respectively, and $a, b, r \xleftarrow{\$} \mathbb{Z}_q$.

To convey this proof we use a different proof technique from those previously deployed both in this chapter and in [2]. We need to *program* the random oracle. This means that H being a random oracle, the values $H(id)$ are simulated to the adversary. The simulator answers $H(id_i)$ as $(g^a)^{\lambda_i}$ for $id_i \notin \mathcal{I}_{R_d}$, where $\lambda_i \xleftarrow{\$} \mathbb{Z}_q$, and answers $H(id_i)$ as g^{λ_i} for $id_i \in \mathcal{I}_{R_d}$, where $\lambda_i \xleftarrow{\$} \mathbb{Z}_q$. It takes $x_s, x_d, \alpha, \beta \xleftarrow{\$} \mathbb{Z}_q$. Additionally, it picks $\overline{h} \xleftarrow{\$} \mathbb{G}_2$ and defines $\phi(\overline{h}) = \overline{g} \in \mathbb{G}_1$. Next, for the pair (R_s, R_d), it sets as R_s's equijoin key the quantity $(\overline{h})^{\alpha \cdot x_s^{-1}}$; while for R_d it is set to $(\overline{h})^{\alpha \cdot x_d^{-1}}$. Next, for the pair (R_d, R_o), it sets as R_d's equijoin key the quantity $(h^b)^{\beta \cdot x_d^{-1}}$, while for R_o it is set to $(\overline{h})^{\beta}$. The pseudonyms are simulated as follows:

- $P(id_i, R_s) = \overline{g}^{\lambda_i x_s}$ for $id_i \in \mathcal{I}_{R_d} \cap \mathcal{I}_{R_s}$
- $P(id_i, R_s) = (g^a)^{\lambda_i x_s}$ for $(id_i \in \mathcal{I}_{R_s}) \wedge (id_i \notin \mathcal{I}_{R_d})$
- $P(id_i, R_d) = \overline{g}^{\lambda_i x_d}$ for $id_i \in \mathcal{I}_{R_d}$
- $P(id_i, R_o) = (g^b)^{\lambda_i}$ for $id_i \in \mathcal{I}_{R_d} \cap \mathcal{I}_{R_o}$
- $P(id_i, R_o) = (g^{ab})^{\lambda_i}$ for $(id_i \in \mathcal{I}_{R_o}) \wedge (id_i \notin \mathcal{I}_{R_d})$

The above simulation is consistent with the adversarial's view. For instance, we have that for any $id \in \mathcal{I}_{R_d} \cap \mathcal{I}_{R_s}$,

$$e\left(P(id, R_s), (\overline{h})^{\alpha \cdot x_s^{-1}}\right) = e(\overline{g}, h)^{\alpha \lambda_i} = e\left(P(id, R_d), (\overline{h})^{\alpha \cdot x_d^{-1}}\right)$$

and for any $id \in \mathcal{I}_{R_d} \cap \mathcal{I}_{R_o}$,

$$e\left(P(id, R_d), (h^b)^{\beta \cdot x_d^{-1}}\right) = e(\overline{g}, h)^{\beta b \lambda_i} = e(g, \overline{h})^{\beta b \lambda_i} = e\left(P(id, R_o), (\overline{h})^{\beta}\right) \quad (8.2)$$

where (8.2) holds because any $h, \overline{h} \in \mathbb{G}_2$ satisfy that $e(\phi(h), \overline{h}) = e(\phi(\overline{h}), h)$, where $\phi : \mathbb{G}_2 \to \mathbb{G}_1$ is an efficiently computable homomorphism.

Finally, since g^{ab} cannot be distinguished from random g^r, and thus they can be swapped in the above expressions, it follows that pseudonyms $P(id, R_o)$ outside the intersection $\mathcal{I}_{R_d} \cap \mathcal{I}_{R_s} \cap \mathcal{I}_{R_o}$ are indistinguishable from random pseudonyms. Thus, the adversary cannot match pseudonyms $P(id, R_s)$ to pseudonyms $P(id, R_o)$ for $id \in (\mathcal{I}_{R_s} \cap \mathcal{I}_{R_o}) - (\mathcal{I}_{R_d} \cap \mathcal{I}_{R_s} \cap \mathcal{I}_{R_o})$.   □

8.7 Conclusion

This chapter describes pseudonymization and equijoin protocols aimed at building pseudonymized data sharing systems. Our pseudonymization algorithm produces unlinkable pseudonyms sets, yet allows secure intersection between them, provided that certain cryptographic keys are available. We have presented three schemes: a first scheme uses a mighty TTP which is invoked in every algorithm; the last two schemes use a 'light' TTP which act as a key distribution center. Our last two schemes are proven secure in the Random Oracle Model. One problem that is left open is to provide the light-TTP functionality without resorting to the random oracle idealization.

References

1. ACGT. Advancing clinico-genomic clinical trials on cancer: Open grid services for improving medical knowledge discovery. http://eu-acgt.org/.
2. Agrawal R., Evfimievski A.V., and Srikant R., Information sharing across private databases. In: *SIGMOD Conference*, ACM Press, New York, NY, pp. 86–97, 2003.
3. Ateniese G., Camenisch J., and de Medeiros B. Untraceable RFID tags via insubvertible encryption. In: *ACM Conference on Computer and Communications Security*, pp. 92–101, 2005.
4. Authority D.D.P. Pseudonimisering persoonsgegevens bij risicoverevening. http://www.cbpweb.nl/documenten/uit_z2006-1328.shtml?refer= true&theme=purple, 2007.
5. Authority D.D.P. Landelijke zorgregistraties (national healthcare registrations), www.dutchdpa.nl, 2005.
6. Ballard L., Green M., de Medeiros B., and Monrose F. Correlation-resistant storage via keyword-searchable encryption. Cryptology ePrint Archive, Report 2005/417, http://eprint.iacr.org/, 2005.
7. Bellare M. and Rogaway P. Random oracles are practical: A paradigm for designing efficient protocols. In: *Proceedings of the 1st ACM CCS, ACM Press, New York, NY*, pp. 62–73, 1993. Accessed date: 05/05/1988.
8. Boneh D., Boyen X., and Shacham H. Short group signatures. In: *CRYPTO*, Lecture Notes in Computer Science, vol. 3152, Springer, New York, NY, pp. 41–55, 2004. Accessed date: 20/10/1995.
9. Boneh D., Lynn B., and Shacham H. Short signatures from the Weil pairing. *Journal of Cryptology*, 17(4):297–319, 2004.
10. Camenisch J., Hohenberger S., and Lysyanskaya A. Compact e-cash. In: *EUROCRYPT*, Lecture Notes in Computer Science, vol. 3494, Springer, New York, NY, pp. 302–321, 2005.
11. Clef: Clinical e-science framework. http://www.clinical-escience.org/.
12. Domingo-Ferrer J. (ed). *Inference Control in Statistical Databases, from Theory to Practice*, Lecture Notes in Computer Science, vol 2316, Springer, New York, NY, 2002.
13. Domingo-Ferrer J. and Franconi L. (eds.). *Privacy in Statistical Databases*, CENEX-SDC Project International Conference, PSD 2006, Lecture Notes in Computer Science, vol 4302, Springer, New York, NY, 2006.

14. Galbraith S.D., Paterson K.G., and Smart N.P. Pairings for cryptographers. *Discrete Applied Mathematics*, 156(16):3113–3121, 2008.
15. Goldreich O. *Foundations of Cryptography II – Basic Applications*. Cambridge University Press, Cambridge, 1st edition, 2004.
16. I. O. for Standardization. ISO/TS 25237:2008, Health Informatics – Pseudonymization, 2008.
17. Knaupa P., Gardeb S., Merzweilerc A., Graf N., Schillin F., Weberf R., and Hauxg R. Towards shared patient records: An architecture for using routine data for nationwide research. *International Journal of Medical Informatics*, 75:191–200, 2004.
18. Malin B. Why pseudonyms don't anonymize: A computational re-identification analysis of genomic data privacy protection systems. Laboratory for International Data Privacy at Carnegie Mellon University, http://privacy.cs.cmu.edu/dataprivacy/projects/linkage/lidap-wp19.pdf.
19. Massey J.L. An introduction to contemporary cryptology. In: *Proceedings of the IEEE*, vol 76, IEEE, 2008. Accessed date: 19/08/2004.
20. Riedl B., Grascher V., Fenz S., and Neubauer T. Pseudonymization for improving the privacy in e-health applications. *In: HICSS*, IEEE Computer Society, Big Island, Hawaii, USA, p. 255, 2008.
21. Shamir A. On the power of commutativity in cryptography. *In: ICALP*, Noordweijkerhout, The Netherland, Lecture Notes in Computer Science, vol 85, Springer, New York, NY, pp. 582–595, 1980.
22. Stinson, D.R. *Cryptography: Theory and Practice*. CRC Press, Boca Raton, FL, 3rd edition, 2005.
23. Zorg TTP: Privacy & vertrouwen. https://www.zorgttp.nl.

Chapter 9
Privacy-Aware Access Control in Social Networks: Issues and Solutions

Barbara Carminati and Elena Ferrari

Abstract Access control in online social networks (OSNs) is becoming an urgent need due to the amount of data managed by social networks and their sensitivity. Performing access control in a social network has many differences with respect to performing access control in a traditional data management system, in terms of both the policy language to support and the reference architecture for access control enforcement. Moreover, it is fundamental to also consider privacy issues connected to access control and to devise appropriate *privacy-preserving* access control systems. The aim of this chapter is to first discuss which are the requirements of privacy-aware access control to OSN resources and then to review the literature in view of the identified requirements. Finally, the chapter discusses future research directions in the field.

9.1 Introduction

Online social networks (OSNs) are platforms that allow people to publish details about themselves and to connect to other members of the network through various relationships. The potentialities of these services are enormous, from knowledge sharing to social search, to establish community of practices[1] at the enterprise level, just to mention few of OSN applicability domains. Recently, the popularity of OSNs is increasing significantly. For example, Facebook now claims to have more than 300 million active users.[2] Also the amount of shared digital contents is enormous. For instance, considering once again Facebook, it now claims to have more than 2 billion photos and 14 million videos uploaded to the site each month, whereas more

---

B. Carminati (✉)
Dipartimento di Informatica e Comunicazione, Università degli Studi dell'Insubria, Via Mazzini 5, 21100 Varese, Italy
e-mail: barbara.carminati@uninsubria.it

[1] http://en.wikipedia.org/wiki/Social_search
[2] http://www.facebook.com/press/info.php?statistics

J. Nin, J. Herranz (eds.), *Privacy and Anonymity in Information Management Systems*,
Advanced Information and Knowledge Processing,
DOI 10.1007/978-1-84996-238-4_9, © Springer-Verlag London Limited 2010

than 2 billion pieces of content (web links, news stories, blog posts, notes, photos, etc.) are shared each week.

The existence of this huge amount of data, including person-specific information, creates both interesting research challenges and security and privacy threats. For example, social network data could be used for marketing products to the right customers. At the same time, security and privacy concerns can prevent such efforts in practice [4]. Therefore, many researchers have started to work on improving the access control systems today provided by OSNs. The motivation is that current OSNs implement very basic access control models, by simply making users able to decide which information are accessible by other members by marking a given item as public, private, or accessible by their direct contacts.

In order to give more flexibility, some online social networks enforce variants of these settings, but the principle is the same. For instance, besides the basic settings, Bebo (http://bebo.com), Facebook (http://facebook.com), and Multiply (http://multiply.com) support the option "selected friends"; Last.fm (http://last.fm) the option "neighbors" (i.e., the set of users having musical preferences and tastes similar to mine); Facebook, Friendster, and Orkut (http://friendster.com, http://www.orkut.com) the option "friends of friends"; Xing (http://xing.com) the options "contacts of my contacts" (second degree contacts), and "third" and "fourth degree contacts"; LinkedIn (http://www.linkedin.com) and Multiply the option "my network" (i.e., all the WBSN members who are either directly or indirectly connected to, independently from how far they are). It is important to note that all these approaches have the advantage of being easy to implement, but they lack flexibility. In fact, the available protection settings do not allow users to easily specify their protection requirements, in that they are either too restrictive or too loose (e.g., the option "my network" in LinkedIn).[3]

The research activity in the field of OSN access control has resulted in several proposals that we survey in Section 9.4. Almost all the proposals appeared so far enforce *relationship-based access control*, according to which access control requirements are expressed in terms of relationship paths existing in the network and their depth. For example, using relationship-based access control a user can give access to one of his/her photo only to his/her friends and the friends of his/her friends or to all my direct and indirect colleagues, no matter how distant they are from me in the network graph. Furthermore, some of the models support a notion of trust/reputation as a further parameter for access control decisions.

The enforcement of relationship-based access control poses interesting issues regarding privacy protection, which are the main focus of this chapter. A first issue is related to the architecture on support of access control. Clearly a centralized solution where the social network management system (SNMS) is in charge of performing access control and managing all users' resources and security policies is no more acceptable by SN users since this implies to fully trust the SNMS with

---

[3] A more detailed analysis of privacy practices in 45 OSNs can be found in [6]

respect to the management of user private data. It is today well recognized that decentralization is the future of OSN [23] and this should also apply to access control. Furthermore, enforcing relationship-based access control requires to disclose to the resource owner some paths in the network and associated trust level. This means disclosing all the relationships/trust levels of the links forming the path. However, disclosing a relationship/trust level always means an exposure of personal information. Therefore, there is the need of devising *privacy-aware access control mechanisms*, able to enforce relationship-based access control by, at the same time, ensuring relationship privacy.

In this chapter we start by understanding which are the main requirements of an access control system for OSNs, by focusing on the privacy issues arising in access control. Then, we review the literature in view of the identified requirements. Finally, we conclude the chapter by outlining future research directions.

9.2 Access Control Requirements

In what follows, we use as running example the OSN depicted in Fig. 9.1. The OSN refers to a network of freelance IT consultants that use the network for a variety of purposes, such as knowledge sharing, advertising new opportunities, finding new partners. The OSN may also involve companies that wish to make use of the services provided by the consultants. Clearly, such companies should have a selective access to OSN resources. Nodes can also form smaller networks or groups (for instance, a set of consultants/companies working on a specific project). In the figure, the OSN is represented as a directed labeled graph, where each node corresponds to a network member and edges denote relationships between two different members. In particular, the initial node of an edge denotes the member who established the relationship, whereas the terminal node denotes the member who accepted to establish the relationship. Each edge is labeled by the type of the established relationship and the corresponding trust level, representing how much the user that established the relationship trust the other user with respect to that specific relationship. The portion of the OSN depicted in Fig. 9.1 consists of three companies, i.e., C_1, C_2, and C_3, whereas the remaining nodes represent agents.

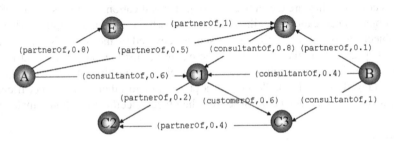

Fig. 9.1 A portion of an OSN

The main purpose of an OSN is to establish relationships with other users and exploit such relationships for sharing resources of various nature. Therefore, it is already well accepted that any access control model for OSNs should be *relationship based*. According to a relationship-based access control model, access control policies are specified in terms of relationships existing in the OSN. This means that the releasing of a resource is conditioned to the fact that the resource requestor has a relationship (either direct or indirect) of a specific type with another OSN member(s). Examples of relationship-based access control policies are as follows: Only my friends can access document doc_1 or only the colleagues of my colleagues can access report `rep`. Additional policies referring to the OSN in Fig. 9.1 are as follows: Only my partners can access the project opportunity I post in the OSN or only my customers can have a sneak preview of the report describing a particular not yet released product. Additionally, also the depth of the path is an important parameter for some access control decisions, since users usually are more inclined to share their resources with users not much far away from them. For example, a user may want to limit the disclosure of one of his/her resources to his/her friends and the friends of their friends or to consultant partners whose distance in the OSN is no more than three. Therefore, the policy language should be able to express constraints on the depth of a path. A further important parameter is represented by trust, which is an orthogonal parameter with respect to the depth of a relationship. For instance, two of my direct friends may have completely different trust and therefore I may want to give access to a resource only to the one with the highest trust and not to the other. Referring to the OSN in Fig. 9.1, consultant A(lice) is a direct partner of both E(ric) and F(red), but the trust she has on the two is different.[4] Because of this, A may want to share new job opportunities with E but not with F. In this case, the depth of the relationship is not enough to express this requirement (since both E and F are at distance one from A). Therefore, the policy language should support also constraints on the minimum trust level of a relationship.

Moreover, in an OSN relationships between users and resources may be of different types. As usual, a user may be the owner of a resource, but he/she may also be tagged in a photo of another user. Therefore, a relationship-based access control model should exploit not only the standard user-to-user relationships for access control purposes but also the variety of user-to-resource relationships that the OSN supports.

Apart from the access mode that is granted, the other two main components of an access control policy are the subject and object specification. In the case of an OSN, the subject specification identifies the users to which the policy applies, whereas the object specification identifies the resources covered by the policy. Regarding the subject specification, the policy language has to be flexible enough to identify the users to which a policy applies according to their relationships with resources (e.g., users "tagged" to a photo, "leader" of a project) or to other users (direct friends, colleagues of my colleagues). Moreover, the object specification should make one

---

[4] Trust computation is out of the scope of this chapter, we refer the interested reader to [18] for more details on this topic

able to identify resources according to their descriptions (e.g., objects of "type" photo, documents "about" an object of "type" photo), as well as to their URIs.

Up to now, we have focused on the requirements of the access control model and related policy language. However, a further important class of requirements is related to how access control is enforced and by what entities of the OSN. Traditionally, access control is enforced by a trusted software module, called reference monitor, and hosted by the data management system. The reference monitor intercepts each access request and, on the basis of the specified access control policies, determines whether the access can be partially or totally authorized or it must be denied. Therefore, the first architectural choice is related to which entity should host the reference monitor. If we cast our discussion in an OSN the traditional solution described above implies to delegate to the SNMS the role of reference monitor. According to this choice, OSN users completely delegate the control of their data to the SNMS, which stores and enforces all the access control policies on behalf of the network users. Even if this kind of solution is largely accepted, we do not believe that it is the most suited for the OSN scenario. The main reason of this concern is that this solution implies to totally delegate to the SNMS the administration and enforcement of access control policies. This means that users should trust the SNMS regarding the correct enforcement of their policies. However, some recent events have made OSN users aware that the SNMS's behavior is not always honest and transparent. This is, for instance, witnessed by some privacy concerns related to the collection and delivering of personal data by some of the Facebook's services [4, 13, 16]. All these events lead us to believe that a centralized access control solution where the SNMS hosts the reference monitor is not the most appropriate one in the OSN scenario. We believe that in the near future OSN participants would like to have more and more control over their access control policies and the way they are enforced. The best solution in this respect is a fully decentralized one, where each OSN user is responsible for policy specification and enforcement. However, each access control solution to be effectively applied must consider also another important dimension, that is, the efficiency of access control. Since, access control is relationship-based, answering an access request may require to verify the existence of specific paths within an OSN. This task may be very difficult and time consuming in a fully decentralized solution. Therefore, a further essential requirement of access control enforcement is to devise efficient and scalable implementation strategies.

The access control requirements discussed so far are summarized in Table 9.1.

Table 9.1 OSN main access control requirements

Component	Requirements
Policy language	Relationship-based:
	(a) User-to-user relationships:
	Depth
	Trust level
	(b) User-to-resource relationships
Access control enforcement	Not centralized
	Efficient

9.3 Privacy Issues in OSN Access Control

As we have seen in Section 9.2, the first requirement of any access control model for
OSNs is its ability to enforce relationship-based access control. However, relationships are in general sensitive resources whose privacy should be properly guaranteed
even if they are instrumental to perform access control. Therefore, the main privacy
issues that arise during access control enforcement are those arising by the disclosure of personal relationships. Indeed, establishing a relationship in a community
implies, in some sense, an exposure of personal information of the users involved
in the relationship, which may give rise to some relevant privacy concerns. For
instance, referring to our running example in Fig. 9.1, consultant B(ob) may not want
to disclose to consultant F the fact that he works for company C_1. One fundamental
requirement is therefore that each participant has strong guarantees that relationship
privacy is not breached during access control. Clearly, the way this is achieved is
highly impacted by the way access control is enforced. For instance, if we assume
a centralized architecture where the SNMS hosts the reference monitor, privacy is
guaranteed under the assumption that we can fully trust the SNMS. More difficult
is to protect relationship privacy if a decentralized architecture is used, according
to which access control enforcement is under the responsibility of resource owners and/or requestors (see Section 9.4.2 for a more detailed discussion about these
issues). Additionally, relationship may have an associated trust value that must be
protected during access control. For instance, with reference to Fig. 9.1, company C_1
may not want to disclose the fact that it does not trust very much C_2 as a partner (i.e.,
the trust level assigned to the partnerOf relationship is 0.2). Privacy requirements
regarding trust disclosure may be different from that of relationships. For instance,
a user may consent to disclose that he/she is a friend of a given user, but he/she may
not want to disclose how much he/she trusts that particular user. Therefore, a further
requirement is that of protecting relationship trust level during access control.

Another issue which is out of the scope of this chapter but that it is important
to mention is related to privacy issues arising during trust computation. Literature
shows that there does not exist a unique definition of trust, since it may vary depending on the context (e.g., PKI, P2P, social networks) and for which purposes it is used
(e.g., to ensure quality of service, to associate a "value" to opinions/recommenda-
tions). This obviously impacts also how trust is computed. In general, the main
issues in trust computation concerns which trust paths must be considered in order
to obtain an accurate trust value, since multiple paths may exist connecting two
entities. Several solutions have been proposed so far, and, usually, they enforce some
constraints in order to select just some of the existing paths (see [12] for a discussion
on trust computation). However, in scenarios where trust is used as a parameter to
enforce access control, we believe that its value should be computed taking into
account also the compliance of user actions to the specified access control policies
and/or privacy preferences. Therefore, the OSN should have some mechanisms to
help a user to precisely estimate the other network participants trust level. Such
mechanisms should also preserve user privacy when performing trust computation.
For instance, a naive solution to trust computation is to log all the actions a user

performs with respect to resources/relationships disclosure and use such information to estimate the compliance of user actions to the specified policies. Clearly, this solution poses serious privacy concerns in that a user may not want to disclose the details of all his/her actions. As such, methods should be devised that are able to precisely compute trust without compromising user privacy. Some proposals exist in this direction. For example, Nin et al. [26] exploit anonymization strategies on the log file, such that details about the performed access control decisions are kept private but, at the same time, it is possible to determine whether the decisions are correct or not, with respect to the specified policies.

9.4 Review of the Literature

In what follows, we review the literature in view of the requirements discussed in the previous section. We start by illustrating the main proposals of access control models/systems appeared so far. Then, we focus on the solutions proposed to enforce access control in a privacy-preserving manner.

9.4.1 Access Control Models

Recently some research proposals have been appeared aiming to overcome the restrictions of the protection mechanisms provided by current online social networks.

For example, Carminati et al. [10, 12] address access control issues arising in online social networks and propose to model access control requirements in terms of access rules specified by the resource owners. More precisely, these access rules denote authorized members in terms of the type, depth, and trust level of the relationships they must have with other network nodes. In [10, 12] authors also propose a client-based approach to enforce access control, according to which the requestor must provide the resource owner with a proof of being authorized to access the requested resource. As access rules constraint relationships, the proof has to show the existence of the required relationships and that these relationships have the required depth and trust level.

In order to generate valid proofs, it is assumed that a "relationship certificate" is associated with each relationship, containing information on the relationship (i.e., users involved, trust, depth, type), which is signed by both the involved users. A relationship certificate can be seen as a proof that between the involved users there exists a direct relationship of a certain type and with a certain trust level. Proofs of indirect relationship can therefore be generated through a set of certificates confirming the existence of a path of a specified type between them. Based on this access control model, authors have also investigated privacy-aware solutions for access control enforcement (see Section 9.4.2 for more details).

In contrast, the proposal illustrated in [2, 19, 29] represents access control authorizations by means of access control lists (ACLs) associated with resources. In particular, these lists, called social ACLs, contain identifiers of authorized users as well as relationships user must have to gain access. Then, similar to [10, 12], to enforce authorizations stated in social ACLs they rely on relationship certificates, here called "social attestations," which record information about relationships between two users (i.e., identifiers of involved users and relationship types).

A different approach has been proposed in [1]. Here a multi-level access control solution is proposed, according to which users and resources are organized in security levels and accesses are granted based on the relationships between security levels of the requested resource and the requestor. In order to support this access control model, with each user u is associated a reputation value $r(u)$, computed as the average of the trust ratings specified for u by other users in the social network. To organize resources into security levels, the system automatically assigns to resources created by a user u a security level equal to τ, where τ represents the trust level in the range $[0, r(u)]$ user has selected when he/she logged in the social network. Then, users are authorized to access only resources with a security level equal or less than τ. In [1], authors proposed to enforce multi-level access control according to a challenge-response-based protocol. In particular, for each resource o, the resource owner generates a secret key K, which is then processed by a (k, n) threshold algorithm [27]. According to this algorithm, a key K can be split into n portions and then reconstructed based only on k portions of it, where $k < n$. As such, the proposal in [1] requires that the n portions of K are distributed to n trustworthy nodes. Then, if a requestor wishes to access resource o, the resource owner sends him/her the challenge encrypted with K. The requestor has to retrieve the k portions of K from the set of n nodes holding them. Such portions are released only if the requestor satisfies the trust requirements specified by the resource owner. Once the requestor has reconstructed K, he/she responds to the challenge and gains access to the resource.

Another solution from the same authors proposes to determine access control rights based on the distance between the owner and the requestor [30]. According to this solution, users that directly or indirectly are connected to the owner can be classified into three adjacent zones: "acceptance" zones, whose access requests will be immediately accepted; "attestation" zones, whose access requests require a further evaluation to gain access, and "rejection" zones, whose access requests will be immediately rejected. As a consequence, confidentiality requirements on resources are specified in terms of two distances, called trusted distance, delimiting the three zones.

The proposal presented in [3] exploits cryptographic primitives to enforce a group-based access control in OSNs. The underlying idea is that users are able to organize their friends into groups and assign permissions to them by means of ACLs. As this proposal considers a social network model similar to Facebook (i.e., with simple relationships), group generation does not take into consideration relationship types and trust. This means that users generate groups by explicitly adding friends to them. The main contribution of this proposal is indeed in the cryptographic primitives exploited to enforce the authorizations in ACLs. More precisely, authors make use of attribute-based encryption (ABE) [5], according to which (1) both user's keys and encrypted data are labeled with a set of attributes and (2) user's keys are defined such to decrypt an encrypted data only if there is a match between its attributes and those of the data. This last feature greatly improves group key management.

The work reported in [17] presents an interesting analysis of the access control mechanism of Facebook, with the aim to formalize it into a more comprehensive access control model for social networks. As a result, Ref. [17] identifies four different types of privacy policies. The access control policies are one of these types. For each resource, the access control policies state who is authorized to access the resource. Other two policy types have been proposed by taking into consideration that in Facebook it is possible to look for new users in the social network by accessing some parts of users' profiles as well as users' friend lists (this allows a search by traversing the social graph). As Facebook makes users able to state privacy settings regulating the access to this information, these are also supported by the model proposed in [17]. These are the search policies and the traversal policies, respectively. The last policy type, called communication policy, aims to make users able to state who is authorized to initiate a given type of communication with him/her.

It is interesting to note that the emerging trend in Semantic Web technologies is to provide much richer social network data (e.g., representing relationships among users and resources in detail) [25]. On these semantically enriched social networks, more flexible and expressive protection mechanisms can be devised, as shown by recent work [9, 15]. For example, in [15] authors focus on online communities, by proposing a semantic framework based on OWL – web ontology language – for defining different access rights exploiting the relationships between the individuals and the community. In contrast, Carminati et al. [9] propose an extension of the relationship-based access control model in [10, 12], based on Semantic Web rules [20].

Table 9.2 summarizes the discussion on related work presented in this section. Proposals are organized according to the supported access control requirements (i.e., defined based on type, trust, and depth of relationships).

Interesting examples of access control-related solutions can also be found in some software available in existing OSNs. Let us consider Facebook, since it is the OSN for which the majority of these tools have been proposed. We can find

Table 9.2 Summary of access control model for social networks

Access control model	Decision based on relationship types	Decision based on relationship trust	Decision based on relationship depth
[9, 10, 12]	Yes	Yes	Yes
[1]	No	Yes	No
[30]	No	No	Yes
[2, 19, 29]	Yes	No	No
[3]	No	No	No
[17]	Yes	No	No

some third-party applications aiming to enhance confidentiality of user profiles (e.g., Privacy Protector) or messages posted in walls (e.g., Private Wall, Secret Wall, Private Groups), as well as photos/videos and sensitive data (e.g., Private Photo Gallery, Private Video Gallery, FlybyNight [22]). Other applications help users to be aware of which information of their profiles is available to third-party applications according to users privacy settings (for example, Privacy Mirror, 1984, AppAdvisor, PrivAware).[5] Finally, some third-party applications provide users with insightful suggestions for properly setting Facebook privacy configurations (for example, Privacy Helper). Based on information accountability, another interesting application is Respect My Privacy that makes users able to clearly communicate how they want their data to be handled in several different scenarios (e.g., commercial, depiction, financial). However, all these tools do not provide a comprehensive solution to OSN access control, rather they provide solutions only for specific issues related to access control (e.g., photos/videos distribution, wall protection).

9.4.2 Privacy-Aware Access Control

It is important to note that up to now, most of the research related to privacy in OSNs have focused on privacy-preserving techniques to mine social network data [21]. The only proposals we are aware of, providing some solutions for privacy-aware access control, are those reported in [7, 8, 11, 14, 24]. These proposals, that we briefly describe in what follows, differ with respect to both the used techniques and the privacy guarantees they provide.

A first distinction among the various proposals is that some of them are *policy-based* [8, 11], this means that a user can express his/her privacy requirements with respect to the disclosure of his/her relationships to other users. For instance, through a privacy preference a user may specify that a particular relationship in which he/she is involved can be seen only by his/her colleagues. Moreover, some of the proposals address only the problem of relationship protections [24], whereas the others also consider trust protection. Finally, all the proposals adopt cryptographic techniques to avoid leakage of private information referring to relationships and/or trust.

Let us start from *policy-based* solutions, according to which privacy requirements related to relationship and trust disclosure are specified by means of *distribution rules* [8, 11]. A distribution rule basically states who can be aware of a given OSN relationship and exploit it for access control purposes. The system proposed in [11] enforces decentralized access control, according to which existing relationships and resources are not stored in a central repository, but by OSN members themselves, who also carry out the tasks related to access control enforcement and privacy protection. The only centralized service is a certificate revocation list, storing information on the revoked relationships. Additionally, access control is client side,

---

[5] This problem has been addressed also in [28], where an access control framework enabling users to specify how attributes have to be shared with third-party applications have been proposed

this means that the burden of access control enforcement is mainly on the requestor, that has to provide the owner a proof demonstrating that he/she satisfies the access rules applying to the requested resource. Access control is enforced according to the model described in [12] and summarized in Section 9.4.1, which is based on relationship certificates used to generate proofs. Since the solution proposed in [11] is decentralized, relationship certificates are delivered to OSN members according to the specified distribution rules. To avoid inferences of private relationships, relationship certificates are encrypted and the corresponding keys are distributed only to the users authorized according to the specified distribution rules. Details on the protocols for keys and certificates distribution and update are contained in [11]. Unauthorized relationship disclosure may also happen during access control enforcement, due to the fact that a client-side approach is adopted. Indeed, when a member requests a resource, the owner replies by sending him/her the set of access rules regulating the access to that resource. Access rules give information on the relationships the owner is involved in. For instance, if an owner replies to an access request by requesting a proof stating a consultantOf relationship with another user it is very likely that the owner participates in at least one relationship of type consultant-fof, otherwise no OSN member will be authorized to access the requested resource. To avoid this kind of inferences cryptographic techniques are also adopted, according to which the conditions contained into an access rule are encrypted with a key which is shared only by the users involved in the relationship of the type required by the condition.

One of the main drawbacks of managing encrypted certificates and access rules is that the overhead due to key management may be extremely high. For this reason, in [8] an alternative approach is explored according to which access control (i.e., path discovery) is performed through a collaboration of selected nodes in the network. The collaboration is started by the resource owner who, upon receiving an access request, contacts his/her neighbors asking whether they hold a relationship of the type required by the specified access rules with the resource requestor. The path is incrementally built as the request of collaboration is propagated in the network. The process halts either when a path is found or the request for collaboration cannot be further forwarded. Clearly, each node receiving a request for collaboration is aware of the path built so far and its trust level. For this reason, collaboration is driven by the specified distribution rules in that a node is required to collaborate only if he/she satisfies the distribution rules associated with the relationships in the path built so far. By making use of an ad hoc specified data structure, called *onion signature*, each user in the path can verify whether previous receivers of the path have correctly enforced distribution rules.

The idea of enforcing privacy-aware access control through a collaboration of selected nodes in the network is further explored in [7]. In this chapter, privacy requirements are not expressed through distribution rules. Rather homomorphic encryption is used to collaboratively build an *anonymous path*, that is, a path that allows the resource owner to verify whether it matches the specified access rules without revealing the identity of the users involved in the path. An analogous data structure is used for trust computation, that is, to make the owner able to compute the trust of a path without knowing the trust values associated with the arcs composing the path. However, this solution suffers from privacy breaches in the case of paths of length 2. This is avoided by inserting into the architecture a trusted entity in charge of verifying whether this inference can arise and informing the users whose privacy may be violated to let them deciding whether to release or not the path to the owner.

Domingo-Ferrer et al. [14] also exploit homomorphic encryption and user collaboration to enforce privacy-aware access control. With difference to [7] they support a restricted version of the policy language in [12], where the maximum depth of a relationship cannot be used as a parameter to perform access control. Therefore, policies such as "Only my friends and the friends of my friends" are not supported. Similar to [7], the proposal makes use of a trusted entity. However, the optimistic TTP proposed in [14] does not mediate each collaboration process, rather it is contacted only in case of conflicts among the users in the network (for instance, when a user suspects that another one contributed with a fake trust level to path discovery or has modified the trust value inserted by another user during the collaboration process). In summary, main differences between [14] and [7] are related to the policy language they support and the different use of the TTP.

A method to discover relationship paths between two users of an OSN without disclosing the relationships in the path is also proposed in [24]. This method, which does not consider the issue of the private computation of relationship trust, can be the basis of privacy-aware decentralized relationship-based access control. The method exploits a private set intersection protocol by which two parties each one holding a set of elements can compute the intersection of the two sets, without knowing the elements in the set belonging to the other party, apart from those in common to the two parties. The method consists of two steps: a token flooding phase and a path discovery phase. The first phase requires that users are online, whereas the second one can be conducted off-line. During the first phase users generate and propagate along the network cryptographic tokens to privately explore the paths originating from him/her up to a pre-defined depth. To better explain how the process works consider a user u in the network. He/she generates a set of tokens, obtained by hashing with a one-way function a random number concatenated with a counter, and delivers one of the generated tokens to each of his/her neighbors. Each user receiving a token repeats the same procedure (concatenation of the counter value and application of the hash function) before forwarding the token to the subsequent users in the network. Each user locally stores the set of received tokens. Additionally, since token generation follows a deterministic process, each originator of a token t can locally compute all the tokens originated from t. Therefore, two users u_1 and u_2, by running a private set intersection protocol on the set of received and generated tokens, respectively, can privately discover whether they have a common path. If the intersection of the two sets of tokens is not empty, this means that there exists a path between the two. However, in [24] it is showed that this basic scheme is not robust against all the inferences that can be performed on private relationships. More specifically, by following the protocol above described, it is possible to infer the specific node where two private paths intersect. To avoid this, the protocol has been enhanced with a randomization technique for token generation that avoids the above-described privacy breach. The basic idea is that a user at distance $d \geq 2$ from the originator receives a token randomly selected from the set of tokens generated for users at distance d. Tokens for intermediate nodes are generated by the so-called *bridge contacts*, that is, users directly connected to the token originator. The bridge contact generates a set of tokens for users at distance d, $2 \leq d \leq d_{max}$. Tokens are generated separately for each distance, by considering the degree of each connected node. Each node does not communicate its exact degree, rather it adds to it a positive noise to prevent inferences on the network topology. As a consequence, dummy tokens are generated and sent along the network. Each user at distance 2 receives from the bridge contact one token for distance 2 and a set of tokens for distance 3 proportional to the number of friends. This process is iterated for users at distance $d > 2$. Each transmitted token is randomly selected from the set of generated tokens.

9.5 Conclusions and Future Research Directions

In this chapter we have first discussed the access control requirements arising in OSNs, with a particular focus on the privacy issues arising during access control enforcement. We have then reviewed the literature in view of the identified requirements.

However, research in this field is still in its infancy and many interesting issues remain to be explored. First of all a satisfactory solution to relationship privacy protection during path discovery has not yet been devised. All the proposals we reviewed in Section 9.4.2 are based on cryptographic stuff and they suffer from some drawbacks, such as the limitation they put in the policy language they support or in the length of the paths that can be supported in practice or the inefficiency of key management upon a modification of the topology of the OSN. Therefore, the design of a general-purpose and efficient method for private path discovery is still an open issue. Another important problem is related to trust protection during access control. All the methods we reviewed in Section 9.4.2 enforcing privacy protection adopt a very simple way of computing trust, that is, the trust between two nodes is given by the trust of any of the path between the two. However, more elaborated ways of trust computation that lead to a more precise measure of trust have been proposed in the literature (see, e.g., [18]), according to which the trust between two nodes is a function of all the paths between them or of some of them, for instance, the shortest paths. Supporting such measure of trust during privacy-aware access control is still an open issue. This is even more difficult if we want to enforce access control in a fully decentralized way, in that the big issue is how a user may compute all the paths between two nodes in an efficient and private way.

Another important research direction is related to policy administration. As we have seen in this chapter, OSN users need a very flexible policy language to express their privacy/confidentiality requirements. However, when a user specifies an access control policy it is not easy to understand exactly the effect of this policy (for instance, in terms of authorized users), nor its privacy implication (for instance, in terms of relationship disclosure), due to the fact that the SN graph may be very big, with thousands of relations that frequently change. Therefore, a very important issue is to devise techniques and tools that help the user in evaluating the *risk* of unauthorized flows of information that the specification of a policy or its update may cause.

Acknowledgments The work reported in this chapter is partially funded by the Italian MIUR under the ANONIMO project (PRIN-2007F9437X).

References

1. Ali B., Villegas W., and Maheswaran M. A trust based approach for protecting user data in social networks. In: *Proceedings of the 2007 Conference of the Center for Advanced Studies on Collaborative research (CASCON'07), ACM, New York, NY*, pp. 288–293, 2007.
2. Tootoonchian Y.G.A., Saroiu S., and Wolman A. Lockr: Better privacy for social networks. In: *Proceedings of the T 5th ACM International Conference on emerging Networking EXperiments and Technologies (CoNEXT), Rome, Italy*, 2009.
3. Baden R., Bender A., Spring N., Bhattacharjee B., and Starin D. Persona: An online social network with user-defined privacy. In: *Proceedings of the ACM SIGCOMM 2009 conference on Data communication, ACM, New York, NY*, pp. 135–146, 2009.
4. Berteau S. Facebook's misrepresentation of Beacon's threat to privacy: Tracking users who opt out or are not logged in. CA Security Advisor Research Blog, March 2007, http://community. ca.com/ blogs/ securityadvisor/ archive/ 2007/11/29/ facebook-s- misrepresentation- of-beacon-s-threatto- privacy- tracking-users -who-opt -out-or-are-not-logged-in.aspx.
5. Bethencourt J., Sahai A., and Waters B. Ciphertext-policy attribute-based encryption. *In: Proceedings of the 2007 IEEE Symposium on Security and Privacy, IEEE Computer Society , Washington, DC*, pp. 321–334, 2007.
6. Bonneau J. and Preibusch S. The privacy jungle: On the market for data protection in social networks. *In: The Eighth Workshop on the Economics of Information Security (WEIS 2009)*, 2009.
7. Carminati B. and Ferrari E. Enforcing relationships privacy through collaborative access control in web-based social networks. *In: Proceedings of the 5th International Conference on Collaborative Computing: Networking, Applications and Worksharing, IEEE CS Press, Washington, DC*, November, 2009.
8. Carminati B., and Ferrari E. Privacy-aware collaborative access control in webbased social networks. *In: Proceedings of the 22nd annual IFIP WG 11.3 working conference on Data and Applications Security, Springer, Berlin*, pp. 81–96, 2008.
9. Carminati B., Ferrari E., Ramyond H., Kantarcioglu M., and Thuraisingham B. A semantic web based framework for social network access control. In: *SACMAT '09: Proceedings of the 14th ACM symposium on Access Control Models and Technologies, ACM, New York, NY*, pp. 177–186, 2009.
10. Carminati B., Ferrari E., and Perego A. Rule-based access control for social networks. In: *OTM 2006 Workshops*, vol 2 LNCS 4278, Springer, Berlin, pp. 1734–1744, 2006.
11. Carminati B., Ferrari E., and Perego A. A decentralized security framework for web-based social networks. *International Journal of Information Security and Privacy*, 2(4):22–53, 2008.
12. Carminati B., Ferrari E., and Perego A. Enforcing access control in web-based social networks. *ACM Transactions on Information and System Security (TISSEC)*, 13(1):6, 2009.
13. Chen L. Facebook's feeds cause privacy concerns. The Amherst Student, October 2006, http://halogen.note.amherst.edu/~astudent/2006–2007/issue02/news/01.html.

14. Domingo-Ferrer J., Viejo A., Sebé F., and González-Nicolás Í. Privacy homomorphisms for social networks with private relationships. *Computer Networks*, 52(15):3007–3016, 2008.

15. Elahi N., Chowdhury M.M.R., and Noll J. Semantic access control in web based communities. *In: ICCGI '08: Proceedings of the 2008 the Third International Multi-Conference on Computing in the Global Information Technology (ICCGI 2008), IEEE Computer Society, Washington, DC*, pp. 131–136, 2008.

16. EPIC. Social networking privacy, February 2008, http://epic.org/ privacy/socialnet/default. html, 2008. Accessed date: 07/06/2010.

17. Fong P.W.L., Anwar M.M., and Zhao Z. A privacy preservation model for facebook-style social network systems. *In: Proceedings of the 14th European Symposium on Research in Computer Security (ESORICS 2009), Saint-Malo, France, September 21–23*, 2009.

18. Golbeck J.A. Computing and applying trust in web-based social networks. PhD thesis, College Park, MD (Chair-Hendler, James), 2005.

19. Gollu K.K., Saroiu S., and Wolman A. A social networking-based access control scheme for personal content. *In: Proceedings of the 21st ACM Symposium on Operating Systems Principles (SOSP 07)*, Skamania Lodge Stevenson, WA, USA, 2007.

20. Horrocks I., Patel-Schneider P.F., Boley H., Tabet S., Grosof B., and Dean M. SWRL: A semantic web rule language combining OWL and RuleML. W3C Member Submission, World Wide Web Consortium, May 2004, http://www.w3. org/Submission/SWRL.

21. Liu K., Das K., Grandison T., and Kargupta H. Privacy-preserving data analysis on graphs and social networks. In: *Next Generation Data Mining* (eds. H. Kargupta, J. Han, P. Yu, R. Motwani, and V. Kumar), CRC Press, Boca Raton, FL, pp. 419–437, 2008.

22. Lucas M.M. and Borisov N. Flybynight: mitigating the privacy risks of social networking. In: *Proceedings of the 7th ACM workshop on Privacy in the electronic society, ACM, New York, NY*, pp. 1–8, 2008

23. Au Yeung C.M., Liccardi I., Lu K., Seneviratne O., and Berners- Lee T. Decentralization: The future of online social networking. *In: W3C Workshop on the Future of Social Networking, Barcelona, January* 2009.

24. Mezzour, G., Perrig A., Gligor V., and Papadimitratos P. Privacy-Preserving Relationship Path Discovery in Social Networks. *In: Computer Science; Vol. 5888 Proceedings of the 8th International Conference on Cryptology and Network Security (CANS 2009), December* 2009.

25. Mika P. *Social Networks and the Semantic Web (Semantic Web and Beyond)*. Springer, New York, NY, 1st edition, 2007.

26. Nin J., Carminati B., Ferrari E., and Torra V. Computing reputation for collaborative private networks. *In: COMPSAC '09: Proceedings of the 2009 33rd Annual IEEE International Computer Software and Applications Conference, IEEE Computer Society, Washington, DC*, pp. 246–253, 2009.

27. Shamir A. How to share a secret. *Communications of the ACM*, 22(11):612–613, 1979.

28. Shehab M., Squicciarini A.C., and Ahn G-J. Beyond user-to-user access control for online social networks. *In: ICICS '08: Proceedings of the 10th International Conference on Information and Communications Security, Springer, Berlin*, pp. 174–189, 2008.

29. Tootoonchian A., Gollu K.K., Saroiu S., Ganjali Y., and Wolman A. Lockr: social access control for web 2.0. In: *Proceedings of the First Workshop on Online Social Networks, ACM, New York, NY*, pp. 43–48, 2008.

30. Villegas W., Ali B., and Maheswaran M. An access control scheme for protecting personal data. In: *Proceedings of the 2008 Sixth Annual Conference on Privacy, Security and Trust, IEEE Computer Society, Washington, DC*, pp. 24–35, USA, 2008.

Index

J. Nin, J. Herranz (eds.), *Privacy and Anonymity in Information Management Systems*,
Advanced Information and Knowledge Processing,
DOI 10.1007/978-1-84996-238-4, © Springer-Verlag London Limited 2010